Top 100 Pro Wrestlers of all Time

Ric Flair   Lou Thesz   Rikidozan   Antonio Inoki   Hulk Hogan   Andre the Giant   El Santo   Giant Baba   Steve Austin   Buddy Rogers   Frank Gotch   Jim Londos   Ed "Strangler" Lewis   Stan Hansen   Bruno Sammartino   The Rock   Gorgeous George   Bruiser Brody   Riki Choshu   Mitsuharu Misawa   Verne Gagne   Jumbo Tsuruta   Terry Funk   Mil Mascaras   Bret Hart   Dory Funk Jr   Tiger Mask (Satoru Sayama)   Blue Demon   Perro Aguayo   Nick Bockwinkel   Dusty Rhodes   Johnny Valentine   Freddie Blassie   Vader   George Hackenschmidt   Jushin Liger   Toshiaki Kawada   Keiji Muto   Jack Brisco   Harley Race   El Hijo del Santo   Tatsumi Fujinami   Danny Hodge   Akira Maeda   Chigusa Nagayo   Ricky Steamboat   Shawn Michaels   Shinya Hashimoto   Ray Stevens   Randy Savage   Gene Kiniski   Nobuhiko Takada   Mick Foley   Genichiro Tenryu   The Crusher   Dick the Bruiser   Canek   Antonino Rocca   The Sheik   Don Leo Jonathan   The Dynamite Kid   The Undertaker   El Solitario   Superstar Billy Graham   Jerry Lawler   Roddy Piper   Ultimo Dragon   Billy Robinson   Jaguar Yokota   Lioness Asuka   Bobo Brazil   Karl Gotch   Bert Assirati   Gori Guerrero   Bill Longson   Killer Kowalski   Mildred Burke   Abdullah the Butcher   The Destroyer   Atsushi Onita   Ted DiBiase   Earl McCready   Pat O'Connor   Fritz Von Erich   Wahoo McDaniel   "Whipper" Billy Watson   Leroy McGuirk   Mad Dog Vachon   Yvon Robert   Bronko Nagurski   Dos Caras   Edouard Carpentier   Rayo de Jalisco Sr.   Stanislaus Zbyszko   Sting   Pat Patterson   Masahiro Chono   Dara Singh   Jesse Ventura   Eddie Graham

WrESTLiNgObserver's

Top 100 Pro Wrestlers of All Time

by **John F. Molinaro**
edited by **Jeff Marek** & **Dave Meltzer**

WINDING
STAIR
PRESS

Dedication

This book is dedicated to my brother Anthony, who was responsible for getting me hooked on wrestling when I was six; to my parents Frank and Josie, my brother Paul and my entire family for all their love and support; and to Sharon Valentine – widow of Johnny Valentine – for being a constant source of inspiration as the toughest person in the wrestling business I've ever met.

Acknowledgments

This book couldn't have come to fruition without the help of so many people, including everybody at Thin Data, Stewart House Publishing and Live Audio Wrestling. However, a few individuals need to be singled out for special thanks.

First, thanks to Chris Carder and Arthur Stern for giving me the opportunity to write this book.

To Jeff Marek, for always believing in me, and for helping me to believe in myself. Your overwhelming, and continual public praise of my work over the years has meant the world to me and has made me realize – finally! – that I am not without some talent. Thanks for helping my voice be heard.

To Dave Meltzer, whose editorial contributions and guidance on this project was simply immeasurable. Working with you on this book has been the highlight of my professional career. Thanks so much for your friendship and for inspiring me to cover the wrestling industry the way I do.

To John Powell and Greg Oliver, my former partners in crime at SLAM! Wrestling, for taking a young, wide-eyed journalism school graduate and helping to mold him into the poised reporter I am today. The influence the both of you have had on my career is staggering. This book is as much yours as it is mine.

To colleagues in the wrestling business like Mike Tenay, Mike Mooneyham, Bill Apter, Jim Ross, Dan Lovranski and Dave Schearer for their encouragement, their support, and most of all, their friendship over the years.

To friends Chris Persia, Lee Versage, Chris Harris, Gerard Doyle, Mike Shaye and Adrian Bromley, for never looking down their noses at me because I was "just writing about wrestling," and telling me that I would be writing books long before this came around.

And to Mick Foley, the late Lou Thesz and Gary Will and Royal Duncan for paving the way by publishing thoughtful and intelligent books that engaged readers in an insightful dialogue on the subject of pro wrestling and its rich history.

Text copyright © 2002 by John F. Molinaro

ISBN 1-55366-305-5

Cataloguing in Publication Data is available

Winding Stair Press
An imprint of Stewart House Publishing Inc.
290 North Queen Street, Suite #210
Toronto, Ontario
Canada, M9C 5K4
www.stewarthousepub.com

Design and photo research: Counterpunch / Peter Ross
Developmental editor: David Bernardi
Special thanks to Dr. Michael Lano for his dedicated enthusiasm and expert wrestling knowledge.

This book is available at special discounts for bulk purchases by groups or organizations for sales promotions, premiums, fundraising and educational purposes. For details, contact: Peter March, Stewart House Publishing Inc., Special Sales Department, 195 Allstate Parkway, Markham, Ontario. Tel: (866) 474-3478.

Printed in Canada

1   2   3   4   5   06   05   04   03   02

Contents

State of the Wrestling Industry   VII

Foreword   IX

The Top 100

1   Ric Flair   1

2   Lou Thesz   8

3   Rikidozan   14

4   Antonio Inoki   20

5   Hulk Hogan   26

6   Andre the Giant   33

7   El Santo   38

8   Giant Baba   44

9   Steve Austin   50

10   Buddy Rogers   56

11   Frank Gotch   62

12   Jim Londos   64

13   Ed "Strangler" Lewis   66

14   Stan Hansen   68

15   Bruno Sammartino   70

16   The Rock   72

17   Gorgeous George   74

18   Bruiser Brody   76

19   Riki Choshu   78

20   Mitsuharu Misawa   80

21   Verne Gagne   82

22   Jumbo Tsuruta   84

23   Terry Funk   86

24   Mil Mascaras   88

25   Bret Hart   90

Famous Holds and Finishers   92

26   Dory Funk Jr   96

27   Tiger Mask (Satoru Sayama)   98

28   Blue Demon   101

29   Perro Aguayo   102

30   Nick Bockwinkel   104

31   Dusty Rhodes   106

32   Johnny Valentine   108

33   Freddie Blassie   110

34   Vader   112

35   George Hackenschmidt   114

36   Jushin Liger   116

37   Toshiaki Kawada   118

38   Keiji Muto   120

39   Jack Brisco   122

40   Harley Race   124

41   El Hijo del Santo   126

42   Tatsumi Fujinami   128

43   Danny Hodge   130

44 Akira Maeda **132**

45 Chigusa Nagayo **134**

46 Ricky Steamboat **136**

47 Shawn Michaels **138**

48 Shinya Hashimoto **140**

49 Ray Stevens **142**

50 Randy Savage **144**

51 Gene Kiniski **146**

52 Nobuhiko Takada **146**

53 Mick Foley **147**

54 Genichiro Tenryu **150**

55 The Crusher **150**

56 Dick the Bruiser **151**

57 Canek **152**

58 Antonino Rocca **153**

59 The Sheik **153**

60 Don Leo Jonathan **154**

61 The Dynamite Kid **155**

62 The Undertaker **157**

63 El Solitario **158**

64 Superstar Billy Graham **159**

65 Jerry Lawler **161**

66 Roddy Piper **162**

67 Ultimo Dragon **165**

68 Billy Robinson **165**

69 Jaguar Yokota **166**

70 Lioness Asuka **167**

71 Bobo Brazil **169**

72 Karl Gotch **169**

73 Bert Assirati **170**

74 Gori Guerrero **171**

75 Bill Longson **171**

Ring of Friendship **172**

76 Killer Kowalski **176**

77 Mildred Burke **176**

78 Abdullah the Butcher **177**

79 The Destroyer **179**

80 Atsushi Onita **181**

81 Ted DiBiase **183**

82 Earl McCready **183**

83 Pat O'Connor **184**

84 Fritz Von Erich **186**

85 Wahoo McDaniel **187**

86 "Whipper" Billy Watson **189**

87 Leroy McGuirk **190**

88 Mad Dog Vachon **190**

89 Yvon Robert **191**

90 Bronko Nagurski **192**

91 Dos Caras **193**

92 Edouard Carpentier **193**

93 Rayo de Jalisco Sr **195**

94 Stanislaus Zbyszko **196**

95 Sting **196**

96 Pat Patterson **197**

97 Masahiro Chono **198**

98 Dara Singh **199**

99 Jesse Ventura **199**

100 Eddie Graham **200**

The Next Ten

Jun Aklyama **201**

Kurt Angle **202**

Chris Benoit **202**

Triple H **204**

Chris Jericho **205**

Kenta Kobashi **206**

Satoshi Kojima **206**

Yuji Nagata **207**

Kazushi Sakuraba **208**

Manami Toyota **208**

Index **210**

Photo credits **212**

The State of the Wrestling Industry

At the time of this writing, the prognostication for the long-term health of pro wrestling couldn't be worse, either in North America or in any other part of the wrestling globe.

The biggest mainstream star of the past 15 years, The Rock, has become a superhero in Hollywood and has left wrestling behind him. Outside of the occasional big money show (WrestleMania, Summer Slam), Dwayne Johnson will probably never be a full-time wrestler again. Consensus is that he'll be one of the only (and certainly the most successful) wrestlers to leave the sport for the greener pastures of Hollywood, where stunt men take your bumps for you (something neither Hulk Hogan nor Roddy Piper could do). And as The Rock goes, so goes much of the mainstream focus on pro wrestling, which has enjoyed a brilliant resurgence since 1997.

The WWE, desperate to create any buzz about the product, is taking the absolute worst route possible: nostalgia, which is one of the concepts that led to the slow death of the WCW promotion. Yet, McMahon seems content to ignore his own industry's history and go down this same road himself.

Despite the fact that the WWE had ridiculed the thought of Hulk Hogan as champion in the past, Hogan was hotshotted to the top of the WWE heap after his return and was soon crowned WWE Champion. It was a terrible waste, and did nothing to replace The Rock, and the mainstream stardom he had achieved. In fact, quite the opposite happened. Fans, and even casual observers, openly ridiculed the WWE for the decision to go with the '80 nostalgia act, proving that you never really can go home again. Hogan proved to be great for the live crowd, but it was soon made clear that his years as a vibrant TV character and PPV draw were behind him.

To make things even worse, the World Wrestling Federation* is in the process of re-branding itself "World Wrestling Entertainment" after losing a court battle with The World Wildlife Fund over the initials "WWF." The price of this exercise will undoubtedly eat into a large chunk – if not gobble up all – of McMahon's profits from WrestleMania x8.

Looking around, competition is coming from nowhere. Australian rock promoter Andrew McManus seemed to be the most successful earlier on, but his World Wrestling All Stars ultimately went nowhere, by making the most basic of wrestling mistakes. The same goes for Jimmy Hart and his XWF promotion, which turned out to be nothing more than a pipe dream for a handful of wrestlers looking for a quick payday.

Jeff Jarrett and his father (long time wrestling promoter Jerry) have an interesting concept in the works with NWA Total Non-Stop Action, which shuns TV as a marketing tool and instead chooses to broadcast wrestling PPVs weekly at $10 per show. The upside is potentially huge, but the key is whether or not they can combine the right product and the right concepts with a reasonable price tag. You can argue that the price point is there, but as for content – using WWE rejects like Scott Hall, Buff Bagwell, Brian Christopher and Road Dogg – the promotion's future is hardly bright.

*When referring to the company prior to the name change, we have used the World Wrestling Federation (WWF) throughout the book in order to be historically accurate.

Perhaps by the time this book is launched the company will already be toast.

Strong network television is the key to making wrestling work in the current environment, however, today's wrestling fan has an expectation of what wrestling is supposed to look like, both in the ring and on the screen. Fans have been educated to expect a big, expensive show with pyro, slick video packages, polished stars (an arguable point, granted), soap operatic drama, surgically enhanced women, and mind-numbing violence. All of this comes with a steep price tag. This is the main hurdle when it comes to providing any serious competition for Vince McMahon and the WWE. McMahon has essentially priced his competition out of the marketplace. Without a dump truck full of money you can't beat Vince at the game of TV wrestling.

But even Vince is feeling the heat. Live event attendance is down, and so are merchandise sales and TV numbers. Much like they did in the early '90s, when business slipped domestically, the WWE is taking the show overseas. England, Germany, Japan, and Australia will now be new destination points as the company tries to keep the green flowing at the same $400 million per year levels they've been at for the past couple of years.

In Mexico, another traditional wrestling hotbed, there's nothing going on outside of some great TV produced by EMLL. The deflated local currency has put wrestling in a precarious spot down there, with no serious money available to either wrestler or promoter. However, the argument has been made by numerous wrestling analysts (most notably Bryan Alvarez), that Mexican Lucha Libre could be the next breakthrough in North America. Latinos are the fastest growing demographic in the U.S., and Lucha is a style that many Americans haven't seen. The rise of Latinos in pop culture can only be ignored by wrestling promoters for so long.

And finally Japan, where promoters have always looked for new concepts, has sadly run out of viable ideas for the North American appetite. The past few years have seen the closing of Frontier Martial-Arts Wrestling (where ECW and ultimately the WWF "borrowed" concepts to carve out a niche in American wrestling culture), taking with it former owner Shoichi Arai (who hanged himself after the company shut down and the debts piled up). Also, the forerunner to the hybrid shoot/worked style of pro wrestling, Akira Maeda's Rings, closed down for good in the past year. New Japan,

traditionally the powerhouse of Japanese wrestling, is facing enormous problems, as they have found themselves losing key talent to rival promotions (earlier this year Keiji Muto, Satoshi Kojima, and Kendo Ka Shin jumped to rival All Japan) and have seen their legends leave for good (Riki Choshu bailing after a 15 year relationship went sour). Furthermore, the use of the Mixed Martial Arts promotion Pride to establish their pro wrestlers as legitimate fighters has been a disaster, to say the least. Taking a quick peek at other companies, Baba's All Japan seems to be on somewhat of a comeback trail, and Pro Wrestling Noah, lead by Mitsuharu Misawa, is more of a complement to the scene than a leader.

So we ask, What's next? The answer is, Who knows? Will it be Lucha Libre, as some claim? How about "reality fighting," like the Ultimate Fighting Championship and Pride? We don't know, but what we can be sure of is that for any new concept to work it has to begin with "the star" – that one wrestler who breaks through, connects with the audience in a profound way, and sends the industry off into new territory – much like the wrestlers you're about to read about in the following pages.

Jeff Marek

Foreword

Pro wrestling is a strange business. Every era is completely different from the one that preceded it, and the companies themselves have been radically different from one another. It is an evolving industry: in the beginning, it attempted to pass itself off as legitimate sport, despite the fact that finishes had always been predetermined. As time went on, more color was added, and the hype increased. Once pro wrestling became a fixture on the new medium of television, the color and the hype took center stage above any remnant of sport. There have always been, and probably always will be, numerous companies all over the world, all with very different ideas of what pro wrestling should be, many of which have proven successful.

Wrestlers today are bigger, stronger, and faster than they were decades ago – like athletes in all sports. Part of this is due to better training, part is simply that people are bigger nowadays, and part is because physiques are so important in winning fan support that chemicals are used to achieve that "larger-than-life" look. Furthermore, each company and wrestling region approaches the sport in a slightly different way. In North America – which has long been dominated by the World Wrestling Federation – it is fast-paced entertainment, with no real pretense at sport. In Mexico, the two major promotions are completely different. The traditional EMLL is the last of the old-school promotions, featuring two-out-of-three-falls matches and a fast-paced style. The gimmick of the mask is still a part of its culture, and because the wrestlers are much smaller, high-flying and acrobatics are more important than power moves and high impact bumps. The newer AAA is what is referred to as "garbage wrestling," focusing on brawling, weapons, wild

costumes, and characters, with no emphasis on believability. The Japanese have every form of wrestling possible, from pure entertainment, to actual sport. And while many of their matches actually are real, the ones that aren't are made to look as legitimate as possible, as realism is more important to the average Japanese fan than entertainment. In professional wrestling, the style of the day is based on what the public is buying – nothing works forever, and wrestling trends have historically been cyclical in nature. Even after periods where it seems a company can do no wrong, if it doesn't keep changing and catching the attention of new fans, its popularity wanes.

Considering the multitude of styles and promotions in wrestling's history, picking the greatest becomes even more difficult. There are no statistics as there are in other sports. We can cite the number of championships a wrestler has won (which, despite being predetermined, can be a relevant indicator of a wrestler's greatness, since great care is usually taken in selecting champions). We can look at attendance figures to determine a wrestler's drawing power, which is also very relevant, since wrestling is foremost an entertainment industry. But there are also the things that can't be measured with numbers, like the ability to put on a great match every night. Some great artists in the ring, perhaps because they weren't in the right place at the right time, may not have been the greatest drawing cards. There are men on this list who, if wrestling were real, would likely not even have been in the business. There are others who, if it were, would have been as dominant as any athlete of their era. The question, "Who is the greatest wrestler of all time?" is often asked, and with the death of Lou Thesz in

April of 2002, the question has come up a lot recently. This listing was put together before Thesz' death, and consideration was given to several wrestlers when deciding on the number one pick.

Why Ric Flair? Flair is not the biggest star, even of his era. Hulk Hogan was a bigger name and a bigger drawing card, and others of his era gained more mainstream recognition. What Flair was, was the best performer inside the ring over a longer period of time than anyone of the past 20 years. When it comes to Flair and Hogan, few will argue these specific points, but people will argue until the end of time over which of the two was the greater wrestler. Throw in Thesz, Rikidozan, Antonio Inoki, and Andre the Giant, and the arguments really begin to heat up.

From following the business for more than 30 years, and from studying its history, I think it's safe to say that every one in this top 100 was a huge star and deserves consideration. There is nobody in the top 40 that could be not included in a list of the top 100. But there are 50 guys not on this list who could easily take the places of spots 51 through 100. For the most part, the people in the top 15 were easy to pick, because they all had special qualities that made them stand out. But the order of the top 15 can be argued forever. Ric Flair, for his longevity, for his ability to make opponents look better than they really were, and for putting on probably as many great wrestling matches over a lengthy period of time as anyone in history, has been chosen as number one. Many also consider him the greatest talker the business has ever produced.

The others in the top 15 could also be considered for their own merits. Lou Thesz had even more longevity than Flair, and had a career that spanned even more eras. He was also a champion when promoters needed a guy who could actually *wrestle*, so that he could handle himself in bad situations (because with a conglomeration of promoters there was always the chance that somebody would try to double-cross you and steal the belt). Rikidozan created Japanese wrestling. When considering a wrestler's impact on his own culture, nobody was ever in his league. Antonio Inoki took the baton from Rikidozan, becoming an enormous television star and an icon to an entire generation. In many ways, Hulk Hogan learned from people like Inoki, as well as Superstar Billy Graham, and became pro wrestling's biggest gate attraction ever. Andre the Giant was the world's biggest gate attraction prior to Hogan, becoming a

household name despite little media exposure. El Santo was more than a wrestler. He was probably the most beloved wrestler ever within his own country, thanks to his long career in the ring and in film. Giant Baba also achieved a name-recognition within his own country above that of anyone in U.S. wrestling history.

Steve Austin is rapidly moving up on this list, as well. Besides being among the best wrestlers inside the ring and an excellent talker, he was the premier drawing card during a period when pro wrestling became bigger financially than any other time in its history. He is the only man in the top 15 who is still active and under the age of 40. Buddy Rogers is considered by virtually everyone to be the greatest performer wrestling had ever seen up to that point in time. Frank Gotch, as an historic figure, is probably the most important wrestler in the U.S., as he popularized wrestling as a sport. While his name has been largely forgotten, his influence is probably greater than any other wrestler's. Gotch was one of the biggest sports stars of his day, and turned Iowa into a wrestling hotbed. Jim Londos was an incredible drawing card. He was the first true matinee idol draw, combining good looks and charisma to draw some of the biggest stadium crowds before the 1980s, and he did so during the Depression, at a time wrestling by all rights should have been dead. Strangler Lewis was the game's biggest star of the 20s, which may have been the sport's hottest period before television. Stan Hansen was Japan's foreign legend. While not as big a star in the U.S., in the post-1970, when wrestling was a huge fixture on network television in Japan, there is little doubt that he was the country's top foreign star. And of course, there is Bruno Sammartino, who was a wrestling god to everyone growing up in the Northeast during the '70s and '80s.

Flair got the nod as the number one wrestler because of his consistency in the ring as well as his longevity. There have been men who were his equals in the ring on their best days, and many were athletically superior. But none were as consistent, night after night, or had the longevity of Ric Flair. Flair scored highly on all of the criteria upon which this list is based. Among them are: professional success, importance to history, how good they were in the ring, their drawing power, and the mainstream status they achieved. For wrestlers prior to 1960, how good they were reputed to be legitimately (although this is always based on rumor, and subject to debate) was also a factor.

You can argue every position endlessly (and they were argued, as this list was not based on one person's opinion, but was the collaboration of several wrestling experts). I might argue some of the picks myself, but I wouldn't say that any fall into the categories of outrageous or stupid. It is also important to remember that many of the best wouldn't necessarily have been as successful in other eras. For example, it's doubtful that the Lou Thesz of 1950 would be a star in the WWE of 2002. For that matter, neither would Andre the Giant, as the fascination with slow-moving giants is long past (as we have seen with The Big Show, a bigger and more athletic version of Andre that has been the WWF's single-biggest marketing disappointment of the past several years). Santo and Rikidozan were cultural heroes at a time when their countries needed them. What they did in their day wouldn't have any relevance to wrestling today, but each performer's influence still remains strong. The popularity of Santo in the '50s led to the popularization of the mask, which is still the most important element of Lucha Libre 50 years later. Rikidozan exuded real toughness which, in Japan, is extremely important. You can be the flashiest wrestler or the best talker around, but if the people don't think you are legitimately tough, you'll always be missing one of the most important ingredients for stardom there.

In the U.S., with the advent of Hulkamania, you had to look like a star, complete with the tan and the physique. While appearance was important beforehand, it took on far greater importance after 1984, and would exclude many wrestlers prior to this era from today's version of the sport. Certain wrestlers, such as Hogan, Flair, Austin, Rock, and Bruiser Brody would probably have been stars at any point and anywhere in the modern history of wrestling had they been given a fair chance. Today, someone who is both a great talker and great wrestler in the ring, but who has only a mediocre build, is immediately disregarded as a main-event candidate. However, on occasion, a Mick Foley comes along and changes the rules once again. No matter what you consider the necessary attributes of a wrestling superstar, someone missing one or many of those attributes will turn up and become one anyway.

The one thing I've learned about people's choices for the greatest wrestler of all time is that they are usually their favorite wrestlers when they were children. When and where you grew up plays an enormous role in picking the all-time greats in so-called legitimate sports. But in wrestling, where wins and losses are predetermined, it's even more of a factor.

Let the arguments begin.

Dave Meltzer

The Wrestling Observer Newsletter

The No. 1 insider pro wrestling publication in the world, is available either by ordering through the mail or through credit card orders. The mailing address is Wrestling Observer, P.O. Box 1228, Campbell, CA 95009-1228.

You can send credit card orders to dave@wrestlingobserver.com You can order by mail via check or money order made out to Wrestling Observer, or via cash. For credit card orders, send your name, address, phone number, credit card information and an expiration date. There will be a $1 processing fee for all credit card orders.

Rates for the Observer are (in $U.S.):

UNITED STATES
$11 for 4 weekly issues, $28 for 12, $54 for 24, $90 for 40

CANADA AND MEXICO
$12 for 4 weekly issues, $30 for 12, $57 for 24, $95 for 40

For more information about *The Wrestling Observer Newsletter* and daily wrestling news, interviews and features visit www.wrestlingobserver.com.

Ric Flair

"It is through Art, and through Art only, that we can realize our perfection."

— OSCAR WILDE, 1891

"If wrestling can be considered an art form, then [Ric Flair] is using oils, and the many others merely water colors."

— JIM ROSS, STARRCADE 1988

Rembrandt. Picasso. van Gogh. Renoir. Matisse. Dalí.

And Ric Flair.

Yes, Ric Flair.

For 29 years, the wrestling ring was Ric Flair's canvas; he used his vast repertoire of unique brushstrokes and a palette of brilliant colors to create masterpieces the likes of which pro wrestling had never before seen.

He is a wrestler of unequalled vision and artistic genius – his enduring bouts against Ricky Steamboat, Bruiser Brody, Harley Race, Terry Funk, and countless others standing as breathtaking compositions that have earned him his undeniable place in the wrestling pantheon.

He is the embodiment – the very definition – of pro wrestling: a performer of unparalleled work ethic, one of the best promo men in history, a man dripping with charisma, a master psychologist and a compelling storyteller possessing the ability to carry even the most hapless opponent to a five-star classic.

Combining a persona that borrowed heavily from "Nature Boy" Buddy Rogers and a working technique influenced by Ray Stevens, Nick Bockwinkel, Harley Race, and Dick Murdoch, Flair constructed a revolutionary ring style that changed the face of pro wrestling. His emergence as one of wrestling's biggest stars not only set the proverbial bar to unreachable heights, but also inspired a generation

I'm a kiss-stealin, wheelin dealin, jet-plane flyin, limousine-riding, sonofa-gun. I am the Nature Boy! – Ric Flair

of fans to take up the sport.

And while there were a handful of wrestlers that were better inside the ring at their peak, none could claim to be one of the top-five workers in wrestling for 20 years, and none consistently had the best matches in the world for a longer stretch of time than Flair. Wrestling over 300 times per year and appearing everywhere in the world as the National Wrestling Alliance World Champion, Flair's matches and interviews are required study material for every wrestler who has ambitions to master the art of "getting over."

Because of his ability to consistently perform at a peak level while maintaining a barnstorming travel schedule, his finest work inside the ring, although ignored by the traditional sports media, ranks alongside the legendary accomplishments of Babe Ruth, Muhammad Ali, Wayne Gretzky, Michael Jordan, and Jack Nicklaus.

It is for these reasons that Ric Flair heads our list of the Top 100 pro wrestlers of all time.

Richard Morgan Fliehr was born on February 25, 1949, in Memphis, Tennessee, but grew up in Edina, Minnesota. A wrestling fan since childhood (when he was Mad Dog Vachon's paperboy), Fliehr was an amateur wrestler while attending military prep school in Wisconsin, winning state honors in 1967. He moved on to the University of Minnesota, playing offensive guard on the football team, before losing

facing page: Ric Flair against Sting.

his academic eligibility in 1970.

A friend from college, Greg Gagne, son of the legendary American Wrestling Association World Champion Verne Gagne, suggested he try pro wrestling. Fliehr started training under Gagne, Wahoo McDaniel, and Billy Robinson in 1971. The camp proved to be too grueling for Fliehr, and he dropped out twice. Fortunately, he returned, completing his training in 1972 alongside fellow trainees Jim Brunzell, The Iron Sheik, Ken Patera, and former Olympic wrestling bronze medallist Chris Taylor.

On December 10, 1972, Ric Flair made his in-ring debut in the AWA, wrestling George Gadaski to a 10-minute draw in Rice Lake, Wisconsin. By 1973, Flair was being used as a jobber to put over Verne's son Greg.

Mike Mooneyham, a reporter and columnist with the Charleston Post and Courier. "Flair was supposed to have been in [Valentine's] seat. He [was originally] in the seat next to the pilot but Johnny said [Flair] was kind of scared to be up there. He said Flair kept whining until Johnny said 'You get in the back, I'll sit up here in the front.' So really it could have changed the future of wrestling."

Prior to the crash, Flair was being groomed by Crockett to become the promotion's top star. He also had long-term aspirations of becoming the NWA World Champion and knew that prolonged inactivity would hurt his career. In the aftermath of the accident, Flair was hospitalized with a broken back and was told by doctors he would probably never wrestle again.

After years of playing a tweener, Flair became a full-fledged heel on September 29, 1985, turning on Dusty Rhodes in Atlanta. A replay of the famous '70s angle that saw Ole Anderson turn on Rhodes, it was the birth of Flair's legendary heel run in the '80s.

Midway through 1974, Flair left Minnesota for Jim Crockett's Mid-Atlantic territory, on the recommendation of McDaniel. After bleaching his hair and winning the Mid-Atlantic tag titles with veteran Rip Hawk, Flair turned to singles competition in 1975. Developing the cocky attitude and punctuating his interviews with the "wooo" that would become his trademark, Flair began building his reputation as an exceptional heel, capturing the Mid-Atlantic Television title from Paul Jones as his star began to rise.

And then, just as quickly, his star plummeted from the sky.

On October 4, 1975, a twin-engine Cessna 310 plane carrying Flair, Johnny Valentine, Bob Bruggers, Tim Woods, and promoter David Crockett crashed en route to Wilmington, North Carolina. As they approached the runway the plane ran out of gas, cutting across treetops and a utility pole before crashing nose-first into a railroad embankment. The crash took the life of the pilot, while leaving Valentine paralyzed for life and Bruggers unable to wrestle ever again.

Ironically, had it not been for a simple twist of fate, it could have been Flair's career that ended.

"I talked to Johnny Valentine about the crash and Johnny was next to the pilot, he was up front in the plane," reveals

Despite the prognostications, Flair returned to the ring in February 1976, and started his legendary feud with McDaniel. Flair, now billing himself as the "Nature Boy," defeated Wahoo in a hair vs. title match to win the Mid-Atlantic Heavyweight Championship, establishing himself as Crockett's top heel and getting ready to set the territory on fire.

In late 1976, Flair formed a killer tag-team with Greg Valentine (drawing comparisons to the famous Ray Stevens and Pat Patterson duo) and captured the NWA World Tag titles while feuding with fellow heels Gene and Ole Anderson. After winning his first of five United States Heavyweight titles in 1977, he began feuding with Ricky Steamboat.

It was in the Carolinas, a full 12 years before their famous national run, that Flair and Steamboat were first matched against each other. Their stellar program not only sold out the territory, but also set a new standard for in-ring athleticism and match psychology in the U.S. Together, Flair and Steamboat taxed their bodies to the point of exhaustion, inextricably tying their careers together with their legendary matches.

Because of his exemplary heel-work, people started mentioning Flair as a potential NWA world champion. By 1978, Flair began his crusade for the title, accepting book-

facing page: Ric Flair takes care of Hollywood Hogan.

Ric Flair at the Richmond Coliseum before a bout against Tony Atlas.

ings in St. Louis. By appearing in St. Louis – which was considered the wrestling capital of the world – Flair's stock rose, and the bulk of the NWA promoters sat up and began to take notice. In addition, Flair became a regular in Toronto, an NWA stronghold, and began appearing on *Georgia Championship Wrestling* on TBS out of Atlanta, garnering national television exposure that bolstered his campaign to become champion.

After legendary feuds with Roddy Piper, Jimmy Snuka, Blackjack Mulligan, and Greg Valentine, Flair's dreams were fulfilled when he defeated Dusty Rhodes for the NWA World title on September 17, 1981, in Kansas City.

And with that, the Ric Flair era was born.

As champion, Flair split his time between wrestling in Mid-Atlantic and globetrotting around the world, appearing in most territories as the heel champion and feuding with Harley Race, Tommy Rich, and Kerry Von Erich. In June of 1982, he completed his first tour of All Japan as the world champion before returning to the U.S. and battling

WWF champ Bob Backlund to a double count-out.

Flair's program with Von Erich heated up as the two battled in a memorable cage match on Christmas Night in Dallas. The finish saw Terry Gordy turn heel and slam the door on Von Erich's head, costing him the title and sending the packed arena into a state of pandemonium. In the aftermath, the legendary Freebirds vs. Von Erich feud was born, giving the World Class territory three years of main event sellouts.

Flair's first reign ended on June 10, 1983, when he dropped the title to Harley Race. At the time, critics questioned the decision, but the move paid off huge dividends as Crockett proceeded to book him into a textbook world title chase program, culminating in Flair regaining the belt on November 24 at the inaugural Starrcade.

After exchanging the title with Race in a pair of hushed-up title changes, Flair dropped the belt to Kerry Von Erich at Texas Stadium on May 6, 1984. The show drew state records for attendance (32,130 fans) and gate receipts ($400,000). After regaining the title on May 24 in Japan, Flair finished out the year as champion, defeating Dusty Rhodes at the second annual Starrcade.

By 1985, the promotional war between Crockett and Vince McMahon was in full swing, as the cartel of NWA promoters came under attack by the WWF's national expansion. Crockett, by this time NWA President, cut back Flair's dates outside of Mid-Atlantic and went national himself, purchasing the WWF's timeslot on TBS for $1 million.

After years of playing a tweener, Flair became a full-fledged heel on September 29, 1985, turning on Dusty Rhodes in Atlanta. A replay of the famous '70s angle that saw Ole Anderson turn on Rhodes, it was the birth of Flair's legendary heel run in the '80s. By the end of the year, the Four Horsemen (Flair, Ole and Arn Anderson, Tully Blanchard, and manager J.J. Dillon) were assembled, quickly establishing themselves as the dominant heel clique and feuding with the top babyfaces in the company.

Crockett enjoyed banner years in 1985 and 1986 due to the exposure TBS granted him. He began to promote shows across the country with Flair engaging in a series of hot programs with Rhodes, Ronnie Garvin, and Barry Windham. The highpoint of the Flair-Windham series came on February 14, 1986, when they battled to a classic 41-minute double count-out in Orlando.

In 1987, Crockett's national push stumbled as house show attendance dropped due to Rhodes' repetitive booking and subsequent diluting of Flair as champion. By the end of the year, as the company grew deeper in debt due to escalating salaries, Crockett and Rhodes decided to stage their first pay-per-view event, that year's Starrcade, in hopes of generating some much-needed revenue.

The event, which saw Flair regain the world title from Ronnie Garvin, was a financial flop, as McMahon fired a crushing blow by staging his Survivor Series pay-per-view event on the same day and successfully strong-arming the majority of cable operators into not carrying Starrcade. Crockett took a financial bath and, nearing bankruptcy, he sold the promotion in 1988 to Ted Turner, ensuring that

shows and on television that enthralled fans. The artistry, athleticism and psychology displayed was simply awe-inspiring, as Flair and Steamboat staged, arguably, the greatest series of matches of all time.

The Flair-Steamboat feud produced no less than three match-of-the-decade candidates: the Steamboat title win in Chicago, an epic 55-minute best-of-three-falls encounter in New Orleans televised live on TBS, and the Flair title win on May 7 in Nashville, considered the greatest match of the '80s.

In one of the all-time superb angles in history, Terry Funk attacked Flair in the fallout of the Nashville match, setting up their milestone program which saw them criss-cross the U.S. in an unbelievable series of death matches.

Ric Flair in Japan promoting the first-ever combined NJPW/WCW Tokyo Dome show against Tatsumi Fujinami.

wrestling remained a staple of TBS programming.

Before that, Crockett staged the first Clash of the Champions special live on TBS the afternoon of the WWF's WrestleMania IV. Heralded as one of the best shows of the year, Flair faced Sting in the main event, carrying the young upstart to an incredible 45-minute draw. The bout won match of the year honors and instantly elevated Sting to national star status. That quickly, Flair had made his career.

By the end of 1988, tensions between Rhodes and Flair boiled over, as Flair grew irate with Rhodes' repetitive booking. Flair began to negotiate with McMahon and came close to joining the WWF, but the sale of the NWA finally went through, on the condition that Flair stayed. Flair finished the year as champion while Rhodes was quickly pushed out.

Flair was rewarded for staying as 1989 proved to be the zenith of his career. Steamboat came out of retirement and the two titans quickly renewed their legendary feud. On February 20, Steamboat defeated Flair for the world title in Chicago in a 23-minute classic, picking up where they left off in the late '70s. They continued to recreate their magic, embarking on an incredible series of matches in house

The apex of the groundbreaking feud came on November 15 with their landmark "I Quit" match, broadcast live on TBS. For 18 minutes Flair and Funk battled it out in one of wrestling's greatest brawls, set up by the late Gordon Solie's now-classic line: "Five letters. Two words. I quit."

Coming off his best year in wrestling, Flair's career was sabotaged in 1990 by then-WCW Executive Vice President Jim Herd, who thought Flair, at age 41, was too old to carry the promotion. Sting was crowned world champion after beating Flair for the strap on July 7, while Flair was demoted to supporting player. The move turned out to be a disaster as Sting faltered at the box-office. He dropped the title back to Flair on January 11, 1991.

But by this time, Rhodes, back from his WWF tenure, was named WCW booker and returned to his old ways. No finer example of his booking ineptitude exists than March 21, 1991, when Flair defended his WCW World title against New Japan Pro Wrestling's Tatsumi Fujinami. The bout saw the two battle-weary warriors put together a 23-minute classic before Rhodes' fingerprints on the match became embarrassingly evident.

After a ref bump, Fujinami tossed Flair over the top

rope. A second ref entered the ring and moments later counted a pin on Flair. Fujinami was crowned the new WCW World Champion in the middle of the ring and the 64,500 fans (paying $3,160,000) in the Tokyo Dome left the building thinking they had seen an historic title change. Little did they know that Fujinami was about to be stripped of the title by WCW for throwing Flair over the top rope. Flair returned to the U.S. with the title, and although Fujinami was billed in Japan as the world champion, Japanese fans received a taste of how diehard Mid-Atlantic fans felt after being burned countless times during Rhodes' term as booker for Crockett.

After the "Dusty Finish" debacle in Japan, Flair's career took an earth-shattering turn. Herd pegged Lex Luger as the next world champion and savior of the company. Tensions came to a head when Flair refused to drop the title unless he was given a contract extension. Herd, meanwhile, wanted to renegotiate Flair's contract to one year, with a pay-cut. Plans changed and Herd insisted Flair to drop the title to Barry Windham at a TV taping. When they realized Flair had no intention of doing so, WCW fired him and stripped him of the title. Flair retained possession of the belt – having paid a deposit on it in 1982 – and was recognized by the NWA as World Champion.

His unfathomable dismissal sent shockwaves throughout the business, as fans and critics struggled to understand WCW's decision to fire its franchise player. For the next two years, WCW fans disrupted house shows, TV tapings and pay-per-views in his absence with the now legendary chants of "We Want Flair." The chant picked up more momentum when they started taking place at WWF house shows. Such was the devotion and adulation that Flair inspired.

After being fired, Flair sat out for several months before landing in the WWF with the belt, billing himself as the "real world champion." (WCW filed a lawsuit to get the title back before Flair eventually sold it back to them in 1992.) Flair was immediately programmed with Roddy Piper, rekindling their famous Mid-Atlantic feud before eventually being set up in the dream feud that fans had wanted to see for years: Ric Flair, the flag-bearer of the NWA vs. Hulk Hogan, the indomitable star of the WWF.

The first Flair-Hogan match came on October 22, 1991 in Dayton, Ohio. The series lasted throughout the fall and into 1992, as the two icons battled it out on house shows before above-average crowds. Flair's greatest moment in the WWF

came on January 19, 1992, when he won the Royal Rumble. The match was a brilliantly booked masterpiece, as Flair entered the match at number three and lasted 59 minutes in the ring to claim the vacant WWF World Title.

Flair held the title until WrestleMania VII, when he dropped it to Randy Savage. After regaining it in September, Flair lost the title to Bret Hart on October 12 in Saskatoon, Saskatchewan. With Hart selected as the long-term champion in the wake of the steroid scandals that rocked the company, Flair was phased down. McMahon agreed to let Flair out of his contract and, after wrestling his final match in the WWF, he resurfaced in WCW in February 1993.

After Sid Vicious was fired for his scissors attack on Arn Anderson, Flair replaced him in the main event slot at Starrcade, defeating Vader for the WCW World title in his hometown of Charlotte. The entire pay-per-view was built around Flair having to retire if he didn't regain the belt and was bolstered by a series of classic interviews that played on Flair's genuine emotion. After being shunned by WCW two years earlier, Flair was world champion once again.

In 1994, Flair was set up as the top heel as he prepared for his run with Hogan. Flair dropped the title to Hogan on July 17 and finished out the year by jobbing to him at house shows and on TV. Hogan's jealousy of Flair's legendary career led to one power play after another, with Hogan burying Flair whenever the chance presented itself. After agreeing on and then backing out of dropping the title to Flair at an August Clash of the Champions, Hogan's envy led him to bury and tarnish Flair's reputation one more time, defeating him in an embarrassing retirement match in October.

But, like all wrestling retirements, it didn't last. After wrestling Antonio Inoki before 170,000 fans on April 28, 1995, in North Korea – the largest crowd in wrestling history – he returned to WCW in May after being "reinstated."

He renewed his feud with Randy Savage, now in WCW, delivering solid pay-per-view buy rates and increased house shows business, while starting the incredible turnaround the company enjoyed as a result of the NWO angle in 1996. His stay in WCW moved along nicely, for a while. He collected two more WCW World Titles before becoming embroiled in a heated dispute with Eric Bischoff that saw him suspended in 1998. After several months on the sidelines, Flair returned on September 11 at a Monday Nitro in Greeneville, South Carolina. Playing on the legitimate heat between him and Bischoff, a teary-eyed Flair delivered what is considered to

Flair dominates the match against Fujinami, Tokyo, March 21, 1991.

be the greatest interview in history. It was one of those moments that stood still in time, so fraught with sincere emotion that it is pro wrestling's equivalent of Lou Gehrig's famous "luckiest man alive" speech.

wcw failed to capitalize on Flair's newfound momentum, and for the next two years he was systematically buried by Vince Russo and a parade of bookers in one embarrassing angle after another. As wcw unraveled due to the growing backstage politics, an endless string of questionable business moves, and an obsession with booking fake shoot angles, the company began to disintegrate.

By 2001, with the company on its last legs, Time/Warner sold wcw to Vince McMahon. The last wcw event, a Monday Nitro on March 26, saw Flair face off against Sting in the main event, one day short of the 13th anniversary of their legendary encounter at the first Clash of the Champions.

The wwf bought him out of his Time/Warner contract and on November 19, 2001, Flair returned to the wwf during a raw taping in Charlotte, assuming 50 percent ownership of the company, according to the storyline. After trading jibes with McMahon, Flair wrestled his first wwf match in nine years, defeating McMahon at the 2002 Royal Rumble. The match saw Flair carry McMahon to an entertaining match, solidifying his reputation as wrestling's greatest in-ring worker to a whole new generation of fans.

In the final analysis, what Ric Flair is, in essence, is an artist. He is a gifted visionary dedicated to his sport, his craft, his profession, his trade – his art. He is a man who has used the wrestling world as his canvas – molding, sculpting, and stretching the sport in ways never thought possible. In a business where grandiose metaphors such as these are commonplace, Flair, perhaps more than anyone else, is truly deserving of them.

2

Lou Thesz

The greatest wrestler of all time. Lou always kept himself in phenomenal shape, the consummate professional and no argument about it, the all-time best. He was pro wrestling, and the flagbearer for this business throughout the world, and he leaves a void we will never be able to fill. I know he might not have liked what we're doing now, but what an honor to have him in our sport.

— RIC FLAIR

To a generation of fans he will forever be known as "The Champ."

To promoters, he was the indomitable spirit that made pro wrestling glitter – both the mortar and the bricks that held the National Wrestling Alliance together. To historians and critics, he was the greatest World Champion ever, a throwback to a time when the industry was ruled by hookers, shooters, and "legitimate" wrestlers.

But to those who knew him best, he was simply, "Lou."

Lou Thesz distinguished himself during a career that spanned seven decades with a majestic air of professionalism, seriousness, durability, and strength. Thesz was the consummate pro wrestler, possessing a complete set of wrestling skills and an arsenal of maneuvers that enabled him to wrestle his way out of trouble in any situation.

Who is the greatest pro wrestler of all time? Ask historians, longtime fans, ex-wrestlers, promoters, or anybody that has studied wrestling history. The name that inevitably pops up more often than not, with the exception of Ric Flair, is Lou Thesz.

But more important than all the world titles, and all the memorable matches, more important than being the direct link between the era of Frank Gotch, Joe Stecher and "Strangler" Lewis and the explosion of wrestling on televi-

Lou Thesz shows off his World Title belt in Mexico.

sion in the late '40s, Lou Thesz brought legitimacy and credibility to the *sport* of pro wrestling.

There was no showmanship to the ring work of Lou Thesz. Prizing wrestling skill over performing ability, Thesz was a traditionalist – far more of a wrestler than an entertainer. Blessed with great nimbleness and dexterity, excellent conditioning, and amazing reflexes, Thesz was the pinnacle of pro wrestling in his day: a true ring technician.

"Lou Thesz was perhaps the most important figure in American pro wrestling of the last 50 years," states noted wrestling historian Sheldon Goldberg. "He had an extraordinary career that was unusual both for the sheer length of his career and the fact that he spent most of his career at or near the top."

Born Lajos Tiza on April 24, 1916, in Banat, Michigan, Thesz grew up in St Louis, where he attended pro wrestling cards with his father, a shoemaker and former Greco-Roman wrestler in his native Hungary. As a teenager, he trained in amateur wrestling at the local high school, and later with the wrestling coach from the University of Missouri, before making his pro debut at the age of 16 in September of 1932 in East St. Louis, Illinois.

Thesz continued to wrestle in Tom Packs' St. Louis territory and train with Ray Steele, Ad Santel, and former Greek

Lou Thesz backstage in Toronto with the referee and Bulldog Brower on the eve of an important title match.

Olympian George Tragos, before a workout session with Ed "Strangler" Lewis in 1935 changed his life. For 20 minutes, Lewis grinded him into the mat so badly that Thesz actually retired from wrestling for a short stretch. It was only after Lewis called him and convinced him to come back that Thesz returned to wrestling. Lewis took Thesz under his wing, and taught him the art of hooking; the two forged a bond that would see Lewis become the guiding influence in Thesz' career.

By 1937, Thesz had worked his way through the ranks in St. Louis and Packs began to promote him as the new superstar of the territory. On December 29, 1937, he defeated Everett Marshall in St. Louis for the World Heavyweight title (the same title held by Gotch, George Hackenschmidt, and Thesz' mentor "Strangler" Lewis). By virtue of his win he was also awarded the American Wrestling Association World title (Boston). At only 21 years of age Thesz was the youngest World Champion in history.

Between 1939 and 1948, Thesz collected one version of

the World Title after another. Defeating such stars as Yvon Robert, "Whipper" Billy Watson, Bobby Managoff, and Bill Longson, Thesz captured three World titles in the National Wrestling Association (the precursor to the National Wrestling Alliance that was formed in 1948) and the American Wrestling Association (Montreal). By 1947, Thesz had become the dominant power in St. Louis wrestling, headlining as World Champion for the bulk of the year. Taking over the old Packs promotion with the help of his father, Thesz became engulfed in a promotional war with famed promoter Sam Muchnick over the St. Louis territory.

Soon, Muchnick was coming out on the losing end of the battle, with Thesz routinely drawing twice as many fans to his shows. Midwest promoter Al Haft sent Buddy Rogers to work for Muchnick in order to give him an edge and turn his box-office woes around. The idea worked to perfection. Rogers became an instant hit in St. Louis as the main-event feature at the Kiel Auditorium, drawing one sellout after another. This allowed Muchnick to overcome

Thesz' group and become the top promotion in the city. A year later, Thesz and Muchnick merged their groups, setting up a worked promotion vs. promotion feud. With Thesz as the in-ring muscle and Muchnick pulling the promotional strings, they helped turn St. Louis into the wrestling capital of the world.

The wrestling world changed dramatically on July 14, 1948, when a group of promoters gathered in a hotel in Waterloo, Iowa, to create the National Wrestling Alliance. Formed to avoid stringent U.S. anti-trust laws, the NWA became the most powerful cartel in wrestling, despite being divided into separate territories. The idea was for territories around North America to co-exist under the NWA banner and recognize one world champion. Promoters in the NWA came from a legitimate athletic background (hence, the selection of Jack Brisco and Gene Kiniski), and was kept away from showmen who were more about gimmick and style than substance in the ring. The crowning of men like Brisco, Kiniski, Pat O'Connor, Dory Funk Jr., Harley Race, Terry Funk, and Ric Flair in subsequent eras can be traced back directly to Lou Thesz.

With the explosion of wrestling on network television, the powerbrokers within the NWA came up with a blueprint for eliminating all the existing branches of the World title, in order to create one unified World Champion. The man they envisioned making this happen was Lou Thesz, the premier hooker of his era. Because of his mastery of the art of hooking (which allowed him to look out for himself

Thesz was a traditionalist – far more of a wrestler than an entertainer. Blessed with great nimbleness and dexterity, excellent conditioning, and amazing reflexes, Thesz was the pinnacle of pro wrestling in his day: a true ring technician.

agreed to work together, exchange talent, and look out for one another against competing promoters who would encroach upon their fiefdom and dare to oppose them. P.L. "Pinkie" George was named the first president of the NWA and Orville Brown, the reigning Midwest Wrestling Association World Heavyweight Champion, was recognized as the first NWA World Champion. Hence, the modern era of pro wrestling was born.

Six days after the National Wrestling Alliance was formed, Thesz won the National Wrestling Association World title from Longson. NWA promoters began to build towards a unification match between Thesz and Brown, with the goal of creating one undisputed World Champion.

On November 1, 1949, Brown was injured in a career-ending automobile accident – a mere three weeks before the unification match was scheduled to take place in St. Louis. Brown was forced to retire from the ring and relinquish his claim to the title. On November 27, the National Wrestling Alliance awarded the NWA World title to Lou Thesz at its annual convention in St. Louis, a decision that turned out to have tremendous historical ramifications.

The selection of Thesz as World Champion began a policy that lasted from the '50s all the way into the '80s of having the NWA World title on someone who could handle themselves in the ring in any situation. Preference was given to wrestlers who were amateur standouts in college or in the ring during potential double-crosses and carry out the wishes of promoters), Thesz was pegged as the long-term NWA World Champion. During his first reign, Thesz became the foundation upon which the NWA was built, crisscrossing the U.S. and Canada on a whirlwind tour and facing all the top stars in every major territory. He became one of the top draws in the business and among the highest paid pro athletes in the U.S.

What Lou Thesz gave the NWA, more than anything else, was credibility. Here was a hooker who was as dedicated to the craft of wrestling as anybody had ever been. Promoters' minds were at ease, never fearing that they would be double-crossed in the ring, since Thesz could wrestle his way out of a bad situation at the first scent of danger. Opponents quickly learned that you didn't mess with Thesz and that one way or another, you were going to do the job when you wrestled him. It was either that, or risk being crippled or maimed, which Thesz had the ability to do to you. From 1949 to 1956, Thesz was the "unbeatable" World Champion, disposing of one contender after another while proceeding to unify the different versions of the world title.

The first came on July 27, 1950, when he defeated Gorgeous George for the AWA (Boston) World title in Chicago. Thesz followed that up by defeating Baron Michele Leone on May 21, 1952, in Los Angeles to merge the California version of the World title with the NWA title. The match struck

Lou Thesz with the classic version of the NWA championship belt.

"Whipper" Bill Watson via count out on March 15, 1956 in Toronto. Thesz regained the title eight months later in St. Louis, opening a new chapter in NWA history. Even at age 40, Thesz was still a credible world champion due to his unmatched skill in the ring and his superb conditioning. Yet, his drawing power began to slowly wane and several NWA promoters began to set their sights on Edouard Carpentier, the biggest star in the Montreal territory, as their next champion. On June 14, 1957, Carpentier defeated Lou Thesz for the championship in Chicago after Thesz could no longer continue due to a back injury. However, the NWA stepped in once again, ruling that the title could not change hands because of an injury. Infighting over returning the title to Thesz gripped the NWA, as Carpentier remained recognized as world champion in Omaha and Los Angeles.

Perhaps one of Thesz' greatest legacies is that he was the first NWA World Champion to defend the title on Japanese soil. On October 6, 1957, Thesz traveled to Japan and wrestled Japanese icon Rikidozan to a 60-minute draw before 27,000 fans at Tokyo's Korakuen Baseball Stadium. The match aired live on network television in Japan, drawing an incredible 87.0 TV rating, the largest ever for a wrestling event. The match made Thesz' career in Japan, establishing him as a revered star among Japanese fans – a status he would enjoy for decades to come – and at the same time opening the door for future NWA World Champions to defend the title in Japan on a regular basis.

"Thesz' series of bouts against Rikidozan, the father of Japanese pro wrestling, set television records and were a cultural phenomenon," says Sheldon Goldberg. "Thesz is still a revered figure in Japan and literally helped build pro wrestling into mainstream acceptance in that country."

Having seen first-hand the kind of crowds and huge box-office business he drew while wrestling Rikidozan, Thesz went to the annual NWA convention in 1957 and tried to convince promoters to allow him to defend the title on a regular basis in Japan. The NWA promoters, realizing they'd have a much harder time getting good dates on the champion if he wrestled more often in Japan, dismissed Thesz' suggestion. Thesz, realizing that he could make more money in Japan, resigned as World Champion.

Because he had a lifelong grudge against Buddy Rogers, Thesz balked at the NWA's suggestion that he put over Rogers for the title – in fact, during his entire career, it is believed that Thesz never once put over Rogers. Instead, Thesz dropped the title on November 14, 1957, to his handpicked

box-office gold, drawing 25,256 fans paying $103,277 – the first $100,000 live gate in wrestling history.

By 1954, "Strangler" Lewis was traveling on the road with Thesz as his manager and advisor. Lewis was the set-up man, going into towns before Thesz arrived for a scheduled title bout to hype and promote the match. Thesz put off NWA promoters somewhat by insisting that Lewis be paid 3 percent of the gate on top of his regular cut. While they moaned about it, they had no choice but to pay the fee. Such was the power Thesz had.

Thesz continued to roll through opponents in the mid-'50s, headlining all across the country and defeating Buddy Rogers, Verne Gagne, Pat O'Connor, and Antonino Rocca. The lone blemish on his record came on March 22, 1955, when he was disqualified against Leo Nomellini in San Francisco. Nomellini was given the World title, ending Thesz' unbeaten streak of over 900 matches that dated back to 1948. However, the NWA quickly stepped in and returned the strap to Thesz, ruling that the title could not be won in that manner. The ruling had major historical significance as it established the pro wrestling precedent – one that lives on to this day – that titles cannot change hands on a DQ.

After six years, Thesz finally dropped the World title to

successor Dick Hutton, who ultimately flopped at the gate as champion. When Thesz returned, he cut back his schedule and went into semi-retirement. It wasn't long, however, before the NWA came knocking on his door one more time.

In 1962, rumors began to spread that Joe "Toots" Mondt and Vince McMahon Sr. – two of the most powerful promoters in the U.S., who controlled NWA World Champion Buddy Rogers – were going to break off from the NWA and start their own promotion with Rogers as their world champion. The rest of the NWA promoters began to panic, and the decision was made by Muchnick to get the title off of Rogers as quickly as possible. Muchnick convinced Thesz, living in semi-retirement in Arizona, to come back full-time and replace Rogers as NWA Champion. The NWA tried to set up a title match with Thesz, but Rogers, aware of what was going on, missed their first two scheduled matches due to "injury."

Muchnick eventually got the match in the ring, as Rogers squared off against Thesz on January 24, 1963, in Toronto's Maple Leaf Gardens. The NWA made the match a one-fall affair in order to make it easier for Thesz to win the title in the event that Rogers reneged on his promise to lose it. Legend has it that before locking up Thesz told Rogers, "We can do this the easy way…or the hard way." Even at his age, Thesz still had the ability to get the job done in the ring and "hook" anybody at any given time – a fact not lost on Rogers, who dropped the title to Thesz without incident. Twenty-five years after winning his first world title, and now at the age of 46, Lou Thesz was World Champion again. It was a testament to the longevity of his amazing career that saw him outlast contemporaries such as Everett Marshall, Steve Casey, Frank Sexton, Bronko Nagurski, Bill Longson, and Gorgeous George.

Thesz' third title reign was more of the same, as he toured the country taking on the top stars in each territory. He unified the AWA (Ohio) World title with the NWA World title after defeating Karl Gotch in 1964. Thesz' final run on top of the NWA ended on January 7, 1966, when he lost the title to Gene Kiniski in St. Louis.

Thesz continued wrestling on a part-time basis into the '70s, collecting several regional titles along the way. On August 15, 1978, Thesz won his last world title when Mexico's Universal Wrestling Alliances recognized him as its first World Champion. The following year, he wrestled a "retirement" match against Crazy Luke Graham in Atlanta. During the '80s, Thesz couldn't help but remain involved in the sport, as a promoter in St. Louis, as an active trainer, and as a guest referee in marquee world title matches. He also wrestled the occasional match on independent shows while living in Virginia.

His autobiography, *Hooker*, was lauded by historians and fans as the authoritative book on wrestling history, paving the way for thoughtful and intelligent wrestling autobiographies by Mick Foley and Tom Billington in the '90s. From 1992 to 2000, Thesz was the President of the Cauliflower Alley Club, and was the driving force behind the organization. Thesz made headlines on December 26, 1990, when, at the age of 74, he wrestled protégé Masahiro Chono on a New Japan Pro Wrestling card to become the first man to have wrestled in seven different decades.

He became a trainer for the Union of Wrestling Forces International (UWFI), a shoot-style outfit formed by Nobuhiko Takada in the early '90s. He donated his original NWA world title belt to the promotion to be used by its champion, thus giving the UWFI instant credibility. However, Thesz ended his association with the UWFI and took his belt back in 1995 when the company fell on hard financial times and were unable to pay him.

On April 11, 2002, Thesz underwent open heart surgery in Orlando, Florida. He didn't come out of the operation well, as he developed heart arrhythmia, pneumonia and needed a respirator to breathe. Word of his ailing condition spread throughout the wrestling industry as fans and wrestlers prayed for his recovery.

In the end, however, the prayers weren't enough. With his shoulders pinned to the mat, the man noted for kicking out at two and nine-tenths couldn't kick out. Lou Thesz died on April 28, 2001. He was 86 years old.

Before he died, Thesz spent the last years of his life dedicated to properly honoring his contemporaries and those who came before him in the business.

A supporter of amateur wrestling his entire career, Thesz took it upon himself to form the International Wrestling Institute and Museum in Newton, Iowa, in 1999. The museum serves as a "hall of fame" for former pro wrestling stars who were amateur standouts. Inductees include Danny Hodge, Jack Brisco, Frank Gotch, Verne Gagne, "Strangler" Lewis, and of course, Lou Thesz. And while some found it presumptuous of Thesz to induct himself into the Institute, it is typical of the man who lived life by one simple motto:

If it is to be, it is up to me.

3

Rikidozan

Riki was a great sumo star and a very good wrestler. A good friend too. Several of us went over there to get wrestling off the ground, even though various aspects of wrestling had been in Japan for centuries. I think we did a very good job in getting him over, and it helped that he was a credible athlete. We lost him far too young, but he was very instrumental in American-style pro wrestling catching on in Japan and in developing Baba and Inoki's starts in the business. I missed him quite a bit after he died.

— LOU THESZ

It was one of the largest, most lavish funerals in the history of Japan.

They came from all corners of the island nation and converged into the compound of Tokyo's Ikegami Honmon-ji Temple to pay their final respects to their beloved, fallen warrior. Hundreds of majestic flower arrangements, massive in size and brimming with brilliant, vibrant colors, decorated the walls, bearing a stark contrast to the drab, drizzling heavens above. Like his matches that aired on live network television, his funeral had drawn a huge audience, as thousands upon thousands of grieving Japanese citizens streamed into the temple all afternoon for one final glimpse.

Even in death, he could still draw a crowd.

But this time, there would be no miracle comeback. There would be no vanquishing of an American heel. There would be no heroics. This time, he was down for the count and he wasn't going to get up. Rikidozan, the ultimate Japanese hero and father of pro wrestling in Japan, was dead at the age of 39. And the whole nation was in mourning. If they had only known that their national hero, the man who symbolized Japanese ingenuity and pride as the decimated nation built itself into a social and economic power in the aftermath of World War II, wasn't Japanese at all, but was in fact, Korean.

Rikidozan dressed as a sumo wrestler.

Perhaps the single most historically important wrestler in pro wrestling, Rikidozan was responsible for bringing pro wrestling to Japan in 1954 and popularizing the sport, on his way to becoming the most famous pro wrestling star in Japan and the biggest television star ever in the industry.

Thanks to his epic battles against big, monstrous American wrestlers that were broadcast live on network television, Rikidozan became a cultural icon to millions of Japanese, while at the same time establishing television as the predominant medium during the postwar reconstruction of Japan. Rikidozan's fingerprints are all over Japanese pro wrestling, from instilling its basic tenets and booking philosophies, to handpicking the two performers – Shohei "Giant" Baba and Kanji "Antonio" Inoki – that would carry the industry through the decades following his death. His influence on the landscape of Japanese pro wrestling is immeasurable.

The emphasis on athletically credible and believable matches. The slow promotion of wrestlers up the company hierarchy. The archetypal feuds pitting wrestlers from Japan against the U.S. The focus on producing a quality in-ring product with a disdain for hokey gimmickry. Logical and compelling booking built around angles that followed a natural progression. The systematic, gradual building of

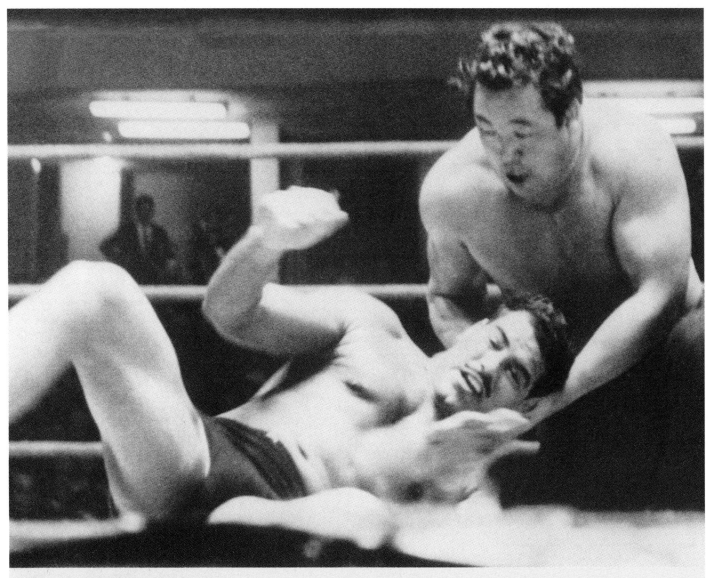

Rikidozan going in for the kill against Dara Singh.

world title feuds that stretched out over years. Live television specials airing in prime time on network television. This was the legacy that he left behind.

Rikidozan (which translates into "rugged mountain road") was born Kim Sin-Nak on November 14, 1924, in North Korea. Like his older brother, he came to Japan at the age of 15 to pursue a career in sumo wrestling, and was first dubbed Rikidozan as he made his debut in the sport. He became an accomplished sumo wrestler, earning the rank of *sekiwake* (junior champion) by age 23. He left sumo in May 1950 after he publicly complained about not being given adequate opportunity to advance through the sumo ranks. After leaving the sport, he took the name Mitsuhiro Momota to avoid prejudice in Japanese society, which still harbored negative feelings towards Koreans from before the war.

After working in construction, Momota received his first taste of pro wrestling when wrestler Bobby Bruns ran a tour of Japan featuring American stars and Japanese natives Masahiko Kimura and Toshio Yamaguchi. Bruns recruited Momota, wanting to capitalize on his name value from his sumo days, and with the help of Kimura and Yamaguchi, began to train him for pro wrestling. On October 28, 1951, Rikidozan made his pro wrestling debut at the Tokyo Memorial Hall, wrestling Bruns to a 10-minute draw. Bruns quickly signed him to a contract and brought him to Hawaii, where Rikidozan would continue to train and learn the fundamentals of the game while gaining experience in front of live crowds.

He was immediately pushed in the U.S., winning his first match on February 17, 1952, after pinning Chief Little Wolf at the Honolulu Civic Auditorium. A month later he won the Pacific Ocean Tag Team titles, with Killer Davies, from Bruns and Lucky Suminovich. He was sent to San

Francisco where he came in as a top star. After only two weeks in the territory he was wrestling in the main event, teaming with Primo Carnera and battling The Sharpe Brothers.

He returned to Japan after a year spent in the U.S. in which he only lost five matches out of 260. News of his success traveled across the news wires from the shores of the U.S. to Japan, setting up major media coverage of his announcement of the formation of the Japan Pro Wrestling Association (JWA) on July 6, 1953. The new promotion debuted on July 18, 1953, in Osaka. Meanwhile, Rikidozan continued to wrestle in the U.S., including a December 6, 1953, match in Honolulu against NWA World Heavyweight Champion Lou Thesz.

Although the JWA debuted seven months earlier, the unofficial beginning of the promotion can be traced back to a three-night stand from February 19 to 21, 1954, at the Kuramae Kokugikan in Tokyo. All three shows were sellouts as Japanese fans were eager to see the pseudo sport pit American stars against the all-conquering Rikidozan. Historically, the most important fact about the shows is that they were broadcast live on network television – the first night on NHK (a government-run network) and the second and third nights on NTV (Nippon Television Network). Television was still in its infancy in Japan in 1954. The country was still rebuilding from the fallout from the war and lagged behind the U.S. in terms of technological advancement.

All of that was about to change.

Rikidozan, teaming with Kimura, battled The Sharpes for the NWA World Tag Team titles. The match ended in a 60-minute draw, but Rikidozan became a national icon on that first televised show, as the images of him chopping down the big Americans (6'6" and 6'7", respectfully, and Canadian, actually) became emblazoned on the consciousness of a nation still smiting from the defeat at the hands of the Allied Forces ten years earlier. Thousands of fans crowded department store windows and parks that had television screens set up to watch the match live and cheer on their native son as he exacted revenge on the U.S. for leaving their nation poor and devastated.

And with that, the basic formula of Japanese wrestling was born: Rikidozan's brilliantly orchestrated morality play of Japan vs. America would become a staple of Japanese wrestling and a defining theme of Japanese network television for decades to follow. On those first three nights,

Rikidozan popularized the medium of television in Japan, creating a stampede of citizens who rushed out to purchase TV sets in order to watch and cheer him on in his future matches against other monstrous American stars.

On December 22, 1954, Rikidozan faced Kimura in a nationally televised bout to determine the first Japanese Heavyweight Champion. Despite a pre-match agreement between the two that they would work a draw, Rikidozan pulled a double-cross in the middle of the match, firing several shoot-kicks and chops and stunning a bewildered Kimura. Rikidozan eventually wore Kimura down and knocked him out to win the title. Like Vince McMahon in 1997, when he screwed Bret Hart, and Akira Maeda in 1987 when he cowardly shot on Riki Choshu, Rikidozan was the ultimate benefactor of the double-cross, using it to lay claim to the presidency of the JWA and to become the undisputed kingpin of Japanese wrestling.

The Japanese Heavyweight title was dropped a year later, making way for the All-Asian Heavyweight title, a championship Rikidozan won when he brought in Emile Czaya (the most popular pro wrestler in Singapore and Hong Kong at the time) to beat for the title on November 22, 1955.

In 1956, the JWA joined the NWA. Rikidozan had aspirations of staging the biggest pro wrestling match in history up to that point: a bout against NWA World Champion Lou Thesz. Even though he had never wrestled in Japan, Thesz was already a legend there thanks to his lengthy run as NWA Champion and for pinning Rikidozan in Hawaii back in 1953. They built towards the title confrontation slowly before staging it on October 6, 1957. Over 27,000 fans packed Tokyo's Korakuen Baseball Stadium to see the NWA World title defended for the very first time on Japanese soil. Rikidozan and Thesz battled to a one-hour draw, with neither man earning a fall.

The match aired live on network television in Japan, drawing a mind-blowing 87.0 rating, the largest TV rating for a wrestling event in history. (To put that in context, the highest-rated match in U.S. history, the infamous Hulk Hogan vs. Andre the Giant match on February 5, 1988, that aired on prime time on NBC, drew a 15.2 rating.) Thesz went back to the U.S. and dropped the world title to Dick Hutton on November 14, 1957, and then began to book himself around the world, billing himself as the NWA International Champion. He dropped the title to Rikidozan on August 27, 1958, who brought the title back to Japan where it became the most esteemed belt in the country for 14 years. (Today, the NWA International Heavyweight Title is part of All Japan's Triple Crown Title.)

Before he passed on in April 2002, Thesz looked back at his matches with Rikidozan with great fondness, acknowledging his place in wrestling history:

"Rikidozan was one of the most colorful and shrewdest men ever in the wrestling world. He was a competent sumo wrestler and parlayed that into a legendary career as a professional freestyle wrestler. He was like a god in Japan when Japan needed its heroes.... Historically, Rikidozan was the beginning of pro wrestling in Japan as we know it, and his place in world wrestling history is sealed."

The first World League tournament, the predecessor to file his teeth at the airport in front of the media and doing several classic interviews in newspapers and on television to promote the feud. Blassie was so effective that the majority of the shows were sold out before he even wrestled his first match.

On April 23, 1962, Rikidozan pinned Blassie in a bloody match that created new levels of heat in Japan. The tour ended with the final of the World League on May 24, 1962, in Tokyo, which saw Rikidozan defeat Thesz to win his fourth consecutive tournament. Two months later he traveled to Los Angeles and dropped the WWA title to Blassie.

On May 17, 1963 Rikidozan won his fifth and final World League tournament by defeating Killer Kowalski. Two days later, Rikidozan and The Destroyer were on opposite sides

Rikidozan was one of the most colorful and shrewdest men ever in the wrestling world. He was a competent sumo wrestler and parlayed that into a legendary career as a professional freestyle wrestler.

the Carnival Championship in All Japan, took place in 1959 before packed crowds and huge television audiences. In the finals, Rikidozan disposed of masked wrestler Mr. Atomic on June 16, 1959, in a bout noted for being the first blood match in Japan. While on tour in Brazil in 1960, he discovered Kanji Inoki, a 16-year-old national high school champion in shot-put and discus, and brought him back to Japan. Rikidozan trained Inoki and Shohei Baba, a former baseball pitcher, for pro wrestling and tagged them as the future torch carriers of Japanese pro wrestling.

After winning his second World League tournament on May 13, 1960, Rikidozan began teaming with Toyonobori, forming the top tag team in Japan. Together they won the All Asian Tag Team titles four times between 1960 and 1963. At the same time, Rikidozan had memorable singles feuds with Sonny Meyers and Prince Iaukea (King Curtis Iaukea). Unable to convince the NWA to give him a run as world champion, Rikidozan went to Los Angeles where he worked out a deal with promoter Jules Strongbow to buy the WWA Championship. On March 28, 1962, he defeated Freddie Blassie at the Olympic Auditorium to win his first World Title.

The stage was now set for the 1962 World League. Blassie, making his first trip to Japan, was pushed to the moon. Promoted as the Vampire, Blassie became a huge heel in Japan thanks to his biting gimmick, which saw him of the ring as they tussled for the WWA World title (Beyer had actually dropped the belt to Blassie in Los Angeles on May 10). In one of the most legendary bouts of all time in Japan, The Destroyer defeated Rikidozan in the one-fall match with the figure-four. By handing Rikidozan his first clean singles loss on Japanese soil, Beyer was set for life: he went on to enjoy a career that lasted two decades in Japan, as one of the top foreigners in the country.

Rikidozan's stunning loss traumatized Japan, setting the stage for their nationally televised rematch on May 24 in Tokyo. Their best-of-three-falls match ended in a 60-minute draw and drew the largest viewing audience in Japanese television history with a 67 rating (the 1957 match with Thesz drew an 87 rating but by 1963 more people in Japan had televisions, accounting for the larger audience and smaller rating). To this day, the Rikidozan-Destroyer bout is the most watched match in wrestling history. When asked about his legendary series with Rikidozan some four decades later, Beyer admits the Japanese legend wasn't the best of workers inside the ring; but, he was the toughest.

"The matches were very hard. He was not a good worker. He was very stiff. I fought for every hold I had. If I had a headlock, I fought for it. He chopped me on the ropes and knocked two of my front teeth out. So it was a little different working with him. He was tougher than nails, he was a tough son of a bitch and he had great balance because he was a junior sumo champion but he was not a technician and he did not have the basic knowledge of how we wrestled in the States."

On December 7, 1963, Rikidozan teamed with The Great Togo and Michiaki Yoshimura against The Destroyer, Killer Buddy Austin, and Ilio DiPaolo, in Hamamatsu. It turned out to be his last pro wrestling match. The company he kept in his personal life would come back to haunt him in the deadliest of fashions. While Rikidozan was a hero to the people of Japan, away from wrestling he was anything but squeaky clean, living a duplicitous life that betrayed the working-class image he projected inside the ring.

He was an iron-fisted authoritarian who kept his underlings in line. He had a propensity for heavy drinking and gambling. He was a friend and business partner of Nicola "Nick" Zapetti, an infamous leader of the *yakuza* (Japanese mob) who controlled the Tokyo underworld with a comprehensive network of political fixers, shifty crime bosses, corrupt businessmen, and financial con-men. Using their considerable muscle, the yakuza helped Rikidozan keep a tight rein on the wrestling industry, helping to fund the JWA and his outside businesses while squashing anybody who dared to usurp his power and authority.

After the match in Hamamatsu, Rikidozan boarded a train headed for Tokyo where he had a scheduled meeting with officials of the Japanese Sumo Association. While partying in a nightclub in the early morning of December 8, he was brutally stabbed in a mob slaying by noted gangster Katsuji Murata, a member of a crime family at war with Zapetti. The attack was cold and calculated, as Murata had urinated on the knife before meeting Rikidozan in the hallway in order to ensure the stab wound would cause an infection.

Rikidozan actually fought Murata and threw him out of the club. Instead of seeking medical attention, he took to the stage to inform the crowd he had just been stabbed, but that it wasn't serious. He then proceeded to dance and drink the night away. He ended up paying the ultimate price for his decision to shrug off the stabbing and show off for the crowd, as days later he contracted peritonitis and had to have major surgery. On December 15, 1963, Rikidozan, the ultimate Japanese wrestling hero who had fought off the challenges of so many giant American heels in the ring, met the one opponent he couldn't beat. Unable to fight off the ravages of the peritonitis, he died, at the age of 39.

Rikidozan shows off his World Title belt.

In the wake of his death, a void was left in the national consciousness of Japan. Business suffered as many major arenas, shocked by the revelations of his mob connections, closed its doors to pro wrestling. It wasn't until 1965, when the JWA elevated Giant Baba and later Inoki as the top stars, that the industry began to recover.

It's been nearly four decades since his death. And yet, Rikidozan's stature as a national icon is still prevalent in Japanese culture. Like the legendary El Santo in Mexico, everyone in Japan knows Rikidozan's name. Images of his greatest matches are shown regularly on television to this day. His gravesite is a national shrine, with fans and pro wrestlers clamoring to visit his final resting place and have their photos taken. Two of his matches still rank among the top-ten rated television programs of all time in Japan. He was commemorated on a national stamp.

In a January 2000 "Man of the Century" poll covering all aspects of life conducted by Nikkan Sports (one of the largest daily newspapers in Japan), Rikidozan came in 14th place (finishing ahead of such icons as Elvis Presley and John F. Kennedy), serving as a true testament to the indelible mark he left on wrestling and the country of Japan.

4

Antonio Inoki

The great Inoki is one of the top names in the history of Japanese wrestling, and he had impact all over the world. He fought Muhammad Ali in that famous mixed-match with ABC Wide World of Sports coverage leading up to it. Inoki brought a lot of attention of the world press to pro wrestling for this and many other matches, including the most attended wrestling card of all time in Korea I was honored to be in the main event with him in, and Ali was also there. Just one of the best and most influential in the business. Another top legend.

— RIC FLAIR

Few have understood the fine line that exists between perception and reality in pro wrestling better than Antonio Inoki.

Here was the unbeatable star of New Japan Pro Wrestling; the greatest shooter of all-time; a man who defeated Olympic judo gold medallists, karate champions, and boxers; the toughest athlete on the planet; an esteemed, elected politician; a mover and shaker in geopolitical circles.

All this, according to the perception of reality that he constructed.

And if he really wasn't the best shooter in the world; if he really wasn't tougher than the fighters from different disciplines he faced – if he only won because he was the promoter; if he became mired in political improprieties that cost him re-election to the Japanese House of the Councils; if he really didn't help liberate Japanese prisoners from Iraq prior to the Gulf War; well, those were just minor details.

But, all the cons and manipulations aside, the reality is that Antonio Inoki stands as one of the most revered stars in wrestling history, earning name recognition in Japanese society on par with Elvis Presley and the Beatles.

One of the two biggest box-office draws in the history of Japan, Antonio Inoki helped save Japanese wrestling in the '60s, when the stench of mob corruption and the gangland execution of Rikidozan still lingered. He helped to bring the industry back up to staggering heights of popularity and acceptance in Japan, becoming bigger than the busi-

A young Antonio Inoki, June, 1972.

ness itself. He was the first Japanese wrestler of world-class caliber, an expert technician who moved around the ring like a panther – with great speed and superb conditioning – inspiring a generation of teenagers to pursue careers in pro wrestling.

He was the "king of sports."

Born February 20th, 1943, in Yokohama, Kanji Inoki moved to Brazil as a teenager where he became a high school track star. Rikidozan, the father of Japanese wrestling and founder of the Japan Pro Wrestling Alliance (JWA), recruited Inoki and brought him back to Japan in April 1960 to train him. The other star prospect of the training camp was a former baseball pitcher by the name of Shohei Baba. On September 30, 1960 Kanji Inoki – given the name Antonio – and Giant Baba made their pro debuts in Tokyo. It was the birth of a rivalry that defined Japanese wrestling for decades.

After the death of Rikidozan in 1963, Japanese wrestling hit a low period. Shocked by the revelations of his gangster connections and mob control of the industry, major arenas closed their doors to wrestling. In the meantime, Inoki and Baba had been sent to the U.S. to gain experience. Upon their return, Baba was billed as the top star of the JWA and had the company built around him, while Inoki played a supporting role. Frustrated, Inoki befriended Hisashi Shinma, forming a partnership that was the Japanese equivalent of the Vince McMahon Jr.-Hulk Hogan duo, and founded

Famous match with AWA champ The Crusher taking on a young Antonio Inoki.

The first historic matchup between Inoki and Johnny Valentine.

Tokyo Pro Wrestling in 1966.

Tokyo Pro Wrestling, bankrolled by Shinma, lasted less than a year, but not before Inoki defeated Johnny Valentine in a high profile match. Because of Valentine's reputation as one of wrestling's best, Inoki's win established him as one of Japan's top stars when he returned to the JWA.

By 1967, the memories of Rikidozan's mob slaying were long forgotten and Japanese wrestling was enjoying one of its greatest boom periods. At the center were Inoki and Baba, teaming up to win the NWA International Tag Team titles four times between 1967 and 1971 while feuding with The Funks. Although Baba was pushed as the top star, it was generally known that Inoki was the better in-ring worker, evidenced by two legendary 60-minute draws against NWA Champion Dory Funk Jr. in 1969 and 1970.

With business at an all-time high, Inoki and Baba attempted a coup to take over the JWA. When it failed, Baba was welcomed back into the fold with open arms. After being fired in December 1971, Inoki, with the help of Shinma, announced the formation of New Japan Pro Wrestling. Scrambling to put together a line-up for his first show on March 6, 1972, Inoki turned to Karl Gotch.

A former JWA wrestler and trainer, highly regarded among Japanese fans and media, Gotch was brought in by Inoki as the "real" world heavyweight champion. His reputation as one of the greatest shooters of all time lent instant credibility to the promotion, as Gotch pinned Inoki in one of the greatest matches in Japanese history.

The storyline going into the match was that Gotch was in top shape while Inoki hadn't wrestled since leaving the

JWA. It not only set the stage for the rematch on October 4 – when Inoki beat Gotch to win the title – but it was also the birth of the concept of athletic legitimacy and credibility in matches, a defining tenet that became the foundation upon which Japanese wrestling was built.

Meanwhile, Baba left the JWA to form All Japan Pro Wrestling in 1972, and in a major coup secured recognition from the NWA, thus gaining valuable access to foreign talent. Realizing they needed to bring in American stars, New Japan purchased the National Wrestling Federation, a group based in Buffalo and Cleveland. After defeating Johnny Powers for the NWF World Title on December 10, 1973, Inoki toured the NWF territory as champion; but, unlike Baba, who was a tremendous draw in the U.S. dur-

closer, things began to fall apart.

In the days leading up to the match, Ali reneged on his promise to do the job. With millions of dollars on the line, both sides agreed to a shoot fight. A set of archaic rules, including no punches to the face or kicks to Ali's head, were put into place, all but handcuffing Inoki and setting the stage for a colossal disaster. Before a live audience and fans from around the world watching, the Inoki vs. Ali match was a 15-round laughable farce. Ali landed a total of six punches while Inoki lay on his back for the bulk of the snooze-fest and kicked at Ali's legs. When the match mercifully ended, it was ruled a draw and Ali was hospitalized. Most critics believe the match shortened Ali's fight career as Inoki's kicks to his legs severely affected his mobility inside the

Inoki formulated the other promotional ideology that would define New Japan over the following decades: the concept of fake shoots. By setting up worked mixed martial arts matches with fighters from other disciplines . . . Inoki endeavored to create the illusion that pro wrestlers were the toughest athletes in the world.

ing his first run, Inoki floundered at the box-office.

Around this time, Inoki formulated the other promotional ideology that would define New Japan over the following decades: the concept of fake shoots. By setting up worked mixed martial arts matches with fighters from other disciplines that were promoted as real, Inoki endeavored to create the illusion that pro wrestlers were the toughest athletes in the world. The first of these matches dates back to February 6, 1976, when Inoki defeated Willem Ruska, a gold medallist in judo at the 1972 Olympics. He won the bout by "TKO," elevating himself as the top sports star in Japan and creating the illusion that he was a serious shooter.

Inoki's next project was even more ambitious, aiming to be the biggest match in wrestling history: a bout against Muhammad Ali, the world boxing heavyweight champion and the most recognized pro athlete on the planet.

Inoki and Shinma, figuring it would be the highest-grossing event in both wrestling AND boxing history, offered Ali $6 million to do the job. Inoki saw it as money well invested: not only would he get the celebrity rub from defeating Ali, but it would also cement his reputation as an international superstar and lend further credibility to the illusionary world he was building. The match was booked for June 25, 1976, in Tokyo and beamed back to North America via closed circuit television. But as the match drew

ring, making him unable to "dance" like he once could.

The affair nearly bankrupted New Japan, as few U.S. markets outside of the Northeast agreed to promote the show. Inoki was a laughingstock and his reputation, not to mention the credibility of New Japan, was all but destroyed. A series of worked mixed martial arts matches were booked in order to restore Inoki's credibility, including wins over judo Olympic medallist Allen Coage (pro wrestling's Bad News Allen), karate champion Eddie "Monster Man" Everett, boxer Chuck Wepner and karate star Willie William.

New Japan's fortunes improved when they forged a working relationship with the WWF. Vince McMahon Sr. crowned Inoki the WWF World Martial Arts Champion in 1978, creating the illusion that Inoki was a legitimate world champion. But the illusion wasn't enough. Baba had already held the NWA World title twice. So, when New Japan and McMahon Sr. brokered a deal that would allow Inoki to become WWF Champion, he jumped at the chance.

On November 30, 1979, Inoki beat Bob Backlund in Japan to win the belt. The plan was for him to drop the title back to Backlund on the last day of the tour. But, unbeknownst to McMahon, Inoki called an audible. The rematch on December 6 was to have seen Backlund regain the title after Inoki's rival, Tiger Jeet Singh, interfered and cost Inoki the match. However, New Japan pulled a double-cross when Shinma ruled it a no-contest and declared Inoki the champion.

It turned out that Inoki was booked to work Madison Square Garden the following month. The match was to air live in Japan and Inoki wanted to ensure Japanese fans saw him defend the strap in the main event in the U.S. The WWF refused to acknowledge the title switch and a compromise was worked out to get the belt off Inoki. It was announced in Japan that the title was held up because Inoki was already scheduled to defend his Martial Arts Title in New York. Backlund and Bobby Duncum, McMahon's heel foil of the month, battled for the "vacant" title, even though Backlund was billed as champ upon returning to the U.S.

New Japan and All Japan called a temporary truce, staging a joint show on August 26, 1979. Inoki and Baba teamed up for the first time since their JWA days, defeating Tiger Jeet Singh and Abdullah the Butcher in the main event. But the relationship deteriorated once more when New Japan signed Abdullah, All Japan's longtime top heel. By doubling Abdullah's weekly salary from $4000 to $8000 – unprecedented money back then – New Japan fired the first shot in a bitter promotional war that dominated Japan during the '80s and '90s.

It also set off a succession of major stars jumping between both groups. Stan Hansen, New Japan's top foreign heel, jumped to All Japan with a similar deal to Abdullah's after months of secret negotiations with Baba. New Japan signed Dick Murdoch. All Japan inked Tiger Jeet Singh. New Japan signed Bruiser Brody. And so it went, back and forth, for most of the '80s with the biggest blow coming in 1984 when Riki Choshu jumped to All Japan.

In the early '80s, Inoki and Shinma began their biggest con: a fabricated tournament with fictitious matches from around the world, bogus point standings and top stars vying for the IWGP World title. The tournament finals on June 2, 1983, in Tokyo came down to Inoki and Hulk Hogan, the biggest draw in the world at the time. While Inoki was originally booked to go over, things went horribly awry when he learned that he had to take time off due to an exceedingly high blood sugar level.

To cover for his absence, the finish of the match was changed to another fake shoot angle that Inoki and Shinma had become famous for. Hogan knocked Inoki off the apron with a lariat in one of the most famous spots in wrestling history, rendering Inoki "unconscious" after he crashed to the floor. The match was stopped, and as a result

Hogan was declared the champion while Inoki was sidelined for three months.

During his absence, it was discovered that Shinma and Inoki embezzled company funds to bail out Inoki's failing business ventures outside of wrestling. In the fallout, Shinma resigned as booker and chairman of the board while Inoki was forced to step down as president.

On June 14, 1984, a second IWGP Heavyweight tournament final was staged with Inoki booked to go over Hogan. But if the Ali-Inoki match proved anything, it was that even the best-laid plans were susceptible to falling apart. Months earlier, Hogan became the WWF World Champion. As a result, Vince McMahon Jr. did not want his champion to job to Inoki. A compromise was worked out where Inoki would win the match via count-out after interference from Choshu. It turned out to be a huge error: fans at Tokyo's Budokan Hall became so enraged over the non-finish that they rioted for 20 minutes, setting fires inside the building.

When Choshu jumped to All Japan, it tipped the bitter promotional war in Baba's favor and left New Japan in a state of chaos. Inoki exacted a small measure of revenge on All Japan by signing Bruiser Brody to the biggest money deal in history up until that point. The company was saved as the Inoki-Brody feud rejuvenated New Japan's house show business and drew consistent TV ratings.

Inoki eventually returned to the old formula, booking himself against former world boxing champion Leon Spinks. While the Inoki match was a disaster, Akira Maeda earned rave reviews for his match against Don Neilsen, a former kickboxing champion. The calls to build the promotion around Maeda began to grow louder, as promoters saw a potential Maeda vs. Inoki match as money in the bank. It never happened, though, due to Maeda's refusal to work with Inoki and Inoki's refusal to job to Maeda.

With business in the dumps in 1989, Inoki brought in Russian Shota Chochoshivili, an Olympic gold medallist in judo, to challenge for his World Mixed Martial Arts Title. The Inoki hype-machine went to work, managing to convince the public that it would be a real match. The hype paid off as 53,800 fans, the largest crowd in Japanese history (paying a world record $2,781,000), jammed into the Tokyo Dome on April 24 to see Inoki lose his first mixed match. The success of the event paved the way for New Japan to regularly stage shows at the Tokyo Dome in the '90s.

Eventually, as Inoki's standing began to slip, he cut back his full-time schedule and went into politics. On July 24,

Antonio Inoki with NJPW booker and star Riki Choshu at a rare Keio Plaza Press Conference signing.

1989, he was elected as a member of the House of the Councils, the Japanese equivalent of the U.S. Senate. Just as he did in wrestling, Inoki, with the help of Shinma, worked his cons on the political stage. On December 3, 1990, he promoted "Peace Festival" in Baghdad, Iraq, prior to the start of the Gulf War. The event took place simultaneously to the Iraqi government releasing Japanese hostages, allowing Inoki to take credit as their savior.

But the cons eventually caught up with Inoki when Shinma went public with stories of tax evasion and political scandals – later substantiated by his former secretary. Indictments never materialized; however, the mere suggestion of impropriety cost him re-election in 1995.

By 1994, Inoki, a mere figurehead of the company he started, announced his retirement. The "Final Countdown" became a protracted series of retirement matches that dragged on for four years, allowing him to fleece fans for their sentiment and sympathy.

And of course, there was North Korea.

Inoki, working with the North Korean government, staged a pair of wrestling shows as part of the Pyongyang International Sports and Culture Festival for Peace. With wrestling as the featured event, all attendance records were obliterated, as a mind-blowing 170,000 fans packed into Pyongyang Stadium on April 29, 1995, to watch Inoki defeat Ric Flair in the main event.

Inoki continued on the "Final Countdown" before wrestling in his retirement match on April 4, 1998. After forming the Universal Fighting-arts Organization with Satoru Sayama, he turned his attentions to finding a successor to take his place as the "greatest shooter in wrestling." He found a protégé in Naoya Ogawa, a judo silver medallist in the 1992 Olympics. With Ogawa as his puppet, Inoki attempted to recreate his legend for a new generation of Japanese fans. Inoki once again regained power and returned to the old formula of fake shoots designed to prove that pro wrestlers were the toughest athletes in the world.

Times may have changed, but for Inoki, the con remains the same.

5

Hulk Hogan

Hulk Hogan is and has been the biggest name and draw in pro wrestling, no doubt about it. Hulk has done so much for this business and everyone in it, and paved the way for other wrestlers like The Rock and Steve Austin to break into mainstream movies, television and other areas. He helped shape the modern era of pro wrestling. I tip my hat to him.

— RIC FLAIR

"Hulk Hogan made pro wrestling the 'vogue' thing to watch," states long-time wrestling reporter Bill Apter. "In the past if you said, 'I'm a pro wrestling fan' you were looked upon as a weirdo or a creature from another planet. When Hogan came into prominence, being a fan of wrestling became cool."

How true; yet, how ironic then that the one performer who helped wrestling gain mainstream acceptance, taking it to startling heights of popularity and putting it in its rightful place in the strata of pop culture, is usually the wrestler hardcore fans point to as the devil incarnate.

Few can refute Hogan was a wrestler of below-average ability, that he was in the right place at the right time, that he was a man of great ego and selfishness, a master politician and manipulator, and a product of the steroid era of the '80s. The list of criticisms is endless but there can be no denying that Hulk Hogan, love him or hate him, is wrestling's greatest drawing-card of all time.

His name on the marquee during the peak of his WWF tenure was the difference between the company drawing 10,000 vs. 4,000 fans in the same city. His presence in the main event guaranteed nearly double the average attendance of AWA house shows. WCW doubled their pay-per-view buy rates and saw house show attendance increase four-fold upon Hogan's arrival in the company. Nobody in wrestling history consistently sold more tickets during a

The classic Hollywood Hogan look.

longer stretch of time or had a greater impact on attendance than Hogan.

For non-fans and outsiders, Hulk Hogan *is* pro wrestling, the only identifiable face in a culturally diverse and historically rich industry that dates back over one hundred years.

As the centerpiece of Vince McMahon's national expansion in the mid-'80s, Hulk Hogan turned the World Wrestling Federation from a regional fiefdom based in the Northeast into a global wrestling empire. With the backing of McMahon's finely-tuned hype machine, Hogan became the single most recognized wrestler in history, responsible for making "WrestleMania" and the "WWF" into household names.

Together, Hogan and McMahon tore apart wrestling's territorial system by the seams in the '80s, totally changing the landscape of the industry in North America. One by one, promotions bit the dust as McMahon, using Hogan as his heavy artillery, waged an all-out war on promoters, wiping out the territorial wrestling map. The era of the "mom-and-pop" wrestling company that made money by selling wrestling tickets gave way to McMahon's corporate-run merchandising franchise that sold t-shirts, albums, and valuable ad space to an impressive list of sponsors.

While McMahon ripped entire sections of wrestling lore from the record books and replaced it with his own revisionist prose, Hogan authored one of the most important

facing page: Hulk Hogan chokes Lex Luger.

chapters in wrestling history as he led the WWF through a dizzying, awe-inspiring box-office run.

Record attendances and gate figures. Sold out venues in major markets. The explosion of pay-per-view. Astonishing buyrates and huge television ratings. Incredible merchandise sales. Saturday Night's Main Event specials on NBC. All of these were by-products of the Hogan/McMahon colossus.

Where the traditional press once frowned upon doing stories about professional wrestlers, Hogan became the exception. Television shows and other national media sought Hogan as a guest as he parlayed his immense popularity into becoming a cross-cultural icon of epic proportions: Hollywood films, TV roles and commercials, his own cartoon series, a guest host spot on *Saturday Night Live*, the

appearing as Thunderlips in a cameo role in *Rocky III* opposite Sylvester Stallone. In between runs with the AWA, he toured with New Japan Pro Wrestling, feuding with Andre and Antonio Inoki while becoming the top foreign star in the company and the biggest international box-office draw. Back home, his world title chase program heated up as Bockwinkel, for months on end, retained his title via DQ or screw-job ending. The feud climaxed on April 24, 1983, in St. Paul, dubbed "Super Sunday" by promoter Verne Gagne, when Hogan took on Bockwinkel in match where he would lose the title if he were disqualified. Hogan ended up pinning Bockwinkel for the belt, only to have the result overturned because he had thrown Bockwinkel over the top rope earlier in the match.

The only singles match between Hulk Hogan and Bret Hart, San Francisco, 2000.

cover of Sports Illustrated, major print articles, his likeness on lunchboxes and on, and on, and on.

Hulk Hogan was born Terry Bollea on August 11, 1953, in Augusta, Georgia. After toiling in Alabama – where he first wrestled Andre the Giant – and Tennessee, as Sterling Golden and Terry Boulder, he took the name Hulk Hogan and moved on to Vince McMahon Sr.'s WWF.

It was as a heel in New York that Hogan first won notoriety. By bloodying Andre with a loaded elbow pad and body-slamming him during a 1980 TV taping, Hogan became an instant star. Long before their famous run together in 1987, Hogan and Andre barnstormed the U.S. and Canada, taking their feud to major markets and arenas outside the WWF's Northeast territory. The highpoint of their run together came underneath the Bruno Sammartino vs. Larry Zbyszko match on August 9, 1980 that drew 36,295 to Shea Stadium.

"Hulkamania" was born in the AWA, where Hogan first became a top babyface while chasing Nick Bockwinkel for the world title. The seedlings of a marketing phenomenon were first planted, as Hogan became one of the most popular stars in the business during the historic feud.

In 1982, he had his first taste of Hollywood celebrity,

Hogan's career in Japan peaked on June 2, 1983, when he faced Antonio Inoki in the final of the tournament to crown the first IWGP Heavyweight Champion. For two years, Inoki announced fictitious match results and bogus point standings of a worldwide tournament for the express purpose of building himself up as world champion. Ironically, it is Hogan who ended up winning the title, his first world championship (seven months before winning the WWF World title). Inoki had to take time off due to an exceedingly high blood sugar level and booked a fake shoot angle to explain his loss. During the course of the match in Tokyo, Hogan clotheslined Inoki off the apron, sending him crashing to the floor in an "unconscious" heap. The match was stopped and in the ensuing chaos, Hogan was crowned the new champion.

In late 1983, he secretly jumped to the WWF, lured by a big money, guaranteed contract from Vince McMahon Jr. and leaving Gagne to rebuild months of planned storylines and booked shows. It was arguably the most important jump in history, as Hogan's defection signified the first shot fired by McMahon in the fabled wrestling wars that would see him take the WWF national.

On January 23, 1984, Hogan defeated The Iron Sheik before a sold-out Madison Square Garden to win his first of six WWF world titles. With Hogan as its world champion, McMahon's company became a national entity, steamrolling one territory after another in the process. Hogan was promoted as the unbeatable babyface and became the showpiece of the WWF, taking on the top heels in the company. His February 18, 1985, match against Roddy Piper, billed as "The War to Settle the Score" was televised live on MTV and drew an impressive 9.1 rating. WrestleMania I further cemented Hogan's status as a national icon, receiving the celebrity rub from teaming with Mr. T (the biggest TV star in the country at the time) that sent him skyrocketing towards superstardom.

Hogan led the WWF through banner years from 1984 to 1987, headlining major shows across the U.S. and Canada. In 1986, he broke the wrestling attendance record, drawing 64,100 fans (paying $800,000) for a revenge match against Paul Orndorff at Toronto's CNE Stadium on August 28. The record stood for seven months before Hogan faced Andre the Giant in the main event at WrestleMania III.

Seven years after their initial feud in the WWF that set the wrestling world on fire, Hogan and Andre produced box-office magic. With McMahon perpetuating the fairy tale that Andre was undefeated and fans asking themselves whether or not Hogan could hand him his first loss, WrestleMania III was the single most successful show in wrestling history.

Over 78,000 fans (forever recorded as 93,173 by McMahon mythology) filed into the Pontiac Silverdome to watch Hogan beat Andre in the ultimate showdown. When the smoke cleared, the WWF had drawn in $1,599,000 in gate revenues (the first million dollar live gate in wrestling history), another $5.2 million in close circuit revenue, and set the pay-per-view buy rate record with an 8.0.

But it didn't end there.

The rematch came on February 5, 1988, as part of a prime-time special on NBC, the first live wrestling special on network TV since the era of Gorgeous George. Drawing a 15.2 rating (still the most-watched pro wrestling show in U.S. history), Hogan dropped the title to Andre after the famous twin referee finish.

Over the next few years, the Hogan locomotive continued to chug down the track at an incredible pace, featuring the explosion of wrestling on pay-per-view; starring roles in Hollywood films; memorable feuds against Randy Sav-

Hulk Hogan strangles AWA world champ Nick Bockwinkel.

age, Ted DiBiase and Ric Flair; numerous WrestleMania main events before huge crowds; and five more world titles.

But by 1992 the train had run out of steam and was derailed. Where his drug-enhanced body was once his greatest asset, it was now his greatest detriment.

The WWF became mired in steroid and drug scandals brought to light by New York Post columnist Phil Mushnick, forcing McMahon to introduce stringent drug testing that made it impossible for him to push the steroid monsters that built up his company in the first place. Hogan only made matters worse when he lied about his steroid use during his infamous appearance on the *Arsenio Hall Show*.

In the fallout, Hogan went on a hiatus to temper the growing media and government scrutiny bearing down on the WWF. He eventually returned and won the WWF world title, but his comeback was a financial flop, forcing McMahon to take the company in an entirely new direction. After

Hulk Hogan and Ken Patera lock hands as Bobby Duncum Sr. looks on.

close to a decade together, the duo that forever changed the industry parted company.

McMahon wanted him to drop the title to Bret Hart, but Hogan, exerting the authority granted to him by a creative control clause in his contract (the same clause that allowed him to literally take control for the bulk of his tenure in the WWF), nixed the idea. In the ultimate display of the power he had within the company, he handpicked Yokozuna as his "successor," dropping the title to him on June 13, 1993, before wrestling his final match in the WWF in August.

After a brief stopover in New Japan, Hogan found new life in WCW on June 11, 1994, inking the richest deal in wrestling history. Days before making his in-ring debut in WCW in July, Hogan was summoned to testify in McMahon's federal trial for steroid possession and distribution.

Hogan made a deal with the government, agreeing to testify that McMahon supplied him with steroids in exchange for prosecutorial immunity. However, during the trial Hogan testified that McMahon never forced him to take steroids and that his use was his own personal choice.

Over the course of questioning he also admitted that he started using steroids in 1976 and that he lied about his use on the *Arsenio Hall Show* and in the press. While McMahon was acquitted later that month, Hogan's reputation was soiled.

On July 17, 1994, Hulk Hogan, the star synonymous with the WWF, made his in-ring debut in WCW against Ric Flair, capturing the World Heavyweight title. While his presence in WCW gave Eric Bischoff the backing to convince the Turner executives to launch Monday Nitro, the same Hogan magic wasn't there, as fans quickly grew tired of his static personality and backstage politics.

Returning to his early days in the business as a rule-breaker, he reinvented himself as "Hollywood" Hogan in 1996, turning heel in one of the most unforgettable angles in wrestling history. Hogan was reborn as the leader of the NWO, finding new shelf life as a top-drawing heel and helping to turn the company around and lead it through its greatest run of box-office business ever.

But just as quickly as WCW reached never before seen

heights of profitability, it was over. The company became diseased thanks to backstage politicking and self-indulgent maneuvering by Hogan and others, looking to hold onto their top spots at all costs. In the aftermath of the McMahon-Bret Hart screw job in Montreal, Hogan and Bischoff became obsessed with booking fake shoot angles that attempted to fool everybody in the company, but which ultimately did nothing for WCW's bottom line.

In 1998 Hogan and Kevin Nash "worked" a backstage feud, which led to Hogan's "retirement" after Nash became booker. It was an angle designed to improve company morale, as Nash became the company hero to the under-card workers who by this point were sick of Hogan. As it turned out, the angle had catastrophic consequences.

The stage was set for Hogan to take time off and then return months later to regain the title and finish the fake shoot angle. Russo, however, had other ideas, as he had set up the angle as a double-cross to get Hogan out of the company. Hogan, therefore, was unknowingly an accomplice to the fake angle that led to his departure from the company. A month later he filed a very *real* lawsuit against WCW for defamation stemming from Russo's speech.

It was this morbid obsession with fake shoot angles, coupled with the backstage politics and the refusal by Hogan and the older headliners to put over younger talent in order to create the next generation of superstars, that led to the demise of the company.

After sliding down a slippery slope, WCW was bought

"Hulkamania" was born in the AWA, where Hogan first became a top babyface while chasing Nick Bockwinkel for the world title.

With newfound power as booker, Nash ended Bill Goldberg's winning streak at Starrcade to win the WCW world title. One week later, Nash lost the belt to Hogan in the infamous one-finger touch title change at the Georgia Dome, all but destroying the Atlanta market as the 38,809 fans in attendance (paying $930,735) were burned once again. And while the Nash-Hogan feud was a work that allowed Nash to win the belt and then drop it to Hogan without doing a job, it totally killed the value of the WCW title.

The same fake retirement and one-touch title change angle was inexplicably repeated with Sting the following year in October with Hogan laying down for the three-count. While it was the talk of wrestling fans on the Internet and fooled the boys in the company, it did nothing for business. All of this, however, was just a precursor to the famous fake shoot angle between Vince Russo and Hogan that, ironically, led to Hogan's departure from WCW.

In the days prior to Hogan's match on pay-per-view with then-WCW World Champion Jeff Jarrett on July 9, 2000, rumors were spread that Russo wanted Jarrett to go over but that Hogan refused to job. When both got in the ring, Russo came out and told Jarrett to lie down for Hogan. After pinning Jarrett, Hogan delivered a speech before the live crowd bad-mouthing Russo. The angle was furthered along later in the show when Russo came out and delivered an expletive-laced diatribe against Hogan.

out by Vince McMahon in the spring of 2001.

The corpse of WCW hadn't even gone cold before Hogan signed with the WWF in January 2002, returning home to the site of his greatest triumphs and fame. His career had officially come full circle as he feuded with The Rock – the Hulk Hogan of his era – following one of the greatest interviews and mic performances of his entire career, leading up to their WrestleMania 18 main-event match.

Over 68,000 fans packed into Toronto's SkyDome to watch Hogan, wrestling's biggest icon of the '80s, clash with The Rock, the superstar of the new millennium. Although the match left a lot to be desired athletically, it was, nonetheless, an epic battle as the throng of rabid wrestling fans cheered every single move Hogan made in the ring, all but blowing the roof off the SkyDome. In the end, Hogan laid down for The Rock and did the job.

The following month, the comeback was completed when he defeated Triple H to win his sixth WWF World Heavyweight title, 18 years after his first title reign began.

At the age of 48, he proved what was once old could be new again, introducing himself to a new generation of WWF fans who had only heard of Hulkamania. And while the memories of his role in the demise of WCW lingered on, they could not disrupt Hulk Hogan's rank as the premier in-ring innovator in sports entertainment.

6

Andre the Giant

The Big Man. Andre was one of the all-time biggest draws ever in this industry. One of the greats who drew tremendous crowds wherever he went, and a very tough man always in that ring. Andre was a legend inside and outside the ring, and the people loved him. The wrestlers loved him too. He did a lot for wrestling when he went on The Tonight Show *in the seventies, one of the first mainstream appearances for a modern-era pro wrestler.*

— RIC FLAIR

"Bodyslam me, boss."

Killer Kowalski stood in stunned silence in the middle of the ring after Andre the Giant mumbled those words to him.

Moments earlier, Kowalski scaled the turnbuckle to lunge at Andre, only to have the gargantuan superstar grab him off the top rope like a rag doll. Andre clutched Kowalski with his meaty paws and effortlessly tossed him to the other side of the ring, sending him crashing to the canvas in a heap of twisted flesh and aching limbs. As Andre absorbed the applause and adulation of the thousands of fans who had packed into the building that evening, Kowalski slowly picked his battered, withered body off the mat. Andre walked over to him and in a guttural, yet hushed tone, whispered those three simple words that would remain ingrained in the consciousness of Kowalski for over two decades.

"He came over and whispered 'Bodyslam me, boss,'" recalls Kowalski of the match from the mid-'70s. "I took a moment and said, 'Bullshit.' I would have got a hernia. He said it again so I crotched him and he lifted himself and the people applauded me. They thought I did all the work and slammed him. That's the kind of guy he was. If you let him do things to you, he would let you do things to him."

Andre may have been the most feared man in the busi-

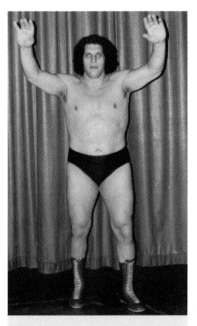

Andre at the Hampton Coliseum in Hampton, Virginia. Andre would go on this night to team with Chief Wahoo McDaniel in a tag bout against the Anderson Brothers.

ness during a storied 28-year career, but the Bunyanesque Frenchman that became known simply as "The Giant" also had an enormous capacity for generosity and humility.

Born Andre Rene Rousimoff on May 19, 1946, in Grenoble, France, he lived the life most people dream of...

A career that took him to every corner of the globe. More money than he could spend. Women hanging all over him. And the reverence of legions of fans.

To promoters, Andre the Giant meant money in the bank. During the '70s, he was unquestionably the most famous pro wrestler and one of the most recognizable sports figures on the planet. At his peak, he was the top box-office draw internationally in the wrestling world and was among the highest paid athletes in pro sports. He was the larger-than-life superstar that traveled the world several times over and headlined in every promotion there ever was. With his monstrous, hulking size, Andre was reputed to be among the largest, most powerful men in the world. Yet, the price of his fame and superstardom was a costly one, one he paid for dearly every day of his wrestling career. It was a price that, occasionally – mostly during quiet and introspective moments – reduced him to a quivering mass of emotions, as he told friends that he just wanted to be "normal," at least for one day.

Andre press slams NWA champ Harley Race as Moondog Mayne and Masa Saito watch.

Andre was born with acromegaly, an odd glandular disease that stems from chronic over-secretion of growth hormone by the body. He eventually became a "victim" of his own body, as his hands, feet, and head thickened at an alarming rate once he could no longer grow in height. His limbs, body, and face would grow to distorted, freakish proportions. Bogged down by a grueling travel schedule as his career progressed, his joints began to creak under the constant strain of his massive bulk. As years passed, the aging process began to accelerate, and doctors told Andre he would never live to see his 50th birthday.

But that did little to dim his spirit. Living each day to the fullest, he was the brightest, most luminous figure in a constellation full of wrestling superstars.

French Alps. Given the name Jean Ferre and billed as 7'4" and 385 pounds, Andre was an instant hit in Montreal, wiping the mat with opponents in handicap matches and teaming with Carpentier in three-on-two bouts. His rare singles matches came against Kowalski and Don Leo Jonathan, the two biggest, most monstrous heels in the territory at the time. His matches against Kowalski set the territory on fire as they wrestled before packed houses all over Quebec and Northern Ontario. Kowalski, no lightweight himself at 6'7" and 280 pounds, recalls being in awe of Andre's size.

"He would go to grab me by the neck and my head would disappear in his hand. When I was in the ring and I tried to grab him, the people on the other side of the ring couldn't

left: Andre against Bobby Heenan and Ken Patera. *middle:* Billy Graham and Andre arm wrestling on Thanksgiving night at the Norfolk Scope in Norfolk, Virginia. Andre won the arm wrestling contest but took a terrible beating afterwards at the hands of Graham with some help from the Anderson Brothers (Gene & Ole). *right:* Hogan and Andre embrace beside the referee, Lord James Blears.

He was, simply, the "Eighth Wonder of the World."

Andre's actual height and weight have been a constant subject of conjecture and wrestling mythology, further lending to his legend and mystique. Billed as 7'4" and 520 pounds for most of his career, Andre's true height was believed to have been between 6'9" to 6'11". A 1984 photo of Andre being "dwarfed" while standing next to a 7'2" Wilt Chamberlain supports this belief. During his physical prime, he weighed 350 pounds, but he was believed to have ballooned up to as much as 550 pounds at the time of his death in 1992 – due to the combination of the ravages of acromegaly and his prodigious ability to eat and drink.

Born into a family of five children, Andre left home at the age of 12. By 1964, already 6'7" and weighing 245 pounds of solid muscle, Andre had his first pro match in France at age 18. After wrestling six years in Europe as Andre "The Butcher" Rousimoff and Geant Ferre (after a mythical French storybook lumberjack), he moved to Montreal in late 1970 to seek fame and fortune in North America.

As the worked storyline went, Edouard Carpentier brought him into the territory after discovering him in the

even see me. I just disappeared. That's how big he was."

A May 1972 match promoted as the "Battle of Giants," between Andre and Jonathan – billed as 6'9" and 320 pounds (although he was closer to 6'5" and 285) – sold out the fabled Montreal Forum to the tune of 16,000 fans, breaking Canada's indoor wrestling attendance record. Andre was a box-office smash. But the magic didn't last long. The following year, Montreal went into a tailspin. Seeing Andre crush his opposition week after week, fans started to believe that there wasn't anybody that could beat him. Overexposure had all but killed his drawing power in Montreal. However, promoters in the U.S. were now getting in line to procure his services.

Frank Valois, a star in France during the '60s, became Andre's steward and road mate. Charged with managing Andre's career, Valois set up a meeting with Vince McMahon Sr. to broker a deal over Andre's bookings. McMahon changed his name to Andre the Giant and, realizing that overexposure had killed him in Montreal, he sent Andre on a globetrotting tour of one-nighters in every territory and city allied with the NWA, WWWF, and AWA.

For ten years, with McMahon Sr. pulling the strings, Andre was booked on a dizzying itinerary, appearing in every major territory for every name promoter in the business and in every imaginable port of call around the world: the U.S. Canada. Japan. Australia. Europe. New Zealand.

He became the hired gun that promoters fought each other over to bring into their territories in order to bury their competition. It was his name they wanted on the marquee when booking a major event. He broke attendance records everywhere he went as fans, reading about him and seeing photos of his exploits in wrestling magazines, packed arenas to see the docile Giant.

As the '70s progressed, Andre was booked more and more in singles matches against the top heels in each territory.

out. The owner came out and told him 'Don't ever come back here again.' He just ate and ate and emptied dish after dish until he emptied everything out."

Cases of wine and brandy were guzzled down with the greatest of ease. Beer was his beverage of choice: he was noted for being able to swig back 50 bottles without feeling tipsy. One classic road story has him drinking 119 bottles in one sitting before passing out in a hotel lobby. Unable to move him, somebody threw a piano cover over him and let him sleep off his hangover.

Because of his sheer size and strength, he was also generally feared by most within the business. It became an understood, unspoken edict among the boys in the locker room that you didn't mess with Andre. Wrestlers looking to

Andre was born with acromegaly, an odd glandular disease that stems from chronic over-secretion of growth hormone by the body. He eventually became a "victim" of his own body, as his hands, feet, and head thickened at an alarming rate once he could no longer grow in height.

While remembered for his matches against massive, villainous heels like "Superstar" Billy Graham, Big John Studd, and a young Hulk Hogan (then billed as Terry Boulder and Sterling Golden), Andre's most memorable feud was with Ernie Ladd, a former all-pro lineman in the NFL (who stood 6'9" and weighed 320 pounds). Billed as "The Battle of the Giants," the feud sold out buildings across the U.S. and drew massive gates.

It was during his days with Valois that wrestling mythology waved its magic wand and expunged his record clean of any losses. For years, Andre was billed as being undefeated – never having suffered a pinfall loss. Promoters, knowing a good hook when they saw one, played into the con and booked him in angles against heels that threatened to end the fictitious winning streak. One by one, Andre knocked off all comers, keeping the streak alive for another day until the next challenger stepped up to the plate.

And so the legend and mystique grew.

One thing promoters didn't have to invent was Andre's propensity for food and drink. Where fact and fiction meet is somewhat blurred but there are endless accounts of classic road stories relating Andre's insatiable appetite and capacity for drink.

"He was at a restaurant buffet one time," recalls Kowalski. "He paid six dollars. All-you-can-eat. He emptied the place

embarrass him in the ring in order to make a name for themselves were quickly brought down to reality by a crashing punch from the Giant. Boozy patrons who challenged wrestlers in bars fled for their lives when they saw Andre with them.

During the late '70s, he split his time between the U.S. and Japan, where he was the top monster heel. He displayed amazing stamina and mobility for his size as he wrestled AWA World Champion Nick Bockwinkel to an entertaining 60-minute draw. Matches against Harley Race showed he was much more than a plodding worker; he also had a very good ring psychology.

And he was everywhere, becoming part of mainstream pop culture: An appearance on *The Tonight Show*. A role in the '70s TV series *The Six Million Dollar Man*, playing a character named "Bigfoot." His photo in major newspapers. A full-length, feature article in the December 21, 1981, issue of Sports Illustrated. A prominent role in director Rob Reiner's *The Princess Bride* in 1987. And all the while, he remained one of the most famous wrestlers in the world.

By 1981, now managed by former referee Frenchy Bernard, Andre's weight ballooned to over 500 pounds. Traveling began to grind away at him. He began to slow down in the ring, and the freight of his enormous mass began taking its toll on his pressured joints and bones. As the simplest tasks became increasingly difficult for him because of his size, Andre turned to food and alcohol more and more as a way of dealing with the aches and pains.

It was from this point on that his career began to slowly spiral downward.

He suffered a broken ankle when he collapsed to the floor while getting out of bed, further hindering his mobility. By 1982, Hogan had became the hottest star in the industry thanks to his runs in the AWA and Japan, eventually unseating Andre as the top draw in the world and most famous star in the business. In 1984, with the national wrestling war in full in tilt, Vince McMahon Jr. put an end to his appearances in other territories and booked him solely in the WWF, while allowing him to continue working tours for New Japan.

In April of 1986, Andre, now weighing in excess of 500 pounds, was involved in one of the most famous matches of his career against Akira Maeda in New Japan. Maeda had just returned to the company after a two-year stint with the original UWF, a promotion that staged worked "shoot matches." Having become a cult star by working a submission style, Maeda had developed a disdain for the phoniness of pro wrestling and often failed to adhere to the spirit of co-operation required in worked matches with American stars. When Andre and Maeda were put in the same ring in a singles match, the result was a clash of egos that resulted in one of the most bizarre chapters in Japanese wrestling history. Andre, unimpressed with Maeda's shooter gimmick, no-sold his offense and began going for his eyes. The match quickly dissolved into one of the most surreal spectacles in pro wrestling history, as Maeda threw a succession of shoot kicks to Andre's battered knees. Andre no-sold them but eventually fell to the mat after losing his balance. Knowing he'd be dead in the water if Andre – unable to get up off the mat – got a hold of him, Maeda just circled around the incapacitated Giant until Antonio Inoki rushed in and stopped the match – with no storyline explanation given.

In 1987, Andre the Giant would participate in the biggest money feud of his career. After turning heel in January, Andre was set up in the famous program with Hulk Hogan that culminated at WrestleMania III on March 29. Even in his condition – immobile and decrepit – Andre proved he still had box-office legs, at the very least. A record crowd of over 78,000 fans (93,173 according to wrestling mythology) packed into the Pontiac Silverdome to watch Hogan

become the first man to pin Andre (or so the WWF hype machine told it).

Sadly, Andre was a mere shell of his former self when the event took place. Gone was the young behemoth that amazed fans in Montreal by throwing dropkicks. In its place: an aged, hunched-over giant.

Nonetheless, the show was a financial windfall for the WWF as it drew the largest paid crowd in history, raking in wrestling's first million dollar live gate ($1,599,000) – including an additional $5.2 million in closed circuit revenue – and set the all-time wrestling pay-per-view buy rate.

The rematch came on February 5, 1988, during a live, prime-time special on NBC, the first live wrestling special on network TV since the days of Gorgeous George in the '50s. Drawing a 15.2 rating (which still holds the record as the most watched pro wrestling show in U.S. history), the program saw Andre "win" the title from Hogan with the help of the famous twin referee finish – an angle that will go down as one of the most memorable in wrestling history.

By 1990, his last year in the WWF, he was a babyface again, but was barely able to wrestle. He worked short matches and had to hold onto the ring ropes for dear life in order to keep his balance. His career in the U.S. over, Andre returned to Japan, where he had ruled the rings as the country's top heel for 14 years. But this time, back with All Japan Pro Wrestling, he was reduced to working mid-card comedy matches with Giant Baba. The man who once struck fear in the hearts of Japanese fans now drew only their sympathy. Andre competed on three tours per year for All Japan between 1990 and 1992 before wrestling his final match on December 4, 1992, at Budokan Hall.

Twelve days after burying his father, who passed away in France, Andre the Giant, one of wrestling's biggest stars, was finally put down for the count. He died in his sleep from heart failure on January 27, 1993. He was 46. His funeral at his 200-acre ranch in Ellerbe, North Carolina, was proof of his lasting impression on those closest to him. Having touched the lives of so many during his career, he reduced several of the approximately 200 guests – among them Hulk Hogan, Vince McMahon, Randy Savage, and Pat Patterson – to tears.

While he may have used the term teasingly to communicate the love and friendship he felt for his closest comrades, there can be no doubt that Andre the Giant himself was the true "boss" of the wrestling world.

Andre the Giant ready to whip Ric Flair out of the corner at the Richmond Coliseum.

7

El Santo

Santo Senior was one of the first Mexican wrestling stars to break into movies, as many had done in this country. He was a smaller athlete from what I've seen (which helps in that style), by American pro wrestling standards even at the time; but he accomplished quite a bit and became a very big mainstream star. There have been some very good athletes there, and he was one of the first in wrestling. I read where he was buried in his wrestling costume and mask which really says something. He was certainly revered by the people there for many years.

— LOU THESZ

On June 28, 1934, Rodolfo Guzmán Huerta, all of 17 years old, made his pro wrestling debut as Rudy Guzmán, teaming with older brother Miguel. At the time, very little was made of the event. After all, wrestling's popularity in Mexico was exploding at the time and Guzmán was just another green, awkward rookie. Nobody could have imagined that he would go on to enjoy a 40-year career and capture the hearts of the nation of Mexico as the masked El Santo (translated into English as The Saint), the most beloved and revered wrestler in history.

It seems odd that a masked wrestler could have such a lasting effect on an entire country, but then, El Santo was far from your average wrestler.

The story of El Santo's incredible career is directly tied to the earliest days of *Lucha Libre* (the Spanish word for pro wrestling which translates into free-fighting in English). In 1933, a Mexican promoter by the name of Salvador Lutteroth brought pro wrestling to Mexico after seeing it while on a trip to Texas. With its fast-paced, athletic style, pro wrestling quickly became one of the biggest attractions in Mexico.

Guzmán was born on September 23, 1917, in Tulancingo, Hidalgo, to Jesús Guzmán Campuzano and Josefina Huerta Márquez, the fifth of seven children. As a child, his family moved to Mexico City, where he became enthralled with

Santo unmasks Gran Marcus as Santo's partner Blue Panther lies on the mat.

Lucha Libre. He trained to become a pro wrestler at a local gym with his brother and made his debut as a *rudo* (Spanish for "heel wrestler"). However, he failed to gain notoriety early on.

In 1934, an American wrestler debuted in Mexico under a black, leather mask. Lutteroth dubbed him El Enmascarado, "The Masked Man." Soon, Lutteroth introduced other masked wrestlers into Lucha Libre, creating super heroes and villains for audiences to identify with. The move was a huge success and the modern era of Mexican wrestling was born.

Guzmán soon recognized the potential of this trend. He put on a mask and called himself Murcielago II (The Bat), but quickly dropped the name when the wrestler playing the original Bat character complained. Needing a new name and gimmick, Guzmán took the name El Santo from a character in Alexandre Dumas' novel *The Man in the Iron Mask*, and donned a long, flowing silver cape and what would become his trademark silver mask.

Still wrestling as a rudo, El Santo debuted on July 26, 1942, in Mexico City, in an eight-man Battle Royal where the last two men in the ring went on to wrestle in a regular two-out-of-three falls match. After splitting the first two falls with Ciclón Veloz, Santo was DQ'd for attacking the referee. And with that a career was born that would see El

facing page: Santo against Black Shadow.

Santo become a staple of Mexican pop culture and a national treasure for over four decades.

"He was such a phenomenon because he touched so many people," says broadcaster Mike Tenay. "There were so many people that identified with Santo and I think that's one of the things that made him the cultural icon he was. He was among the first to take the persona of the masked wrestler and to really gain an identity with it."

Masked wrestlers are not all that uncommon in American wrestling. There have been a host of them over the years. But when they leave the arena after their matches are over, they slip out of character and assume their normal identities and live their regular lives. However, as soon as Guzmán put on that silver mask his life literally changed.

ure for my dad to be a part of it in some way. They went out there and busted their butts and made themselves into something big."

As he grew in popularity as a wrestler, Santo quickly went from a cult figure to a national hero who crossed over into every imaginable form of Mexican culture. In 1951, a weekly comic book was created based on El Santo. The comic was a million-dollar seller as the people of Mexico followed the superhero exploits of El Santo each and every week.

And then the film industry came calling. Mexican cinema was looking for a new film formula to bank on. Producers saw the popularity of Lucha Libre and its masked wrestlers and wanted to capitalize on it. Santo was immedi-

In 1950, Santo embarked on a memorable feud with the Black Shadow, climaxing with their landmark November 7, 1952, bout where Santo beat Shadow in a mask vs. mask match. Considered one of the most historically important moments in Lucha Libre history . . .

He was no longer Rodolfo Guzmán Huerta; he was El Santo.

"He didn't have a secret identity. He was always El Santo," offers David Wilt, a noted El Santo expert. "He wasn't just a fictional character, he was an actual person. He wasn't like George Reeves playing Superman and making a few public appearances, he was actually El Santo."

Santo won his first title on February 21, 1943, when he defeated Veloz to capture the National Welterweight title. By the end of his career, Santo would go on to win four National Middleweight titles, two NWA World Welterweight titles, the NWA World Middleweight title, two National Tag Team titles with Rayo de Jalisco, and the National Light Heavyweight title.

While El Santo was unquestionably the most popular and recognizable Lucha star, he was not as good a worker as Gori Guerrero, whom many consider to be the best Mexican wrestler of all time. Guerrero and Santo teamed in the '40s and '50s as La Pareja Atomica (The Atomic Pair), setting Mexico on fire while feuding with the top babyface tag teams of the time. And although Santo was more popular, Guerrero was by far the better wrestler.

"They grew a really special relationship," says son Eddie Guerrero, a former WCW and WWF star. "They were real good buddies and my dad had nothing but respect for him. When Santo made his name for himself it was a real pleas-

ately cast as a crime-fighting superhero and the Lucha Libre horror genre was born.

"In the '40s and '50s, he was really popular with the wrestling and the comic book," explains Wilt. "But film really brought it to a whole new level for fans who were not wrestling fans and who didn't read comic books. Now, he'd reached the level where he really was a major figure in Mexican popular culture."

As Lucha Libre enjoyed its golden years through the '40s and '50s, the basic struggle in the matches was defined by the battle between the *technicos* (Spanish term for "babyfaces") and the rudos.

This struggle became part of Mexico's cultural make-up in the '60s as more and more Lucha Libre storylines mirrored the real-life corruption and hardship on the streets of Mexico City. Wrestlers like Santo, who were portrayed as law-abiding, honest citizens fighting the evil, corrupt rudos helped to ease the despair, balancing the scales of justice in favor of the working man.

"There are few figures like El Santo who have historically dominated the most popular end of the popular culture spectrum," says David William Foster, a Spanish language professor at the University of Arizona and an expert on Mexican cinema and literature. "In a society like Mexico there is the need for cultural heroes. The idea of someone who is going to avenge the wrongs of the world. There's a lack of a sense of justice and order in society. El Santo caught on and he was absolutely venerated in Mexico for decades."

From 1958 up until his last movie in 1982, Santo starred in 54 films. Extolling justice and the forces of good, these campy movies saw Santo battle vampires, aliens, zombies, and Martians. He was often joined by Mil Mascaras and Blue Demon (two other masked Lucha legends that enjoyed successful film careers) in battling his real-life wrestling opponents, as sequences from Santo's matches were often used in the films.

The formula for classic Lucha Libre films saw Santo and other wrestlers split their time between wrestling and crime fighting. What distinguished the genre from run-of-the-mill superhero films is that instead of having a secret identity, the hero's other identity was as a pro wrestler. The films' plots often spilled over into the arena matches, with Santo taking on the villains in the ring, wonderfully blurring the line between pro wrestling and crime fighting.

In 1950, Santo embarked on a memorable feud with the Black Shadow, climaxing with their landmark November 7, 1952, bout where Santo beat Shadow in a mask vs. mask match. Considered one of the most historically important moments in Lucha Libre history, the match helped to establish the mask vs. mask stipulation match as one of the defining traditions of Mexican wrestling.

After the win against Black Shadow, Santo became embroiled in a feud with Blue Demon over the NWA Welterweight title. A famous match in 1953 pitting Santo and Cavernario Galindo against Demon and Black Shadow won match of the year honors and became immortalized in "Los Luchadores," a popular song recorded at the time that is still played regularly in Mexico today.

In 1962 at the height of his film career and popularity, Santo became a full-fledged technico when he was attacked by tag partners Los Espantos I and II in a six-man match against Rayo de Jalisco, Henry Pilusso, and Rito Romero.

As the legend of El Santo grew, so did the lengths he went to protect his identity. Whenever he went out in public, he always wore his mask.

"El Santo really guarded his secret identity," states Wilt. "Whenever he was in public he always wore his mask. He had different masks for different occasions. When he had to eat he had a mask with a chin cut away, you couldn't eat with a small hole in his mask. He would make public appearances at bullfights and with politicians in his mask."

"Everything he would do to protect his identity – that for me is one of the most amazing aspects about him," exclaims Tenay. "That mask was omnipresent at every public appearance he made. In today's wrestling time it's inconceivable that anybody would care to that degree but I think you could tell he took that care in protecting his identity. I think that was also part of that package that made him larger than life."

"Without the mask he was just Rudolfo," says Rogelio Agrasanchez Jr., whose father helped produce two of El Santo's most popular movies in the '70s. "But when he put that mask and costume on he was El Santo."

"He was in *Misterio en las Bermudas* (Mystery in Bermuda), which my dad was filming in Texas," recalls Agrasanchez. "My brother was driving him and Mil Mascaras up from Mexico into Texas. As they were approaching the Texas border, my brother told them they had to take off their masks when they went through customs. Santo was very leery and told my brother 'OK, but don't look back.' That's how secretive he was."

Santo was so protective of his identity that he would often take a different flight from the production crew to film locations because he didn't want them to see him go through customs without his mask for fear of being identified later on the set.

Through the '60s and '70s, Santo would split his time between wrestling and movies. And so the legend continued to grow.

However, the glory days of Lucha Libre would eventually come to an end. In 1976, a new president was elected in Mexico and a new agency was formed dedicated to Mexican film. The government, not impressed with the genre, quickly pulled all funding, making it impossible for producers to finance their films. This move, combined with the import of foreign kung fu movies into Mexico, all but spelled the end for the genre.

"One of his last films, *Misterio en las Bermudas*, marks the end of the genre," explains David Wilt. "Santo made four more films and there was a brief revival in the early '90s [without Santo], but it was pretty much over."

As Santo continued to wrestle his body began to break down. He was no longer as effective in the ring as he once was and on September 12th, 1982, he wrestled in his last match, teaming with his old tag team partner Gori Guerrero, Huracán Ramírez, and El Solitario to defeat Los

Black Shadow goes for the pin on Santo.

Misioneros and Perro Aguayo. For Santo, the pain of retiring was made easier when his son debuted shortly after, carrying on in his footsteps as El Hijo del Santo (the son of the Saint).

Even in retirement, El Santo protected his identity. He wore the mask on several TV appearances and as he entered a new career as an escape artist. On January 26th, 1984, El Santo appeared on a Mexican talk show and without previous warning he publicly unmasked for the first time in his career. Underneath the legendary silver mask was an old, battered face.

Days later he was performing in a skit at a theatre when he complained of a pain in his arm. He was rushed to the hospital. But it was no use. He passed away on February 5 in his hospital bed. He was 68.

Santo's funeral was among the largest in the history of Mexico. Thousands flooded the streets of Mexico City outside the funeral parlor, wanting to catch a glimpse of their fallen hero. Masked wrestlers Mil Mascaras and Blue Demon attended the funeral, breaking down in front of the coffin as they paid their final respects.

It took hours for Santo's coffin to make it from the funeral parlor into the hearse. He was placed in a mausoleum in Mexico City with a simple plaque bearing a likeness of his silver mask. And of course he was buried with the mask on, choosing to be remembered not as Rodolfo Guzmán Huerta, but as the beloved and revered El Santo. Even in death, he protected his identity.

The wrestling storyline goes that on his deathbed Santo told his son El Hijo del Santo to carry on the tradition and to never lose the mask as part of match stipulation.

Although not an official holiday, the anniversary of Santo's death is marked by nationwide celebrations, memorials and wrestling cards honoring his memory. Fans from all across Mexico regularly make pilgrimage to his mausoleum in Mexico City to pay homage to the biggest wrestler and movie star the country has ever known.

In November 1999, SOMOS, a Mexican film-nostalgia magazine, published photos of El Santo without his mask. El Hijo del Santo was outraged and threatened to sue the publication. As it turned out, one of El Santo's other sons had provided the magazine with the photos, and the lawsuit was quickly forgotten.

Looking back at his storied career, several experts try to contextualize and explain Santo's popularity.

"His impact on the Mexican culture and society was so enormous that his popularity alone catapulted Lucha Libre to an even higher level," states Mexican wrestling historian Jose Luis Fernandez. "And as much as it hurts critics to say, his movies are what kept the Mexican cinema business alive when it was crumbling."

"He totally transcended wrestling," states Dave Meltzer. "He was much bigger than just a wrestling star. I think there have been wrestlers as big as him and as popular as him but none that were known throughout an entire country for 40 years. Santo was more than just a wrestler. Nobody had the enduring popularity he had."

"He was a real person," explains David Wilt. "Here was someone who was not an actor. You see him in the movies and then you could watch him on TV and go to your local arena and see him wrestle in person, and go to your newsstand every week and buy a comic book that had his adventures in it. He's not just a fictional character, but an actual person.... His impact on Mexican culture and society was huge."

To this day, the El Santo legend remains embedded in Mexican popular culture, having left an indelible mark on the nation. His legacy is unmatched in wrestling history, and it is doubtful that we will ever see someone of his incredible stature again.

8

Giant Baba

Giant Baba was one of the first Japanese promoters I worked for. I knew of him and respected him before I went over, and I always enjoyed working there and for him. He had already made his legend around the world as a great athlete, and one of the best and most-trusted promoters of all time along with Sam Muchnick. His word was his bond and he helped the wrestling business immensely. He could really move around for a very big man.

— RIC FLAIR

Giant Baba was much more than the founder of All Japan Pro Wrestling. He was a cultural icon in Japan. A national hero to generations of Japanese citizens, Baba was one of only a small handful of wrestlers in history that were larger than the business itself in their respective cultures. His name became known by everybody in Japan – his face instantly recognizable.

In an industry full of con men and backstabbers, Baba distinguished himself as one of the most honest promoters in the business. As wrestling companies evolved into corporations, he and wife Motoko remained the last holdouts, continuing to run their "mom and pop" outfit with the same quaint, folksy and down to earth principles they had adhered to since the beginning.

Baba's was a company where written contracts were unheard of – Baba's word was his bond; where the entire crew traveled on the bus to the next show; where rookies slowly worked their way up the company hierarchy; where athletic credibility was prized above all else; where traditional angles were favored over gimmickry; and, first and foremost, where the entire roster, from top to bottom, out-worked and out-hustled every other wrestling locker room in existence.

At 6'9" and 260 pounds, Shohei Baba may have been remembered as a giant in the wrestling world. But his real

Giant Baba at Kiel Auditorium St. Louis, 1975.

legacy is his overwhelming capacity for generosity and his love of the business, making him a giant among men.

Shohei Baba was born on January 23, 1938, in Sanjyo, Japan. An ace pitcher in high school, Baba dropped out at age 16 and signed a contract with the Yomiuri (Tokyo) Giants, the powerhouse franchise of Japanese baseball.

He trained with the club for several years before making his debut in the 1957 season, while still a teenager. The Giants cut him loose at the end of the 1959 season and his baseball career came to an end when he crashed through a glass door, cutting several nerves in his arm.

After turning down offers from Japan's television and movie producers, who wanted to capitalize on his freakish size and make him a star, Baba turned to pro wrestling. He began training under Rikidozan and became the hot prospect of the camp in April 1960, joined by another promising hopeful by the name of Kanji Inoki.

Together, the two future stars trained under Rikidozan before making their pro debuts after a mere five months. Baba was eventually sent to North America to gain more seasoning, along with handler The Great Togo.

Because his gargantuan size belied the build of the average Japanese person, Baba, playing a monstrous heel, instantly became a huge box-office draw and the first Japanese wrestler to become a legitimate main-event star in North

facing page: Giant Baba against Jack Brisco for the NWA title.

Giant Baba locks up Jack Brisco in an armbar.

America. His physical stature allowed him to break the mold of the stereotypical sneaky, salt-throwing Japanese heel that flourished in post-World War II America, and his success paved the way for another freakish star (Andre the Giant) to be pushed in a similar fashion a decade later.

Towards the end of his American sojourn in 1964, he took on three different world champions (Lou Thesz for the NWA World title in Detroit, Bruno Sammartino for the WWWF World title at Madison Square Garden and Freddie Blassie for the WWA World championship in Los Angeles) within the space of a month – a startling indication of just how big he had become.

While in Los Angeles, he feuded with The Destroyer (Dick Beyer), tussling over Beyer's WWA World title in a

trio of legendary matches in February 1963.

"[Los Angeles promoter] Jules Strongbow came into the dressing room and asked me what I was going to do with this guy," remembers Beyer. "I asked, 'How's the crowd?' and he said 'We're going to sell out.' He told me the ringside seats were solid with Japanese and that this was going to be televised back in Japan."

"So I told Jules that Giant Baba is going to look like the greatest wrestler in the world tonight. We wrestled one hour and I gave him 90 percent of the match. At that time he could only wrestle a little bit. He beat me one fall and had me beat in the second fall when the time limit ran out."

"Three weeks later they brought it back again and Jules asked me what I was going to do. I told him we were going to do the same thing where Baba would take a fall and it's going to look like he had me beat only I'm going to get disqualified so I can't lose the belt....The last time I wrestled him in L.A. we went an hour again. When Baba went back to Japan, he was getting bigger cheers in the ring than Rikidozan."

Back home, the JWA was in dire trouble. The industry was in rough shape after Rikidozan died, with the revelations of his mob connections leading to the majority of venues shutting its doors to pro wrestling. The promotion was in need of a savior.

Enter Giant Baba.

As the perennial International Heavyweight Champion, Baba literally saved pro wrestling in Japan from extinction. By holding the same belt that Rikidozan made famous, Baba lifted the shroud of death that hovered over Japanese wrestling and ushered in a new boom period.

Baba's straightforward, clean-living persona sanitized the corrupt image of the industry that Rikidozan had left behind, opening the doors of Japan's major venues to pro wrestling once more. With Baba as its top drawing-card, the JWA enjoyed a renaissance, successfully renewing the archetypal Japan vs. America morality play made famous by Rikidozan.

Baba was the new wrestling hero of the nation, and all of Japan rallied behind him as he vanquished the top American stars. On August 14, 1967, he wrestled then-NWA World Champion Gene Kiniski to a 65-minute draw in an historic title vs. title match that drew a whopping 25,000-plus fans to the Osaka Baseball Stadium.

But perhaps the best indicator of his popularity came on January 24, 1968, when he defended his title against The Crusher on prime-time network television, directly opposite a Lou Thesz-Danny Hodge match on a rival network. In the first major prime-time war (predating the historic RAW vs. Nitro battles by some 27 years), the Baba-Crusher match drew a 48 rating, nearly double the 26 rating the Thesz-Hodge match garnered.

In 1967, Baba began teaming with Inoki, drawing monster TV ratings and selling out house shows. The two held the NWA International Tag Team titles four times between 1967 and 1971. By 1971, the JWA was in financial trouble. Backstage chaos and dissonance quickly became the order of the day as Baba and Inoki attempted a coup. When it failed, Inoki took the fall; he was fired, while Baba was welcomed back.

After Inoki formed New Japan Pro Wrestling in March

1972, Baba quit the JWA and, with the support of Nippon TV, founded All Japan Pro Wrestling, staging its first show on October 21, 1972, at Tokyo's Machida City Gym.

Baba quickly made moves to ensure that his new promotion would flourish. He became business partners with the Funks, letting them handle the booking of foreign talent into the promotion. He then flew to St. Louis to meet with Sam Muchnick and secured NWA recognition, giving him instant access to the top American talent (including dates on the NWA world champion). Freezing New Japan out of the NWA turned out to be the first shot fired in a bitter promotional war that drastically changed the industry in Japan.

In an attempt to deepen his babyface roster, Baba recruited Tomomi Tsuruta, a Greco-Roman wrestler who represented Japan at the 1972 Olympics. He debuted the following year as Jumbo Tsuruta, and went on to become a pillar of All Japan, and arguably the best in-ring performer in the history of Japanese wrestling. In 1973, Baba brought in The Destroyer, signing him to a six-year exclusive contract and partnering with him in an historic "dream" tag team.

Baba wasted no time in establishing himself as the headliner of his promotion. He created the Pacific Wrestling Federation Title, and would go on to hold the prestigious strap (now part of the Triple Crown Heavyweight title), four times between 1973 and 1984, making it the centerpiece of the All Japan promotion.

On January 23, 1974, Jack Brisco became the first NWA World Heavyweight Champion to appear on an All Japan card, battling Baba to a draw in a double title match. In December of that year, Baba won his first of three NWA world titles, defeating Brisco in Kagoshima before dropping the belt a week later in Toyohashi. He would also enjoy one-week title reigns in 1979 and 1980 after defeating Harley Race.

Business began to lag in Japan in the wake of the Inoki-Muhammad Ali debacle and in 1979 the two groups forged a brief working relationship. On August 26, the Tokyo Sports Newspaper hosted "The Dream Card" at Tokyo's Budokan Hall, a joint All Japan-New Japan show that featured Baba and Inoki teaming up for the first time in eight years to defeat Tiger Jeet Singh and Abdullah the Butcher.

On May 8, 1981, Abdullah The Butcher, Baba's top foreign heel and main-event star of the '70s, jumped to New Japan after Inoki doubled his weekly salary to $8,000 per week (one of the richest contracts in wrestling at the time). A huge blow for All Japan, New Japan's signing of Abdullah took the promotional war to new heights of ferocity, with Baba and Inoki scrambling to get the upper hand on each other.

After Inoki pilfered Abdullah and Dick Murdoch, Baba responded by stealing Tiger Jeet Singh and Umanosuke Ueda, New Japan's top heel tag team. This back-and-forth game set the stage for one of the biggest coups in wrestling history, as Baba was set to take the wrestling war to an entirely new level. A scant two days after finishing up a tour with New Japan, Stan Hansen, Inoki's top in-ring rival, jumped to All Japan, accompanying Bruiser Brody and Jimmy Snuka to the ring during the final of the Real World Tag League on December 13, 1981. He attacked Baba in a post match brawl, setting up a legendary singles feud

promotion. As a result, the legendary Choshu's Army vs. All Japan feud, coupled with the debut of the RoadWarriors, helped Baba enjoy banner years from 1985 to 1986.

With Choshu introducing a faster-paced ring style in All Japan, Baba realized that he could no longer keep up. He began to phase himself out of the main-event picture, passing the torch of leadership to his young stars. In the wake of Choshu's departure in 1987, Baba struck box-office gold by turning Genichiro Tenryu heel and having him feud with Tsuruta, Bruiser Brody, and Abdullah. In the late-'80s his relationship with the NWA totally disintegrated after Crocket pulled Flair from several advertised All Japan tours. Baba could see the handwriting on the wall. He had to create his own world champion.

Because his gargantuan size bellied the build of the average Japanese person, Baba, playing a monstrous heel, instantly became a huge box-office draw and the first Japanese wrestler to become a legitimate main-event star in North America.

between the two over the PWF Title.

Similar to Lex Luger's jump from the WWF to WCW in 1995 (when he secretly left the WWF and appeared on the first edition of Nitro) Hansen's surprise defection to All Japan shocked the wrestling world. The jump was planned out months in advance by Baba, The Funks, and Hansen in a secret meeting in Hawaii. Baba gave Hansen a lifetime deal and doubled his salary, further escalating the war.

And yet, despite having exclusive access to most of the top American stars (including NWA World Champion Ric Flair), All Japan still trailed New Japan at the box office. New Japan was enjoying its boom period from 1981-1984 thanks to the creation of Tiger Mask and the landmark Ishingun vs. Seikigun feud.

In late 1984, Baba succeeded in another major raid of Inoki's roster, taking Riki Choshu (the key player in the Ishingun vs. Seikigun feud), Masa Saito, Animal Hamaguchi, Yoshiaki Yatsu, Kuniaki Kobayashi, Super Strong Machine, Hiro Saito, Dynamite Kid, and Davey Boy Smith. With Inoki's roster decimated, the balance of power had dramatically shifted.

Baba now held all the cards, as the influx of new talent put a fresh coat of paint on All Japan and offered fans exciting new main-event matches. Borrowing from the invasion angle that worked so well in New Japan, Baba immediately set up Choshu as the number one heel in the

And so the Triple Crown was born.

On April 18, 1989, Baba's dream of creating his own world championship was realized, when Tsuruta (the All Japan International Champion) defeated Hansen (the PWF and United National Champion) to unify the three titles and create the Triple Crown. The selection of Tsuruta, arguably the best wrestler in the world at the time, helped put the title on the map, as he embarked on a classic series of title defenses against Hansen and Tenryu.

From 1988-1989, Akira Maeda's Universal Wrestling Federation became the hottest wrestling promotion in the world, renowned for having every match end in a clean knockout or submission. Even the company's top stars were not immune from doing jobs. This formula not only sent the UWF on an incredible box-office run, but also forced Baba to change his booking philosophy in 1989, towards almost all clean finishes (and 100% clean finishes in the main events). It was the wisest decision he ever made, as it resulted in All Japan's next boom period.

Just as the promotional war with New Japan settled down, Tenryu left All Japan in April 1990 and signed a contract with Megane Super (the second biggest eyeglass company in Japan) to form the SWS promotion.

Tenryu's departure left a gaping hole in All Japan's main events. But as it turned out, it was the best thing that could have happened to the company as it forced Baba to elevate his younger talent. A new boom period began as mid-carders Mitsuharu Misawa, Toshiaki Kawada, Kenta Kobashi, and Akira Taue were instantly elevated.

Despite the new infusion of talent at its topmost level, All Japan remained the last citadel of old school wrestling: it was a promotion that featured lengthy main event matches, a ring style that put athleticism and ring psychology at a premium, a policy of 100% clean finishes, finishing moves that worked against the top stars and all ego denied for the good of the company. All Japan was reborn and a new golden era was ushered in with the Triple Crown and Misawa promoted as the focal points. As a result, Budokan Hall became the hottest wrestling building in the world. All Japan sold out over 200 consecutive house shows in Tokyo over the next few years, capping off one of the most amazing box-office runs in history.

It was after the boom period peaked that Baba, finally, followed New Japan's lead and promoted his first show at the Tokyo Dome. On May 1, 1998, over 58,300 fans filed into the Dome to watch Kawada capture the Triple Crown from Misawa. It turned out to be the most successful show Baba ever promoted.

By the end of the year, Baba's health began to deteriorate. Rumors speculating on his condition spread when he missed two dates in December (since, between 1964 and 1984, he wrestled over 4100 consecutive matches without missing a booking). He returned on December 5, teaming with Rusher Kimura and Mitsuo Momota against Haruka Eigen and Masa Fuchi at Budokan Hall, wrestling the same comedy match he had done for years.

It turned out to be his last match.

Baba was diagnosed with cancer. Following surgery to remove the tumor from his bowels, he was given a hopeful prognosis; however, when he returned for a routine check-up on January 8, 1999, it was discovered that the cancer was still there. He underwent a second operation and celebrated his 61st birthday in a Tokyo hospital on January 23. Eight days later, Giant Baba passed away.

The reaction to Baba's death in Japan was equal to that of Frank Sinatra in the U.S. in 1998, as the entire nation mourned the loss of their fallen warrior. News of his death was splashed on the front page of every major newspaper and was the lead story on most television and radio newscasts. Major network television specials commemorating his career were quickly put together. VAP, the company that sold All Japan's home videos, couldn't keep product on the

Giant Baba promotional photograph, 1963.

shelves, selling several millions of dollars' worth of tapes each day of the week he passed away. By February 4, over 100,000 letters of condolence poured into the offices of All Japan. The demand of mourning fans to send telegrams of condolences to the offices of All Japan was so great that there wasn't enough telegram paper to be found in all of Japan.

After a private ceremony for the family, a public funeral was held at Budokan Hall on April 17. One of the largest funerals in the history of Japan, over 28,000 fans visited the arena, one by one, to pay their final respects. On May 2, 1999, the Giant Baba Memorial Show was staged at the Tokyo Dome, drawing over 55,000 fans paying $5,000,000.

Even in death his presence was felt on the Japanese wrestling landscape, his spirit kept alive in the arenas and offices of All Japan where he had spun his promotional magic. Pro wrestling forged ahead in Japan, but it was clear that Baba was still watching every match from the aisle.

The outpouring of emotion from the nation of Japan solidified his standing alongside Rikidozan, his mentor, and Mexico's El Santo as one of the select few performers in wrestling history who managed to transcend the sport and achieve the status of cultural icon.

9

Steve Austin

Stone Cold Steve Austin is a huge name in modern professional wrestling. I watched him grow when he got his first big shot in WCW and later he helped WWF explode as a super performer. He has definitely paid the price after his neck injury and recovery to be a dominant force and double-tough.

— RIC FLAIR

"Stunning" Steve Austin was at the crossroads of his career in 1995.

A year after Hulk Hogan signed with World Championship Wrestling, Austin, at one time an integral cog in the promotion, now found himself mired in mid-card purgatory. Although touted by many as the next Ric Flair, the company was holding him down in favor of aging stars who had "name" value.

Not knowing what to do with him, WCW sent him to New Japan where, already suffering from knee problems, he tore his tricep. He returned to the U.S. dejected and disconsolate. Then Eric Bischoff fired him over the phone in September, telling him the company didn't know how to market him and that because of his style they'd never be able to sell any dolls of his likeness.

How ironic that just a few years later, the "unmarketable" and bland "Stunning" Steve would be reborn as "Stone Cold" in the WWF, the biggest merchandise seller and marketing phenomenon in wrestling history. How ironic that the same mid-carder who was held down under the Hogan-regime in WCW would surpass the stardom achieved by Hogan in the '80s and become the biggest wrestling star in the world during the '90s. And how ironic that the man that was deemed "expendable" by WCW would become indispensable to the WWF during the bitter promotional war between the two companies in the late '90s,

Young Steve Austin.

helping Vince McMahon to spike the final nail in WCW's coffin in 2001.

If Bischoff had only known that his actions that fateful September day would go down in history as wrestling's equivalent of the Boston Red Sox trading Babe Ruth to the New York Yankees in 1919, then perhaps WCW would still be alive today.

The tale of Austin's rise from a struggling rookie earning $25 payoffs on the indy circuit to the industry's biggest star, winning the WWF World title in the main event of WrestleMania, begins with Austin as a child growing up in a small town in Texas.

Born December 18, 1964, and given the name Steve Williams after being adopted, Austin became an avid pro wrestling fan after stumbling upon Paul Boecsh's Houston wrestling on television. Austin was a top athlete in high school where he ran track and played baseball and football before going to North Texas State University on a football scholarship, where he was a defensive end. After finishing his eligibility, he saw a TV ad for Chris Adams' wrestling school and enrolled in 1989, becoming the star pupil of the training camp and catching Adams' eye.

After graduating later that year, he made his pro debut under his real name in World Class Championship Wrestling, defeating Frogman LeBlanc in his first match. Soon after, he changed his name to Steve Austin, to avoid confusion with Steve "Dr. Death" Williams.

facing page: Stone Cold Steve Austin attacks Kurt Angle while disregarding the referee's warning.

Although green at first, Adams recognized the star potential in Austin. In 1990, he booked himself in a headline feud with the rookie that pitted him and his wife Toni against Austin and Jeannie Clark, Adams' ex-wife. Austin, barely out of wrestling school, now found himself in the main event at the Dallas Sportatorium, the same building he watched the Von Erichs in as a high school and college student, when he regularly attended World Class shows.

The feud, playing on the real-life emotions of Adams' divorce, briefly revitalized what was a dying territory by drawing some of the biggest crowds at the Sportatorium in years. The feud thrust him into the spotlight. Austin quickly became recognized as a good worker, winning acclaim from critics who were impressed with his progress in light

comed by wcw's older established stars, who felt threatened by their rising success. From there Austin returned to singles action and became the heel U.S. Heavyweight Champion, engaging in a classic feud with Ricky Steamboat over the belt. However, the feud abruptly stopped after Steamboat suffered a career-ending injury during one of their matches in 1994.

As Hogan was brought into wcw, Austin's stature in the company took a nosedive. His career was all but sabotaged by a bungling collection of bookers who couldn't figure out how to use him properly. After being sidelined with a litany of serious injuries, Bischoff fired him in 1995, explaining that he was not a charismatic star that they could market.

He briefly resurfaced in ecw before moving on to the

A tag match with Steve Austin and The Rock against Kurt Angle and Chris Jericho, September, 2001.

of the fact he had only been in the business for less than a year.

Word of Austin's outstanding work in Dallas spread – heralded in several wrestling newsletters at the time – and reached the wcw brain trust in Atlanta by 1991. In the spring, he signed with the company and was given a strong heel push just below the main event slot. After winning two wcw World TV titles between 1991 and 1992, Austin's career stalled, as he was unable to break into the main event picture. In 1993, he was thrown together with Brian Pillman, and the Hollywood Blondes were born.

After winning the wcw and NWA World Tag Team titles on March 3, Austin and Pillman quickly established themselves as the best tag team in the U.S. on the strength of their superb matches and entertaining interviews that got them over as charismatic heels. Seen as a modern-day version of the famous Pat Patterson and Ray Stevens duo in the '60s, Austin and Pillman were winning widespread acclaim from fans and critics who believed they had the potential to be the tag team of the decade.

Just as the duo was at its creative best, they were inexplicably disbanded by the company – a move that was wel-

WWF, where he debuted as the forgettable Ringmaster with Ted DiBiase as his manager. The Austin-DiBiase pairing and the Ringmaster gimmick floundered. Austin, with his career and the WWF going absolutely nowhere, appeared to be victimized by another company that didn't have a clue how to market him.

And then it happened.

Just as the same dark cloak of booking ineptness that choked his career in wcw was now suffocating him in WWF, a blinding lightning bolt of promoting genius struck. And in its wake emerged a character that became a marketing phenomenon so overwhelming, that it sent Austin skyrocketing into mainstream superstardom as the single greatest performer of the '90s and into the new millennium.

The birth of "Stone Cold" Steve Austin came on June 23, 1996, after he defeated Jake "The Snake" Roberts in the finals of the King of the Ring tournament. In the buildup to the final, the Bible-referencing Roberts quoted a verse from John 3:16 that stated, *"For God so loved the world that he gave his one and only Son, that whoever believes in him shall not perish but have eternal life."*

After winning the King of the Ring and accepting his

crown, Austin cut a promo making fun of Roberts' religious reference stating, "Austin 3:16 says I just whooped your ass!" And with that simple phrase, a new era in wrestling had begun.

Over the next few months, Austin was transformed from mid-card also-ran into a kick-ass, blue-collar, trash-talking heel. He worked a program with Bret Hart, leading to a memorable match at Survivor Series on November 17, where he received a modest amount of cheers from the Madison Square Garden crowd. He moved on to a house show program with Shawn Michaels where the cheers grew and grew in numbers to the point he became a babyface by default.

Austin had established himself as one of the top stars in the company and on March 23, 1997, he wrestled Bret Hart in an I Quit match at WrestleMania 13, now considered one of the greatest matches in the modern era of the wwf. The match, renowned for its brilliant storytelling and flawless execution in switching Austin and Hart's heel/babyface roles, set Austin on course to becoming the industry's unquestioned leader.

For the rest of 1997, he feuded with Bret and Owen Hart and Shawn Michaels in singles programs. Receiving a major push from the company, Austin proved to be a bankable commodity as "Austin 3:16" shirts became the hottest-selling merchandise item in wrestling. He became the best promo man in the business as his catch phrases – "I just whooped your ass" and "Austin 3:16" – became ingrained in the wrestling vocabulary of fans.

Just as his stock was about to shoot through the roof, Austin's push took a tumbling crash. On August 3, 1997, he wrestled Owen Hart at SummerSlam and was going to win the Intercontinental title. They were on their way to having the match of the night when things suddenly turned horribly wrong.

Austin suffered a career-threatening neck injury when Owen Hart did not properly protect his head during a tombstone piledriver spot. Austin lay motionless on the mat as he was momentarily paralyzed from the waist down. Hart stalled for several minutes before Austin somehow maneuvered into position and scored a quick, unconvincing pin. Austin, who was already suffering from neck problems, was rushed to the hospital and five days later had an MRI that showed severe trauma to his C-4 and C-5 vertebrae. The bad news was further compounded when one of the leading neck specialists in the U.S. told him that if he didn't retire he would run the risk of permanent paralysis.

Undeterred, he sought out a second opinion from a Philadelphia doctor who gave him a similar prognosis.

Although unable to work, and with the wwf on the losing end of the promotional war with wcw, Austin, the hottest star in the business before the injury, remained the focal point of wwf programming. Week in and week out, he appeared on RAW in order to lend the show some much-needed star power during its ratings battle with Nitro. He eventually made his return to the ring – working a smarter style without taking any dangerous bumps – defeating Owen Hart at Survivor Series to win his second Intercontinental title.

With the wwf on the mend in the aftermath of the "Montreal Screw job," Austin became the focal point and was the catalyst behind the promotion's incredible turnaround, thanks to a program with Mike Tyson leading up

Stunning Steve Austin!

to WrestleMania 14 in 1998. In the main event, Austin defeated Shawn Michaels to capture his first WWF World Heavyweight title with Tyson as the special referee. In the process, Austin got the celebrity rub from Tyson and WrestleMania rung up three cherries in the form of 730,000 buys, the largest pay-per-view audience in wrestling history up until that point.

The angle with Tyson was a huge success as it set Austin on a course to become the biggest star in the industry and help the WWF surpass WCW in their historic promotional war. Austin's feud with Vince McMahon on RAW helped the program break Nitro's 83-week winning streak in the ratings war, and soon, Austin vs. McMahon on RAW became a Monday night institution.

trailing only Hogan on the all-time list of shows headlined that drew greater than a 1.0 buyrate.

The money-machine kept rolling on into 2001. On April 1 at the Houston Astro Dome, he won his fifth WWF World title from The Rock in the main event of WrestleMania 17, again setting the record for the biggest revenue-producing show in the history of pro wrestling, as well as breaking records in just about every other category.

Following WrestleMania, Austin was programmed in a memorable feud with Kurt Angle, where they had several match of the year caliber bouts. After dropping the title to Angle in September, Austin won it for the sixth time on October 8, surpassing The Rock and Hulk Hogan as the most decorated WWF World Champion in history.

After winning the King of the Ring and accepting his crown, Austin cut a promo making fun of Roberts' religious reference stating, "Austin 3:16 says I just whooped your ass!" And with that simple phrase, a new era in wrestling had begun.

Despite battling persistent knee and neck injuries, Austin revitalized the WWF. While feuding against Mick Foley, Kane, and the Undertaker, he built the WWF's pay-per-view business and house show attendance to incredible heights, becoming the top merchandise seller in the history of the business and, with the exception of Hulk Hogan, selling more wrestling tickets than any previous WWF World Champion.

After dropping the world title to Kane, Austin regained the strap from The Rock on March 28, 1999, at WrestleMania 15. The culmination of the Austin-McMahon program (Rock was McMahon's heel champion) drew 800,000 pay-per-view buys, breaking the record he set one year earlier against Michaels.

The grueling road schedule and years of punishment inside the ring caught up with Austin in late 1999, when he aggravated his neck once again. An examination revealed spinal stenosis and doctors once again told him to retire. He underwent neck surgery in January 2000 and made a special appearance on the WWF's *Backlash* pay-per-view where he interfered in The Rock vs. Triple H main event.

He returned to action full time in September and resumed his place in the main event picture, feuding with Triple H, The Rock, and Kurt Angle. By the end of 2000 he had cemented his legend as one of the best pay-per-view draws in history, moving past Flair into second place and

As Senior Vice President of Talent Relations for the WWF, Jim Ross was responsible for bringing Austin into the company and played a substantial role in fostering and nurturing the professional environment in which he flourished. A wrestling fan since growing up in his native Oklahoma and someone who has been employed in the industry his entire adult life, Ross considers Austin to be "the greatest WWF Champion that the business has ever had."

"He's one of those once-in-a-lifetime talents," states Ross. "The biggest 'up-period' in our business's history, the most significant years for the WWF were with Austin as the featured performer. That is significant. I can only look at how many tickets were sold, and how many pieces of merchandise were sold during those time frames, and the numbers are staggering."

Staggering. Mind-blowing. Unreal. Overwhelming.

You could dig deep in your thesaurus for adjectives that properly encapsulate the remarkable career of Steve Austin and his influence on the wrestling industry.

Perhaps none are more appropriate than "stunning."

Indeed, if only Eric Bischoff had known.

First in WCW, Stunning Steve Austin, 1994.

10

Buddy Rogers

Nature Boy Buddy Rogers was the very first Nature Boy in our sport. An all-time best in the ring, an NWA and WWF champion, a true gentleman and one of the absolute tops who broke records everywhere. A legend who I had the pleasure of working with in the Carolinas for Jim Crockett. He was always in immaculate shape and a great, great athlete.

— RIC FLAIR

The master showman of his era and one of the greatest drawing-cards of all time, Buddy Rogers made an indelible impact on wrestling in the television era of the '40s and '50s, inspiring wrestlers for decades to come, most notably, Ric Flair.

He was the original "Nature Boy," popularizing all the mannerisms that today's fans associate with Flair: The strut. The cocky attitude. The bleached-blond hair. The fancy robes. The figure four leglock. The tanned, muscular physique. He was the original hard-bumping, heel World Champion who cowardly begged for mercy in the corner when in trouble.

A retired Buddy Rogers can still do the strut.

An NWA World Heavyweight Champion from 1961 to 1963 and the first WWWF World Heavyweight Champion in history, Buddy Rogers was one of wrestling's biggest stars in the U.S. from 1948 to 1963, captivating audiences with his unique mix of brashness, showmanship, boastful interviews, and heated matches.

Over his historic career, Rogers won acclaim from fans and critics alike for changing the complexion of wrestling and modernizing it in so many ways. Even Lou Thesz, who carried a real-life grudge against Rogers until the '90s (over degrading comments he made about Thesz' trainer and mentor Ed "Strangler" Lewis), conceded that Rogers was the top worker and performer of the post-World War II era.

Bill Apter has been reporting, writing, and photographing professional wrestling since 1970 and is currently the senior editor of *Power of Wrestling* magazine. As a teenager who saw Rogers wrestle at Madison Square Garden, Apter pinpoints what made Rogers such an influential in-ring performer.

"He stood out from the pack. Buddy Rogers had a special look – the bleached, golden-blond hair, the well-cut and bronzed muscular body. He made the presentation of a pro wrestler slick and classy-looking. The bland look of the stereotypical wrestler that the business was so overrun with was experiencing a change, with many now dying their natural hair color and trying to emulate Rogers' style, which was making a big hit at the box-office."

Gary Will, author of *Wrestling Title Histories*, agrees stating, "[Rogers] had the most complete package of wrestling skills in history."

Born Herman Rohde in Camden, New Jersey, Rogers debuted in 1939 as Dutch Rhode while working as a police officer. Years later, while working in Texas, he took the name "Nature Boy" Buddy Rogers – "Nature Boy" being a hit song at the time and Buddy Rogers a popular science fiction character of the '40s. His first big push came in 1945-1946 while working for famed promoter Morris Sigel in Houston. There, he won the NWA Texas Heavyweight

title four times and feuded with Jim Casey, Dave Levin, and most notably, Thesz.

Rogers eventually made his way north, and by the late '40s he had become a regular competitor on the Dumont Network out of Chicago. Television was still in its infancy at the time and was enjoying its first boom. Thanks to the exploits of Gorgeous George (not to mention the cheap production costs) wrestling became an early staple of network programming during this initial "golden era." Because of the national television exposure it granted him, Rogers quickly became one of the top wrestling stars in the country. Rogers seemed custom-made for television, using the medium to solidify his signature cocky attitude.

"Much like Gorgeous George, Rogers benefited enor-

match against Don Eagle. Prior to Rogers' arrival, Muchnick was getting buried at the box-office, with Thesz regularly drawing more than twice as many fans to his shows. Rogers changed all that and immediately helped Muchnick outdraw Thesz.

Rogers had such influence in St. Louis that Thesz, coming out on the losing end of the promotional war, and Muchnick, fearing business would die back down after Rogers left for another territory, merged their groups in 1949. Although publicly they were presented as two different companies, Thesz and Muchnick worked side-by-side and helped turn St. Louis into the "Wrestling Capital of the World," a title it enjoyed for nearly four decades.

While maintaining Ohio as his home base, Rogers also

He stood out from the pack. Buddy Rogers had a special look – the bleached, golden-blond hair, the well-cut and bronzed muscular body. He made the presentation of a pro wrestler slick and classy-looking.

mously from being in wrestling as television was taking hold in America," says wrestling historian Sheldon Goldberg. "The tanned, muscular body, bleached-blond hair and cocky strut were made for the small screen and Rogers was one of the first to really utilize the medium to its fullest. Really, Rogers was one of the first wrestlers of the TV era who made charisma as important a credential in wrestling, as, well, being able to wrestle."

However, the overexposure of wrestling on network television eventually led to a down period, and the business struggled at the gates. Rogers ventured to Columbus, Ohio, to work for promoter Al Haft in the Midwest Wrestling Association. In addition to being its main-event star as U.S. Heavyweight Champion, Rogers was also the promotion's booker, helping to revitalize the Midwest and turn it into one of the hottest and most profitable territories in the country.

In 1948, promoter Sam Muchnick was engaged in a promotional war with a rogue group run by Thesz and his father. Muchnick was on the losing end of the battle and needed something to turn the tide. That something turned out to be Buddy Rogers. As an NWA member, Haft routinely sent Rogers to St. Louis to help Muchnick's cause.

The charismatic icon immediately became a main event star and huge draw in St. Louis, giving Muchnick his first sellout at the Kiel Auditorium on February 4, 1949, in a

became an institution in Chicago, the city where he tasted his first fame in the late-'40s. During the '50s, his weekly main event matches at the venerable International Amphitheatre drew consistent sellouts of 11,000 fans, who came to watch him tussle with the top babyfaces in the business.

By the late-'50s, Rogers was one of the top stars in the country, and was being controlled more and more by Northeast promoters that included Joe "Toots" Mondt and Vince McMahon Sr. Sam Muchnick, the leading powerbroker in the NWA, put the belt on Rogers as a way to pacify Mondt and McMahon (who controlled the lucrative New York market) and keep them as strong members of the NWA.

The bulk of the NWA promoters were against the move, fearing that Mondt and McMahon – who already controlled Rogers – would make it impossible for them to get good dates for the World Champion in their own territories. Muchnick, however, used his power and defied the wishes of the disgruntled NWA promoters, putting the world title on Buddy Rogers anyway.

In one of the most famous matches in wrestling history, Rogers defeated Pat O'Connor for the NWA World Title on June 30, 1961, in Chicago's Comiskey Park. The match drew 38,622 fans (an attendance record that stood until 1986) and took in $148,000 in gate receipts, a U.S. record that lasted

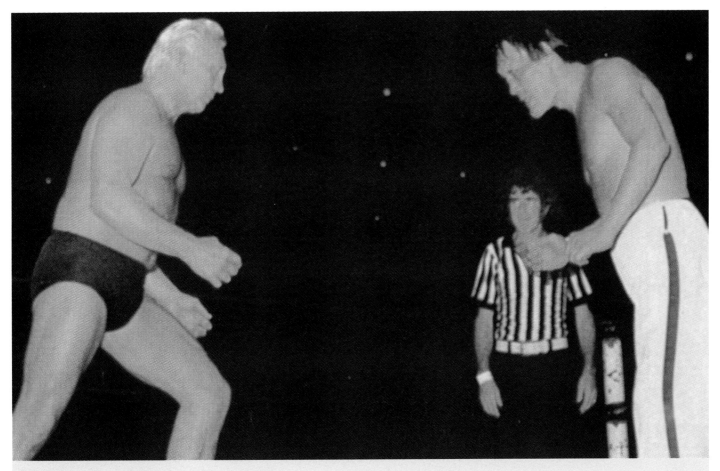
Buddy Rogers against Pak Song.

almost twenty years. They went on to wrestle in a legendary series of matches, including a rematch in Comiskey Park months later that drew 30,000 fans.

Rogers was wrestling's biggest draw in the U.S. at the height of his reign, building on his legendary status by becoming the first 100% heel NWA World Champion (and laying the groundwork for Ric Flair to follow some two decades later in the same role). Yet, despite his success, controversy always lingered close behind him. The Northeast promoters controlled Rogers and booked him into as many dates in their territories as possible, making it increasingly difficult for promoters from other parts of the country to get good dates – especially on weekends – with the World Champion.

Then, in 1962, he was dogged by a series of peculiar episodes. First, he became entangled in a war of words with shooter Karl Gotch after Gotch publicly claimed Rogers was afraid to wrestle him. Rogers, unimpressed with Gotch's tough-guy reputation, laughed off the charge. The situation came to a boiling point on August 31 when Gotch, with the help of Bill Miller, cornered Rogers in a locker room in Columbus, Ohio, and slammed a door on his hand

as he tried to escape. Rogers was sidelined in the fracas and missed several lucrative title matches.

Then, on November 21, Rogers broke his ankle during the first minute of a title match against Killer Kowalski in Montreal. Kowalski won the first fall by pinning Rogers, but the match ended before the start of the second fall due to the injury. The NWA had a problem on their hands, since Kowalski wasn't supposed to go over on Rogers and win the title. In a face-saving move, they continued to recognize Rogers as champion, claiming that Kowalski had to have won two falls cleanly in order to win the title. Despite the decision by the NWA, and with Rogers on the shelf due to injury, Kowalski was recognized as the World Champion in several key markets, most notably St. Louis.

By this time, rumors began to spread that Mondt and McMahon were going to break off from the NWA and start their own promotion with Rogers as their World Champion. The rest of the NWA promoters, already irate over how the Northeast coalition made it impossible for them to book Rogers into their own territories, began to panic. They knew if Rogers left while still World Champion, the credibility of the NWA would be totally destroyed (since the

Buddy "Nature Boy" Rogers.

world title meant so much to promotions in those days). Muchnick made the decision that Thesz, now 46 years old and living in semi-retirement in Arizona, would replace Rogers as NWA Champion.

However, there was still the small matter of Rogers dropping the NWA World title. The NWA tried to set up a title match with Thesz, but Rogers, missed their first two scheduled matches due to "injury" (in a scheme that bears startling resemblances to the ploys Shawn Michaels used to get out of dropping the WWF World title over 30 years later). Fortunately for Muchnick, he had a trump card. All World Champions were required to remit a performance bond to the NWA before having the title put on them. This guaranteed that they would "do the job" when the time came and not run off with the belt. Muchnick threatened to give Rogers' $25,000 bond to charity if he didn't show up and drop the title to Thesz.

With newfound incentive to "do the right thing," Rogers dropped the title to Thesz on January 24, 1963, in Toronto's Maple Leaf Gardens. The NWA made the match a one-fall affair in order to make it easier for Thesz to win the title in the event Rogers reneged on his promise.

McMahon and Mondt seized on the opportunity granted to them by the NWA. Citing the fact Thesz was 46 years old and semi-retired (ignoring the fact that he was still capable of shooting on Rogers if the situation called for it) and that the title switch was based on only one fall, they refused to recognize Thesz as champion. Weeks later, Mondt and McMahon's World Wide Wrestling Federation was born, with Rogers as its inaugural World Champion.

After losing to Thesz, Rogers suffered a mild heart attack that ended his career as a serious, top caliber performer (although many of his contemporaries are skeptical that he even had a heart attack, suspecting that he concocted the story to save face). While still recovering, he was rushed back into the ring for a series of short tag-team matches, a build-up to him losing the world title to Bruno Sammartino. On May 17, 1963, in Madison Square Garden, Sammartino beat Rogers a mere 47 seconds into the match, and would go on to hold the title for nearly eight years.

Battling health problems dating back to the early part of his world title reign, Rogers retired in the summer of 1963. He returned to action briefly in 1967 to work in Detroit and in Montreal, but was gone just as quickly as he reappeared. He wasn't seen or heard from in wrestling circles again until 1978, when he turned up in Florida working for Eddie

Graham. In 1979, he ventured to Jim Crockett's Mid-Atlantic territory in the Carolinas where he became a heel manager (during a time when being a manager meant something in the business), assembling a heel stable that included Jimmy Snuka, John Studd, and Ken Patera.

It was in the Carolinas that he had his last major run in the ring, against a young Ric Flair. Rogers debuted on Mid-Atlantic TV and took aim at Flair, claiming he had stolen the name "Nature Boy" from him and lifted his entire repertoire of moves. Rogers insisted that Flair demonstrate his version of the figure four, to which Flair immediately responded, making a beeline for the interview podium. As Flair applied the hold on a jobber, Rogers became irate and attacked the young superstar, setting up the inevitable feud.

Rogers tussled with Flair in the "Battle of the Nature Boys," a three match series that culminated in a July 9, Greensboro match, where Flair beat Rogers using the figure four, embarking on the path towards wrestling immortality.

In the early '80s, Rogers ended up in the WWF hosting an interview segment called "Roger's Corner" and managing (and occasionally teaming with) a babyface Jimmy Snuka. By 1984, he retired from wrestling and opened up the Monster Factory with Larry Sharpe in his native New Jersey.

In January 1992, Rogers was back in the public eye, as he agreed to wrestle Buddy Landel, an '80s star who also used the moniker "Nature Boy," on an indie show in Philadelphia. By wrestling in the match, Rogers – now in his seventies but still in tremendous shape – would join Lou Thesz as the only men to have wrestled in seven different decades. Unfortunately for Rogers, the encounter never took place, as the Philadelphia-based promotion folded days before the match was scheduled.

In June of 1992, Rogers slipped and fell in a grocery store, breaking his arm in three places. While in rehabilitation, he suffered the cruelest of fates: he had a mild stroke that impaired his speech and left the previously golden-tongued star – who used classic heel interviews to get over to a generation of wrestling fans – slurring his words.

On June 22, 1992, he was hospitalized in Ft. Lauderdale, Florida, after suffering a major stroke. While in the hospital that same day he had another stroke, which left him blind and completely paralyzed on one side of his body. Four days later, the charismatic "Nature Boy" was silenced, passing away at the age of 71.

11

Frank Gotch

World Heavyweight Champion from 1908 to 1913, Frank Gotch is credited with popularizing pro wrestling in the U.S. and is considered by many historians to be the greatest wrestler of all time.

Gotch was the most famous athlete in the U.S. from the turn of the century until his death in 1917. He was a huge box-office hit – his historic matches with George Hackenschmidt, Stanislaus Zbyszko, and Tom Jenkins regularly outdrew heavyweight title fights in boxing – and he helped to establish pro wrestling as a big-time sporting event.

He was a remarkable physical specimen, standing 5'11" and weighing 210 pounds at his peak. In an era when wrestling was part-shoot and part-work, Gotch was renowned for his tremendous natural strength, his unmatched conditioning and endurance, his quickness inside the ring, and his technical ability.

Gotch's place within American culture and his standing as the greatest historical figure in pro wrestling was recognized by Sports Illustrated when they named him among the greatest athletes of the century in their December 27, 1999 issue. Sports Illustrated also named Gotch among the top 50 athletes in Iowa state history. And while pro wrestlers Danny Hodge (Oklahoma) and Verne Gagne (Minnesota) also made the list for their respective states, they were chosen for their credentials as amateur wrestlers. Gotch's selection was based solely on his performance as a pro wrestler.

Because of Gotch, the state of Iowa has remained the beacon of amateur wrestling in the U.S. to this very day. Even more so than Dan Gable – the former Olympic gold medallist and legendary wrestling coach at Iowa University

Imperial Tobacco trading card issued by Ogdens.

– Gotch is considered to be the most influential amateur wrestler of all time in the U.S.

Noted wrestling writers George Barton, sports editor of the Minneapolis Tribune, and Nat Fleischer, publisher of The Ring magazine, heralded Gotch as the dominant wrestler of his era. Barton, having witnessed several of Gotch's matches from ringside, believed he was responsible for establishing the industry's fan base and for influencing a generation of amateur wrestlers in college to take up pro wrestling.

Frank Alvin Gotch was born on April 27, 1878, the youngest of nine children to German immigrants. Growing up on a farm in rural Iowa, Gotch earned a tough-guy reputation by beating locals in wrestling contests while still a teenager. On June 18, 1899, he wrestled in his first real match against Dan McLeod, former American Heavyweight Champion, in Luverne, Iowa. The two wrestled for close to two hours, with the young Gotch holding his own before McLeod eventually won. McLeod was so blown away with Gotch's ability that he told Martin "Farmer" Burns, the former American Heavyweight Champion, that Gotch was the real deal and that he would be champion one day.

On December 18, 1899, Gotch traveled to Fort Dodge, Iowa, where Burns was offering $25 to anybody who could last 15 minutes with him without getting pinned. Gotch challenged Burns and lasted 11 minutes before finally being pinned. Burns was instantly impressed with Gotch and offered to train him, becoming the guiding light in his career in the same way that "Strangler" Lewis was for Lou Thesz.

After winning several matches in Iowa, Gotch went to Alaska, where he appeared on a traveling wrestling and boxing circuit through mining towns. During his six-month run there, he wrestled under the name Frank Kennedy, piling up one victory after another while being billed as "The Champion of the Klondike."

Gotch returned to Iowa and immediately challenged the muscular Tom Jenkins, the reigning American Heavyweight Champion who had a reputation for roughing up opponents. Gotch, who by this time was a major star, lost his first match against Jenkins in 1903, but rebounded to win the title on January 27, 1904, in Bellingham, Washington. He would go on to exchange the title back and forth with Jenkins and Fred Beel over the next two years.

Gotch continued to dominate the industry, and by 1908 he was set for his historic showdown with George Hackenschmidt. History records that Hackenschmidt, a muscular Adonis from Estonia who was the biggest drawing card in Europe at the time, was undefeated when he faced Gotch, winning the bulk of his matches in less than ten minutes. The heavily-hyped match was to take place in Chicago on April 3, 1908.

The match would turn out to be one of the most important in wrestling history. Gotch beat Hackenschmidt for the world title in a two-and-a-half hour marathon that was reputed to be a shoot. Hackenschmidt lost the first fall when Gotch forced him to submit using an ankle lock. After the fall, both wrestlers went to their dressing rooms for a ten-minute break, but Hackenschmidt refused to return to the ring for the next fall. Gotch was awarded the match and became the World Heavyweight Champion, unifying the world title with his American title.

Gotch continued his supremacy in the ring, defeating high profile challengers Yussiff Mahmout, B. F. Roller, Jess Westergaard, and Jenkins. On June 1, 1910, he beat the great Polish star Stanislaus Zbyszko in Chicago. The top star in Europe at the turn of the century, Zbyszko was reputed to have been undefeated in over 900 straight matches before losing to Gotch.

By the time 1911 rolled around, fans were clamoring for a Gotch-Hackenschmidt rematch. The "dream bout" took place on September 4 at Chicago's Comiskey Park, drawing 28,757 fans for a gate of $87,000 (a record at that time). Gotch won the match, retaining the title. The match is now legendary in wrestling circles as reputedly the first double-cross in history. Weeks before the match Hackenschmidt

tore up his knee during a training session (with either Ad Santel or Ben Roller), putting his bout against Gotch in doubt. It was later revealed that either Santel or Roller was paid off by Gotch to injure Hackenschmidt.

Hackenschmidt wanted to pull out of the match, but was persuaded to go ahead when he was conned into believing that Gotch had injured his neck in training. According to many historians, the two combatants agreed to work a match where Gotch would retain the title but where Hackenschmidt would win a fall, thus appearing strong in defeat. Gotch had other ideas. Once the match started he allegedly started to shoot on Hackenschmidt, quickly winning two straight falls in less than half an hour. By all accounts, Hackenschmidt had no business being in the ring at all, due to his knee injury, and was easy prey for Gotch.

Because Hackenschmidt couldn't move in the ring and was destroyed rather easily by Gotch, fans in attendance felt cheated. As a result, wrestling was all but killed off in Chicago and in many other parts of the country.

Gotch went into semi-retirement in 1912, refusing to meet Zbyszko, who was hounding him for a rematch. However, he came out of retirement to defeat Russian George Lurich on April 1, 1913, and retired again with the title.

By 1915, promoters built up to a match between Gotch and then-world champion Joe Stecher, but the bout never happened as Gotch broke his leg while in training. The following year he fell deathly ill, reputedly from uremic poisoning. He remained bed-ridden in his home in Humboldt, Iowa for two months, growing considerably weaker as each day passed, before finally passing away on December 17, 1917. He was only 39 years old.

As the state of Iowa mourned the death of its native son, the news of his death made the front pages of sports sections all across the country. Even in death, Gotch continued to win accolades and respect. He was a member of the first class of the Des Moines Register Sports Hall of Fame, and was the first inductee into the Professional Wrestling Writers Hall of Fame in 1972. He was also the first inductee into the George Tragos and Lou Thesz-established International Wrestling Institute and Museum in 1999, located in Newton, Iowa.

12

Jim Londos

A former world champion who earned mainstream celebrity equal to that of Hulk Hogan's in his prime, Jim Londos was one of wrestling's biggest stars from the late-1910s to the early-1950s.

Nicknamed the "Golden Greek," Londos was wrestling's first sex symbol, attracting hordes of swooning women to his matches who wanted to catch a glimpse of his well-muscled physique and matinee idol looks. Londos parlayed his popularity and vast wrestling skills into becoming wrestling's most recognizable star in the U.S. during the era of the Great Depression and the New Deal.

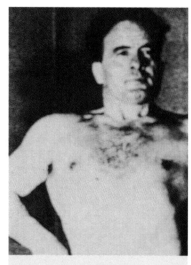
Jim Londos later in his career.

From 1930 to 1932, Londos was the single greatest gate attraction at Madison Square Garden, drawing one sellout after another and revitalizing a New York territory that had been left for dead during the simultaneous rise in popularity of baseball and boxing.

He first became one of the top five stars in the industry after wrestling Ed "Strangler" Lewis to a draw on January 1, 1918, in Canton, Ohio. Because of his capable in-ring skills and handsome features, Londos was given a major push by promoters, who hoped to capitalize on his potential marketability. This became a constant source of resentment for Lewis, who was a former world champion and top star during the '20s. Lewis, one of the greatest shooters of all-time, became Londos' greatest rival both in and out of the ring, as they engaged in a series of highly publicized matches that defined the industry in the '30s.

Born Christopher Theophelus in the 1890s in Argos, Greece, Londos immigrated to the United States at age 13, arriving in New York City. After "riding the rails" across the country to San Francisco, Londos worked several different

jobs while taking up weightlifting, bodybuilding, and wrestling. By 1914, he was working on the carnie circuit, performing a weightlifting act in Portland, Oregon, where he would wrestle shoot matches with "marks." As his popularity rose, he started appearing in major arenas.

"Jim Londos is an interesting study. By all accounts, he was a highly skilled carnival wrestler who had engaged in many wrestling cons back in the days when such things were commonplace," states noted wrestling historian Sheldon Goldberg.

After a decade of working as an undercard performer, Londos began a long association with several versions of the world title that highlighted his storied career. On August 23, 1929, German wrestler Dick Shikat defeated Londos in Philadelphia to become the first world champion recognized by the National Wrestling Association.

After years of being held down by the Ed Lewis and Joe Stecher factions, Londos became the number one man in the industry with the backing of several promoters who recognized his star potential and wanted to push him to the top. Being booked by Joe "Toots" Mondt at this time, he won his first world title on June 6th, 1930, defeating Shikat in Philadelphia. In addition to the NWA's recognition, Londos' victory also brought him world title recognition from the New York State Athletic Commission.

It was during his first title reign that Londos solidified his status as the biggest drawing card of his era. He represented box-office gold for East Coast promoters with his matches at Madison Square Garden, first putting the venerable building on the map. He single-handedly turned the

New York market around, consistently drawing huge sell-out crowds everywhere he went. Londos' incredible box-office run continued into 1931. On June 29, over 21,000 fans (paying a whopping $63,000) filed into Yankee Stadium to watch Londos defeat Ray Steeles.

Londos really hit his stride in late 1931, when four bi-weekly shows at the Garden averaged 15,000 fans with Londos in the main event. The Garden show prior to the four-match run, with a main event featuring Ray Steele vs. Sandor Szabo, drew a paltry 4,000 fans – a true testament to Londos' drawing power and how much he meant to the New York market.

After parting ways with Mondt in 1932, Londos was frozen out of the Garden, and didn't return until 1934. The former partners became bitter rivals when Londos skipped out on a scheduled title defense against Shikat after learning that Mondt had convinced Shikat to shoot on him. Londos was eventually stripped of the New York State Athletic Commission World title in June of 1932 for refusing to defend the belt against Ed Lewis after Lewis defeated Shikat in a number one contender's match. However, Londos continued to reign as NWA World Champion.

After making a deal with Mondt and Lewis, former pro football player Joe Savoldi double-crossed Londos during a match in Chicago on April 7, 1933. Referee Bob Managoff (who also happened to be in Mondt's back pocket) suddenly awarded the fall and the match to Savoldi, making him the new NWA Champion. The match was promoted as a title bout but Londos successfully convinced the Illinois Athletic Commission to rule that they never sanctioned it as such, allowing him to keep the title. On June 25, 1934, Londos won the New York State Athletic Commission World title for the second time, defeating Jim Browning before 20,000 fans in New York. As a result of unifying the NWA and NYSAC belts, Londos began being recognized as the undisputed World Champion in New York.

After Ed White, Londos' original manager, and Mondt called a truce in 1934, Londos was immediately booked into a program with Lewis, culminating in a legendary title match on September 20. Londos retained the title in 49 minutes in front of 35,625 fans in Chicago's Wrigley Field, setting a gate record that lasted until 1951 and an attendance record that lasted until the historic Buddy Rogers vs. Pat O'Connor NWA title match at Comiskey Park in 1961.

The match was such a huge success because it was hyped as a shoot, building upon the legitimate heat between

Wrestling's original Golden Greek.

the two (similar to how the WWF promoted the Shawn Michaels-Bret Hart encounter in Montreal in 1997). The match drew fans from across the country as people wanted to see if Lewis was going to show Londos up in the ring. But of course, Lewis had already agreed to put over Londos.

On June 27, 1935, Londos dropped the title to Danno O'Mahoney in Boston. Londos retired after the match but returned to action in February 1936. He spent most of 1936 and 1937 touring Europe and Africa and continued to draw big at the box-office. By 1938, he had resumed a full-time schedule in the U.S. and reestablished his old drawing power in New York City. In the fall of 1938 he defeated Bronko Nagurski in Philadelphia to win the world title. The win over Nagurski, a former NFL great who was one of wrestling's biggest stars during the late-'30s and early-'40s, demonstrated how much power Londos still had.

He was stripped of the title several times in California and Baltimore in 1944, but was still billed as world champion wherever he traveled. He retired once again at the end of 1952, but eventually returned to tour Australia in 1959, drawing 14,000 fans for a match against former World Heavyweight Boxing Champion Primo Carnera.

Londos died of a heart attack on August 19, 1975, in Escondido, California.

13

Ed "Strangler" Lewis

The biggest wrestling star and most dominant world champion of the '20s, Ed "Strangler" Lewis is one of the seminal figures in wrestling history and is credited with helping to change wrestling from legitimate sport to a complete work.

Lewis, named after 1890s champion Evan "Strangler" Lewis, is remembered for his epic matches against Joe Stecher, Jim Londos, Earl Caddock, and Stanislaus Zbyszko, and is considered one of the best shooters of all time. As one third of the powerful "Gold Dust Trio" with promoter Billy Sandow and Joe "Toots" Mondt (the '20s equivalent of the Hogan/McMahon dynasty of the '80s), Lewis was wrestling's preeminent star and was a mainstream sports figure in the U.S. between 1920 and 1929.

The bulk of historians agree that the "Gold Dust Trio" revolutionized the business between 1921 and 1925 by introducing concepts – such as building storylines through wins and losses and promoting events as entire shows, with undercards and other features, instead of just a one-match attraction – that became fundamental in pro wrestling.

The "Gold Dust Trio" syndicate was a traveling road show that toured the country – the forerunner of the wrestling tour of the modern era. At the center of it all was Ed Lewis.

"Ed Lewis was probably the pivotal figure in the development of professional wrestling as we know it," says noted historian Sheldon Goldberg. "The 'Gold Dust Trio' created the basis for what pro wrestling is today and essentially controlled the industry in this country. Sandow was the business mind. Mondt was the architect of the concept of developing programs and finishes in the matches themselves. Ed Lewis, however, was the crown jewel, because he

Wrestling's greatest shooter, Ed Lewis.

was the muscle that pulled it all off.... The fact that much of the concepts that the 'Gold Dust Trio' developed are still in use today speaks to just how towering and enduring a figure Ed Lewis really is in the history of professional wrestling."

Ed Lewis was born Robert Friedrich in Nekoosa, Wisconsin. Most historians believe he was born on June 30, 1891, while others insist it was in 1890. Growing up as a teenager in Kentucky, Lewis reportedly had his first pro match at the age of 14 in 1904. Lewis challenged World Champion Joe Stecher (renowned shooter and master of the body scissors) on October 21, 1915, in Evansville, Indiana.

On July 4th, 1916, Lewis battled Stecher to a draw in Omaha, Nebraska, that lasted five hours. Some historians point to this match as wrestling's turning point – where it transformed from a legitimate sport to a work – while others say worked wrestling matches date back as early as the 1880s.

Lewis won his first world title (the Olin Title Line) on May 2, 1917, by defeating John Olin in Chicago. He dropped it to Wladek Zbyszko on June 15 in San Francisco, and then won it back a month later in Boston. On December 22, Lewis lost the title for the final time to Zbyszko in New York. This was believed to be the first worked program for the world title.

Over the next few years he would exchange the main branch of the world title with Joe Stecher and Zbyszko. In the mid-'20s, after regaining the world title with the backing of Sandow and Mondt, Lewis began to roll over contenders, becoming so dominant that few fans believed anybody could ever beat him. In 1925, Sandow created the first non-wrestler world champion in Wayne Munn. Sandow believed that Munn, a hulking college football star, had drawing potential and wanted to capitalize on his legitimate athletic background. Even though Munn had no wrestling ability, he defeated Lewis for the world title on January 8, setting up a huge Munn-Lewis rematch, which Sandow hoped to book in a large stadium.

While setting up the title match, Sandow and Mondt booked Munn in a match against noted shooter Stanislaus Zbyszko in order to establish him in the eyes of the public. Unbeknownst to them, Zbyszko had secretly jumped to the Joe Stecher circuit prior to the match on April 15, 1925. In one of the most significant double-crosses in wrestling history, Zbyszko shot on the outmatched Munn and scored so many pins that the referee, despite being in Sandow's pocket, had no choice but to award the title to Zbyszko.

Zbyszko completed the transaction when he dropped the title to Joe Stecher on May 30 in St. Louis, bringing the world title to the opposing syndicate and changing the balance of power in the industry. Tensions furthered between the two groups as wrestlers secretly jumped back and forth in a promotional war that was the equivalent of the '90s WWF vs. WCW feud. By 1928, Stecher wanted out of wrestling and dropped the title to Lewis on February 20 in St. Louis. However, a year later Lewis lost the title to Gus Sonnenberg, another former football player who Sandow thought had drawing potential.

After a tour of Europe, Lewis returned to the U.S. and wrestled a few more matches before retiring and moving back to Wisconsin. It wasn't long before Mondt, now at war with Sandow, called him up for his help when National Wrestling Association World Champion Jim Londos left the syndicate. Mondt booked a Lewis vs. Dick Shikat match for June 9th, 1932, in Long Island, which he billed as a "number one contender match." Lewis won the match, but Londos denied him a title shot. As a result, he was stripped of world title recognition in New York. Lewis went on to win the New York branch of the world title when he beat Jack Sherry on October 10, in New York.

With Lewis back as world champion and Londos gone, the bottom fell out of the New York market. Londos, meanwhile, continued to defend the National Wrestling Association world title around the country. Lewis eventually dropped his world title to Jim Browning on February 20, 1933. As Lewis' numbers at the box-office started to drop,

Ed "Strangler" Lewis demonstrates his crushing full nelson submission grip.

Londos was brought back in to be the number one man in the territory.

Ed Lewis vs. Jim Londos was booked for Chicago's Wrigley Field on September 20, 1934. As the bout neared, the media hype escalated. Mondt did his part by leaking to the press that it was going to be a shoot, even though Lewis had already agreed to the job. Mondt's promotional efforts came to fruition, as 35,265 fans turned up for the show (paying $96,302, a gate record that would stand until 1952). Londos won the match after 49 minutes.

Lewis went into semi-retirement after a tour of Europe in early 1935. He discovered, and gradually took an interest in a youngster named Lou Thesz, and eventually became the guiding influence behind his career.

Lewis came out of retirement in 1942, by this time out of shape and legally blind, and began working for promoter Al Haft in Ohio, where he defeated Orville Brown for the Midwest Wrestling Association title. By 1954, Lou Thesz was NWA World Champion and Lewis was traveling on the road with him as his manager. He lived out his remaining days in Tulsa, Oklahoma, before being permanently hospitalized.

Lewis died on August 7, 1966.

14

Stan Hansen

A four-time holder of All Japan's Triple Crown title and a former AWA World Heavyweight Champion, Stan Hansen was the most popular foreign wrestler in Japanese history.

Hansen was an icon in Japan, thanks to his 120-plus Japanese tours (the most by any foreign wrestler in history). One of the greatest brawlers of all time, Hansen personified toughness in the ring in his legendary matches against Antonio Inoki, Giant Baba, Jumbo Tsuruta, Andre the Giant, Genichiro Tenryu, The Funks, Vader, and Mitsuharu Misawa. In these matches, Hansen brought a level of intensity and believability that Japanese

Stan Hansen with his AWA World Championship.

wrestling had never seen before. Due to his influence, All Japan gained a reputation in the wrestling community as the most physically taxing and athletically credible promotion in the world.

The quintessential *gaijin* wrestler (Japanese for foreigner), Hansen played the role of monster-heel to perfection, paving the road for American heavyweights that would follow him to Japan, including Vader, Bam Bam Bigelow, Steve Williams, Terry Gordy, and Gary Albright.

Trained by Terry and Dory Funk Jr., Hansen was a football standout at West Texas State before entering pro wrestling in 1973. He worked in the Funks' Amarillo territory before they sent him to All Japan for his first tour in 1975. His first big break came in 1976 when he feuded with then WWWF World Champion Bruno Sammartino, when Sammartino suffered a broken neck in a match on April 26 in Madison Square Garden. Hansen's status as a superstar killer heel was established. The rematch on June 25, 1976 drew 32, 000 fans to New York's Shea Stadium, setting the

all-time North American gate record of $400,000 (a record that lasted until August 9, 1980 when the famous Bruno Sammartino-Larry Zbyszko cage match at Shea Stadium drew 36,295 fans and a $537,421 gate).

In 1977, Vince McMahon Sr. sent Hansen to New Japan Pro Wrestling, where he feuded with Inoki for the better part of four years. In one of the most significant moments in Japanese wrestling history, Hansen secretly left New Japan for All Japan and accompanied Bruiser Brody and Jimmy Snuka to the ring during the finals of the Real World Tag League on December 13, 1981. Hansen later formed a groundbreaking tag team with Brody, bringing violence and bedlam to the rings of All Japan for over two years, and changing the perception in Japan that American wrestlers couldn't be main event stars.

Hansen's surprise move to Baba's promotion (similar to Lex Luger's jump from the WWF to WCW 14 years later when he secretly left McMahon and appeared on the very first edition of Nitro) incited a bitter promotional rivalry between New Japan and All Japan that saw the two companies frequently raiding each other's talent rosters. Hansen was a mainstay in All Japan where he became a main event star and the top foreign heel in the country. In between tours he would return to the U.S., where he worked for several territories, capturing the AWA World Heavyweight title on December 29, 1985, from Rick Martel.

When Verne Gagne wanted Hansen to drop the AWA title to Nick Bockwinkel in June of 1986, Hansen refused, as Baba wanted Hansen to wear the AWA title belt on his next tour for All Japan. Because Stan refused to drop the belt in the ring, Gagne stripped Hansen of the title and awarded it to Bockwinkel on June 29, 1986 in Denver, Colorado.

In 1989 Baba turned to Hansen to help him create the Triple Crown title. The April 18 match (where he put over Jumbo Tsuruta), unified the NWA International, Pacific Wrestling Federation and All Japan United National titles. It was a classic match, and immediately established the Triple Crown as the most legitimate world title in all of wrestling.

Later, as Triple Crown Champion, Hansen was part of one of the most memorable title chase programs in history, finally dropping the belt on August 22, 1992, to Misawa. Misawa's title victory was the culmination of a masterfully planned storyline by Baba, which was executed to perfection by Hansen. With great attention to detail and a slow, methodical pace, Misawa chased the title for two years. When Hansen dropped the title to Misawa, he also passed on the mantle of leadership: Misawa would go on to become the cornerstone of the promotion for the next generation.

Hansen's work in losing to Misawa was a perfect example of an older, established veteran losing to an emerging young wrestler, elevating him into the top spot in the process. His selflessness and professionalism earned him worldwide respect from people within the industry, who admired the great pains he took to properly put Misawa over as the promotion's top star.

Years of grueling punishment inside the rings of All Japan began to take its toll on Hansen. His body began to break down and he could no longer compete at the incredible standard he set for himself throughout his career. After a brilliant 27-year career, Hansen retired in 2000 as a result of lumbago, a painful affliction affecting the lower back that he had been suffering with for several years. Looking back at his career, Hansen has no regrets about leaving wrestling when he did.

"I wrestled so long it was time, physically for me to [retire]," recalled Hansen in the spring of 2001. "I think I got out when God was telling me to get out. I feel blessed that I had a great career. Physically I was to the point where I couldn't [go on]. I always said if I couldn't compete on my standards then I would stop. It got to that point and I've never looked back."

Other career highlights include: four Real World Tag Team Championships (in 1983 with Bruiser Brody, 1985 with Ted DiBiase, 1988 with Terry Gordy, and 1989 with

Hansen bloodies Wahoo McDaniel.

Genichiro Tenryu); Carnival Championships in 1992 and 1993; four reigns as PWF Heavyweight Champion; multiple reigns as All Japan and PWF Tag Team Champion; and a run as United National Heavyweight Champion.

15

Bruno Sammartino

A two-time WWWF World Champion, Bruno Sammartino headlined more shows at Madison Square Garden than any other wrestler in history, and was arguably the biggest box-office draw in the business during the '60s and '70s.

For two decades, Sammartino was the backbone of Vince McMahon Sr.'s promotional dynasty in the Northeast, helping to build it into the top-drawing territory in the U.S. As one of wrestling's most popular stars of his era, Sammartino was the focal point of McMahon Sr.'s signature promoting philosophy: a babyface champion marketed to large ethnic populations who feuded against a constantly rotating crop of heel challengers.

Bruno active in retirement at a charity event.

Sammartino's two world title reigns, taking place in an era when titles meant everything, lasted a combined 11 years, a testament to the sheer magnitude and drawing power of the man that truly earned the nickname "The Living Legend."

Sammartino was born in Abruzzi, Italy, in 1935 and immigrated to the United States with his family at age 15. While living in Pittsburgh as a teenager he worked out with weights and wrestled in high school. He wrestled in his first pro match in 1959, and for the next two years he worked for McMahon and Joe "Toots" Mondt's Capitol Wrestling.

In 1961, he left Capitol and went to Toronto, where he received his first big push working for Jack Tunney. In 1963, McMahon brought Sammartino back to New York and on May 17, 1963, he defeated Buddy Rogers for the WWWF World title at Madison Square Garden in 48 seconds.

Sammartino's first world title reign was highlighted by memorable title defenses against Gorilla Monsoon, Killer Kowalski, "Big" Bill Miller, "Superstar" Billy Graham, Waldo Von Erich, Freddie Blassie, Don Leo Johnathan, and Bill Watts. Sammartino became an institution at Madison Square Garden, surpassing the Antonino Rocca era of 1949-1960, and becoming the new top draw at the historic building. By the time his career was over, Sammartino had wrestled in 126 main events at the Garden between 1960 and 1986. With 41 confirmed sellouts, Sammartino tops the all-time list in the history of MSG.

After nearly eight years as World Champion, Sammartino dropped the belt to Ivan Koloff on January 18, 1971.

By 1972, Pedro Morales replaced Bruno as the new ethic babyface world champion, marketed towards New York's large Puerto Rican population. In late 1972, Bruno began touring for the newly-formed All Japan Pro Wrestling, becoming one of the top foreign stars in Japan during the '70s.

With business down slightly during the Morales-era, McMahon convinced Sammartino to come back to New York on a fulltime basis. On December 10, 1973, he defeated Stan Stasiak for the world title before 22,000 fans at the Garden. On April 26, 1976, Sammartino suffered a broken neck during a match against Stan Hansen when he was dumped on his head during a poorly executed slam.

With his world champion on the shelf, McMahon weaved his promoting magic: the word quickly spread that Hansen had broken Sammartino's neck with a clothesline. It turned out to be a stroke of genius. Hansen was dubbed "The Lariat" and became an instant killer heel.

The injury allowed McMahon to build up the feud between Sammartino and Hansen and set up the inevitable

Bruno Sammartino publicity photo showing off his first WWWF title belt.

rematch. On June 25, 1976, Sammartino returned to the ring, defeating Hansen in front of 32,000 fans at Shea Stadium (and setting the all-time North American gate record of $400,000 in the process).

Sammartino's second World Title reign came to an end on April 30, 1977, when he lost to "Superstar" Bill Graham in Baltimore. After dropping the belt, Sammartino began teaming with Larry Zbyszko. Together Sammartino, billed as the mentor, and Zbyszko, tagged as Bruno's eventual successor, became two of the top babyfaces in the promotion. McMahon, sensing he was sitting on something special, split them up in early 1980, turning Zbyszko on Sammartino during a televised one-on-one match that pitted teacher vs. student. Zbyszko's heel turn was one of the most memorable angles of the '80s, and served as the catalyst for one of the biggest matches in history. The bout took place on August 9, 1980, in a steel cage. The 36,295 that passed through the turnstiles at Shea Stadium paid a whopping $537,421, breaking the North American record set four years earlier.

Sammartino retired in September 1981, wrestling his "retirement match" against George Steele before going on one final tour of All Japan in October. While serving as a color commentator for the WWF, he came out of retire-

ment in February 1985, teaming with his son David.

In between announcing duties, Sammartino wrestled the odd match, including a pair of main events in the summer of 1986 at the Garden. Disgusted over the changes McMahon Jr. brought to the wrestling industry and suffering from an ailing back, Sammartino quit the WWF and became a vocal critic of the company.

For all the battles he had in buildings like Madison Square Garden, it is Sammartino's battle against McMahon in the ring of public opinion that garnered the most attention. Sammartino was a constant pain in the WWF's side, attacking McMahon in print and television interviews. Their most famous encounters came on *Larry King Live* and the *Phil Donahue* show in March 1992, as Sammartino accused McMahon of attempting to cover up the steroid and sex scandals that rocked the WWF.

Bruno also testified against the WWF in a 1994 jury trial involving former preliminary wrestler Chuck Austin, who was paralyzed after a 1990 WWF tag team match against The Rockers. Sammartino proved to be the pivotal witness in the trial, and Austin was awarded a $23.5 million verdict.

16

The Rock

A third generation performer who took the business by storm in the late '90s, The Rock skyrocketed to the top of the wrestling world less than three years after making his pro debut, becoming one of the biggest stars in the industry.

During The Rock's rise to superstardom he became known as one of the most charismatic performers of his era, second in popularity only to "Stone Cold" Steve Austin. In his high profile feuds with Austin, the Undertaker, Triple H, Mick Foley, and Kurt Angle, he became wrestling's premier showman, captivating audiences with his boundless personality.

Borrowing heavily from classic Ric Flair interviews, The Rock combined his natural charisma with a healthy dose of exaggerated expressions and mannerisms to become one of the most effective promo men in the business. Pure magic with a microphone in his hand, his sayings were so catchy that they became part of the everyday vernacular of wrestling fans. He had such presence and got over so huge during interviews that it was joked among insiders that he could have stood in the middle of the ring and read numbers from the phone book, and still made it sound entertaining.

The Rock was a major figure in the WWF during its boom period in the late '90s, when it overtook WCW in the aftermath of the historic "Monday Night Wars." He was also one of the most identifiable sports personalities of his time, earning name recognition around the world on par with the biggest stars of major league baseball, the NFL and NBA.

It seemed inevitable that The Rock, born Dwayne Johnson on May 2, 1972, would become a pro wrestler. The son

World Champ, The Rock.

of Rocky Johnson, a popular babyface with the WWWF in the late '70s and early '80s, and the grandson of High Chief Peter Maivia, a main-event star from the '60s to early '80s, Johnson played football at the University of Miami before entering pro wrestling.

After training for wrestling with his father, The Rock secured a series of try-out matches with the WWF in early 1996. He was signed to a developmental contract and sent to Jerry Lawler's Memphis-based United States Wrestling Association promotion to gain experience. He spent the first months of his career working under the name Flex Kavana before he was brought back up by the WWF in November, "debuting" as Rocky Maivia at Survivor Series. Despite his relative inexperience, he was given an immediate push, and won the WWF Intercontinental title on February 13, 1997, from Hunter Hearst Helmsley.

Fans didn't take to him at first because of his white-meat, babyface image, barraging him with choruses of "Rocky Sucks" and "Die, Rocky, Die" chants on a nightly basis. A breakout performance at SummerSlam '98 in a ladder match against Triple H helped him gain acceptance among hardened fans and launched him on his way to the upper tier of the WWF's roster.

He turned heel later that year, becoming a henchman for Vince McMahon in the landmark McMahon vs. Austin feud that helped turn the WWF's fortunes around. Then, on November 15, 1998, he won his first WWF World title at Survivor Series, defeating Mick Foley in the final of a 13-man tournament for the vacant title. The win, however, was

Chris Jericho applies the liontamer on The Rock.

marred by a "screw-job" ending (a takeoff on the infamous Montreal double-cross one year earlier and an obvious thumbing of the nose at Bret Hart and WCW), which saw The Rock lock Foley into a sharpshooter and McMahon immediately call for the bell.

After dropping the title to Mick Foley twice in a four-week period, he appeared in his first WrestleMania main event on March 28, 1999, losing the strap to Austin. It would be another two years before The Rock regained the World title. In the meantime he turned babyface again and continued to have one marquee feud after another with every top star in the company.

By February 2001, The Rock was the WWF World Champion again (for the sixth time) and was headed into a main event match against Austin at WrestleMania XVII on April 1 at the Houston Astro Dome. The Rock dropped the title to Austin in a memorable match that was the climax of the biggest revenue-producing show in the history of pro wrestling (pulling in over $40.6 million in revenues from pay-per-view, merchandising sales, and live gate – records in all three categories).

Almost overnight, The Rock parlayed his popularity from his wrestling career into huge mainstream success. He had a role in *The Mummy Returns*, a Hollywood film directed by Stephen Sommers in 2001. That same year, Universal Pictures inked him to a reported $5.5 million deal to star in *The Scorpion King*, making him the highest-paid actor ever for a debut starring role.

His 2000 autobiography, *The Rock Says*, spent 20 weeks on the New York Times bestseller list, reaching number one and selling over 700,000 copies. On March 18, 2000, he appeared on NBC's *Saturday Night Live*, joining Hulk Hogan as the only pro wrestlers ever to host the popular program. He was a special guest at the 2000 Republican National Convention, where he officially launched a convention session, and he has been the subject of many major media articles, gracing such magazine covers as Newsweek and TV Guide. The June 7, 2001, issue of Rolling Stone featured a full-length cover story on him during the filming of *The Scorpion King*.

On March 17, 2002, The Rock defeated Hulk Hogan at WrestleMania X8 in front of over 68,000 fans at Toronto's SkyDome in an epic battle of two of the greatest icons the wrestling world has ever known.

17

Gorgeous George

Nicknamed the "Toast of the Coast," the "Sensation of the Nation," and the "Human Orchid," Gorgeous George changed the landscape of pro wrestling in the late-'40s and '50s with his outrageous gimmicks. Famous for his bleached-blond hair done up in curls, his fancy sequined robes, and his sissy in-ring mannerisms, George was the biggest star in the U.S. when pro wrestling was first broadcast on network television in 1948.

Thanks to the exposure of national television and his regular appearances with friend Bob Hope, Gorgeous George became a household name and the most famous sports celebrity in the country.

He was believed to have been the highest paid athlete in the world, making in excess of $100,000 a year. He was a tremendous drawing card and meant so much to the business, especially on the west coast, that he often commanded 50 percent of the gate, easily the highest percentage in wrestling history.

Gorgeous George was born George Raymond Wagner in 1915 in Seward, Nebraska, but he grew up in Houston, Texas. He worked under his real name for the first few years, distinguishing himself as a decent junior heavyweight and winning the Pacific Coast Light Heavyweight title, on May 19, 1939, in Eugene, Oregon.

During this time he met Betty Hanson, a cashier in Eugene, and the two were married. By 1940, George began to develop a new gimmick based on Lord Patrick Lansdowne, a '30s star who entered the ring wearing a monocle and a velvet robe.

Don Owen was a legendary promoter in the Portland,

Gorgeous George with wife and valet Cherie Dupree.

Oregon, area for 68 years. His son Barry recalls a story he heard from his dad about how Wagner first got over.

"[Betty] used to make his ring robe and outfits and put a lot of work into them, so he took a long time taking his stuff off in the ring, and really fussed over and took care of them. The outfits got more extravagant as time passed and he ended up taking more time. Now, you can imagine how this went over with an audience full of loggers and lumberjacks. Here was this guy taking his time and they grew impatient and wanted the action to start. So he would use that and take even longer until the point where it became a part of his whole act."

George was on to something; the opening match ritual of disrobing became a regular part of his act, and eventually, promoters started billing him as Gorgeous George.

Wagner's career skyrocketed in Los Angeles in the early '40s when promoter Johnny Doyle gave him a serious push. Looking to add something to his act, George visited a beauty salon where he bleached his hair blond and was advised to let his hair grow out, leading to the long, golden locks he became famous for.

During television's first years, stations around the country looked to fill their schedule with cheap programming. Because it was a spectator sport that could be captured with the unsophisticated cameras of that time, wrestling became a staple of network television. And at the center of it all was Gorgeous George.

On February 22, 1949, George wrestled his first and only match at New York's Madison Square Garden, for promoter

Gorgeous George against Ernie Dusek at Madison Square Garden.

Bill Johnson. This was the dark period of the Garden, as poor attendance and in-fighting between the several warring factions of promoters had kept wrestling out of the building for 11 years. Johnson brought in George, who was a national star by this time, thinking he could sell out the building and bring back wrestling as a regular feature.

Instead, it turned out to be a flop. Only 4,197 fans showed up at the Garden to see George pin Ernie Dusek. The New York newspapers had a field day, labeling the show a fiasco while panning Gorgeous George's act as a pale imitation of men like Jim Londos and Strangler Lewis.

In the early '50s he married his second wife, Cherie Dupree, and she became part of the act as his valet. Cherie would make her way down to the ring, spreading rose petals down the aisle, which was adorned with a long, red carpet. As he made his way to the ring with the strains of "Pomp and Circumstance" blaring over the PA system, he would toss gold-colored hairpins, dubbed "Georgie Pins," to ringside fans.

On May 26, 1950, in Chicago, George was involved in a double-cross of then-AWA (Boston) World Champion Don Eagle in a title match booked by promoter Fred Kohler. Boston promoter Paul Bowser let Kohler book Eagle on the condition he remain champion. With the help of friend Jack Pfefer, a Toledo promoter, they took the title off of

Eagle with a fast count from the referee. George left the building with the title, but was never recognized as the champion.

George's most famous feud came in the late-'50s with former NWA World Heavyweight Champion "Whipper" Billy Watson. Their historic series of matches culminated in 1959, when Watson defeated George in a hair vs. hair match in Toronto's Maple Leaf Gardens, forcing the outrageous star to have his long golden locks sheared. One week later in Toronto, Cherie had her head shaved in a return match. Despite wrestling's low drawing-power in most parts of North America (due to the loss of network TV coverage), both matches drew sellout crowds of over 15,000 fans each. The only other time George had his head shaved came on November 7, 1962, when he lost a hair vs. mask match to The Destroyer at the fabled Olympic Auditorium in Los Angeles. It turned out to be his last match.

During his storied career, George reportedly made close to $2 million, but never saved his money and lived out his final days in destitution while battling alcoholism.

On Christmas Eve 1963, George Wagner suffered a heart attack while in his Hollywood apartment. Two days later he died in Los Angeles General Hospital. He was only 48.

18

Bruiser Brody

One of wrestling's true outlaws who played the game by his own set of rules, Bruiser Brody was the quintessential brawler of his era and among the most influential performers in wrestling history.

At 6'5" and 280 pounds, Brody (born Frank Goodish) managed to bring mayhem, chaos and bedlam with him wherever he traveled. He was the best pure brawler (and arguably the top all-around worker) of the '80s, trailblazing a path for every brawler and big man that followed in his footsteps.

His matches served as the blueprint for the likes of Mick Foley and countless others to copy from. Wrestlers breaking into the business studied tapes of his matches, and promoters held up his ring work as an example of how a big man was supposed to work and get over with fans. Coming out to the ring while swinging a metal chain in his trademark black trunks and furry boots, Brody parted a walkway through the sea of ringside fans with his blood-curdling shouts and instilling the fear of God into them.

From 1978 to 1988, he was among the top five workers in the business, on par with the likes of Ric Flair, The Dynamite Kid, Ted DiBiase and Jumbo Tsuruta. He was easily wrestling's number one star internationally, was the top drawing wrestler on the U.S. independent circuit, and the most popular foreign wrestler in Japan and Puerto Rico at the time of his death.

In the role of the barking madman, Brody carved out a name for himself by carving up the foreheads of opponents like Dusty Rhodes, Terry Funk, Harley Race, Carlos Colon and Abdullah the Butcher.

Brody was a legend both in and out of the ring. In the

Mick Foley's role model, Bruiser Brody, 1974.

seedy world of pro wrestling where promoters rule with an iron fist and make wrestlers toe the line, Brody was a maverick. He was a true free agent, wrestling where and when he wanted, refusing to be tied down to any one promoter or territory. He was a shrewd businessman, setting his own schedule and often times holding up promoters for more pay at the last minute. Brody was notorious for ignoring instructions from bookers, refusing to put wrestlers over when asked and often going into business for himself during the course of a match. Over a six-year period, he did not do one single clean-pin job.

Despite this, promoters couldn't get enough of Brody, as he bounced around North America from territory to territory as a hired gun. Promoters would bring Brody into their territories when attendance was down to help pop a huge gate. Whenever they did, Brody was sure to sell the building out. And like he had done so many times before, he was out the door on his way to the next territory.

Brody played college football at West Texas State and after a failed career in pro football made his wrestling debut in 1973. He shuffled around between Leroy McGuirk's Mid-South office and Fritz Von Erich's Dallas territory before catching his first big break in 1975. While wrestling as a headliner in Florida he caught the eye of Killer Kowalski, who recommended to Vince McMahon Sr. that he bring him up to New York in 1976. McMahon gave him the name Bruiser Brody, programming him in a series of matches against then-wwf World Champion Bruno Sammartino.

Then, while working for Von Erich in 1978, he was booked into Sam Muchnick's St. Louis territory, where he became one of the biggest box-office draws in the country. In January 1979, while still in Dallas, he began competing for All Japan. With his freakish size, Brody was an instant hit in Japan and became a cult hero to fans, breaking the stranglehold Japanese stars had on the business there.

He formed a legendary tag team with Stan Hansen in 1982, feuding with Terry and Dory Funk Jr. They won the Real World Tag League tournament in 1983 and were crowned the first PWF World Tag Team Champions on April 25, 1984. At the height of the promotional war between Baba and Antonio Inoki, Brody left All Japan for New Japan in 1985, signing a $14, 000 a week contract with Inoki, the richest deal in wrestling at that time. Such was his drawing power and influence.

Brody was instantly thrust into a main event program with Inoki, drawing huge crowds and gates all across Japan. But by the end of the year, the two had a falling out over money. His frustration was exacted in the ring when he deviated from the script during a match with New Japan booker Seiji Sakaguchi, nailing him in the knee with his chain. The next day Brody walked out on the tour (and on over $40, 000 in wages).

He returned briefly to New Japan in 1986 and ended up in Dallas as booker for Von Erich before Baba brought him back to All Japan in 1987. At the same time Brody was the top heel in Puerto Rico. Brody started working for Carlos Colon's World Wrestling Council in 1983, helping to make the Caribbean office into one of the hottest territories.

On July 16, 1988 while on tour in Puerto Rico, Brody got into a pre-match argument in a locker-room with wrestler Jose Huertas Gonzales (who was also the territory's booker). After Brody went back into the showers, Gonzales followed him in. Moments later, wrestlers heard screams and watched as Brody stumbled out towards them with several stab wounds while Gonzales left the building.

Brody's liver and lung had been punctured. Medics were called on the scene, but it took them approximately 40 minutes to get him loaded into an ambulance. He died on the operating table in the hospital after bleeding to death at approximately 4:30 a.m., July 17, 1988. He was 42 years old.

"Bruiser Brody was pronounced dead on an operating table in San Juan," wrote Dave Meltzer in the July 16, 1988 edition of the Wrestling Observer Newsletter. "He was the victim of several stab wounds suffered at the hands of another wrestler in the dressing room the previous night before a card in Juan Lobriel Stadium in Bayamon, nine

Part of a six man match where Bruiser Brody teamed with Gene Kiniski and Ed Wiskowski (Col. DeBeers) to defeat T. John Tibedoux and the Funk Brothers, January, 1981.

miles outside of San Juan. The last of the wrestling outlaws had been put down for the count. But this was no angle. And there would be no rematch."

Gonzales was arrested for first-degree murder the following day but the charges were reduced to voluntary homicide at a preliminary hearing in November 1988. He was acquitted of those charges on February 2, 1989.

The two doctors that treated Brody prior to his death testified that Brody told them what happened before he went on the operating table, and, immediately after the incident, wrestler Tony Atlas told police he witnessed the stabbing through a window. Atlas, however, refused to testify at the trial after receiving several death threats, while Colon and Victor Jovica, two of Gonzales' business partners in WWC, testified on his behalf. The judge dismissed the testimony of the two doctors and with no witnesses testifying on Brody's behalf and the police unable to retrieve the murder weapon, the jury acquitted Gonzales, allowing him to escape justice in the eyes of wrestling fans all around the world.

Gonzales may have been able to silence the man, but he couldn't silence the legend or legacy. The spirit of Frank Goodish lived on in countless wrestlers who patterned their careers on the revolutionary and innovative working style of Bruiser Brody, the greatest brawler the wrestling industry has ever known.

19

Riki Choshu

Riki Choshu was the heart and soul of New Japan Pro Wrestling during one of the greatest boom periods in Japanese wrestling, and was arguably one of the most successful promoter/bookers in history.

A three-time IWGP Heavyweight Champion, Choshu's classic matches against Tatsumi Fujinami, Antonio Inoki, Jumbo Tsuruta, Vader, and countless others helped to strengthen his legendary status as one of Japan's biggest stars.

Choshu was born Mitsuo Kwak on December 3, 1951, in South Korea, but grew up in Japan. He represented South Korea in the 1972 Olympics in the freestyle wrestling competition while

Three time IWGP Champ, Riki Choshu.

attending Senshu University in Tokyo. He eventually changed his name to Mitsuo Yoshida, and on December 6, 1973, he became a student at the New Japan training dojo. He made his pro debut on August 8, 1974, in Tokyo.

He changed his name to Riki Choshu three years later, before going to Mexico to gain some experience. While he was there he feuded with Canek in a marquee program, capturing the UWA World title on July 23, 1982.

When he came back to Japan, he turned on Fujinami on October 8, 1982, during a six-man tag match that was the catalyst behind arguably the most important angle in Japanese history. The fake shoot angle saw a frustrated Choshu form Ishingun – a worked promotion within a promotion – to feud with the established stars of New Japan, collectively called Seikigun.

As a result of the heel turn, Choshu was instantly elevated as a headliner and feuded with Fujinami in main events for two years over the WWF International Heavyweight strap.

The Ishingun vs. Seikigun feud, combined with the explosion of Tiger Mask and the subsequent success of its emerging junior heavyweights, helped New Japan enjoy one of the greatest stretches of box-office business in history, with a 90% sellout rate over a one-year period and consistent prime-time television ratings in the 20-25 range. The feud also helped to change the long-established booking philosophy which held that main-event feuds had to pit Japanese stars vs. foreigners.

In the aftermath of Inoki's embezzlement scandal, New Japan promoter Naoki Otsuka secretly negotiated with Giant Baba in spearheading the biggest tactical move in the legendary All Japan vs. New Japan promotional war. In late 1984, a group that included Choshu, Masa Saito, Yoshiaki Yatsu, Animal Hamaguchi, Kuniaki Kobayashi, and The Dynamite Kid jumped to All Japan.

The mass defection of talent – much like Mitsuharu Misawa leaving All Japan in 2000 and taking the bulk of its talent roster with him to form Pro Wrestling NOAH – all but crippled New Japan. All Japan became the battleground of another worked promotion vs. promotion feud, as the landmark Choshu's Army vs. All Japan program set the company on fire. All Japan enjoyed banner years in 1985 and 1986 as Choshu feuded with Jumbo Tsuruta and Genichiro Tenryu.

Choshu jumped back to New Japan in 1987, bringing most of the talent that had gone to All Japan with him. As a result Akira Maeda, the rising star in the promotion, was pushed further down in the pecking order.

Maeda responded by perpetrating one of the single

greatest acts of cowardice in wrestling history, delivering a shoot kick to Choshu's eye during a six-man tag match. Choshu's hands were tied up as he held Osamu Kido in a Scorpion Deathlock, rendering him completely defenseless as Maeda broke his orbital bone and knocked him out cold.

Ten years before the infamous "Montreal screw-job" changed the course of wrestling history, "the shoot kick" became the talk of the industry as one of the biggest in-ring double-crosses ever. As a result of the incident Choshu was sidelined for six weeks.

From 1989 to 1992, Choshu won three IWGP Heavyweight titles, trading the title back and forth between Vader and Fujinami. After Inoki won election to the Japanese senate and became less and less involved in the day-to-day operations of New Japan, Choshu assumed political control of the company along with Hiroshi Hase and Masa Saito. Under Choshu's guidance, New Japan became the hottest promotion in the world and a model of in-ring proficiency. Selling out the Tokyo Dome two to three times a year, he was responsible for booking more shows that garnered $1 million gates than any other promoter in history.

Choshu's booking acumen was the stuff of legends. He created and nurtured an environment where nobody was above doing jobs, and where signature moves and finishers worked on even the top stars. He distinguished himself with his selfless booking, gradually phasing himself out while elevating younger stars to take his place.

No greater example of Choshu's booking style can be seen than at the inaugural G1 Climax tournament in 1991. He went 0-3 in the round robin tournament, putting over Shinya Hashimoto and Masahiro Chono, and booked Chono to beat Keiji Muto in the finals. Strong performances by Chono, Hashimoto, and Muto sent their respective careers through the roof, and they supplanted Choshu as the in-ring leaders of the promotion and became the top stars that would lead New Japan in the ensuing years.

The significance of what Choshu accomplished with the first G1 tournament cannot be understated. He ensured the future of New Japan Pro Wrestling, establishing three of the major stars that would carry the company through one of the biggest box-office runs in wrestling history. Choshu's selflessness was even more astounding in light of the political culture of the U.S. wrestling scene, where older stars blatantly refused to put over the young up-and-comers.

Choshu's booking legacy continued into 1995, when he was the draftsman behind the epic New Japan vs. UWFI

Riki Choshu performs at the Tokyo Japan Egg Dome.

program, a worked inter-promotional feud that was the inspiration behind the NWO angle that turned WCW around one year later. It was the biggest moneymaking feud in wrestling history up until that time, drawing 195,000 people and over $17 million in gate receipts in three consecutive sellouts at the Tokyo Dome within a five-month period. The October 9, 1995 show saw Muto defeat Nobuhiko Takada in the main event before 67,000 fans – the largest pro wrestling crowd ever in Japan up until that point. The show raked in $6.1 million, breaking the all-time gate record for wrestling.

After winning the 1996 G1 Climax, Choshu began to focus more on his booking duties. On January 4, 1998, 65,000 fans jammed into the Tokyo Dome to watch his retirement match.

He came out of retirement on July 30, 2000, to defeat Atsushi Onita in a barbed-wire-exploding-death match in the main event of New Japan's first ever pay-per-view event before going back on the road on a part-time schedule. In 2001, with the company mired in a terrible slump at the box-office, infighting between Inoki and everybody else over the direction of promotion killed the momentum they had built during the '90s. Choshu was fired as booker.

In April 2002, Choshu turned in his resignation and left the company.

20

Mitsuharu Misawa

A five-time Triple Crown Heavyweight Champion and the cornerstone of All Japan Pro Wrestling during the '90s, Mitsuharu Misawa is one of the greatest in-ring performers of all time.

He was the premier worker of his era, elegantly combining compelling ring work, brilliant psychology, and flawless execution of moves into an innovative working style that set new standards of stiffness and athletic credibility. His matches were textbook examples of how to put a match together where each move, each glance, and each gesture was an act of storytelling.

His career is inextricably tied to that of Toshiaki Kawada's – dating back to their high school days when they were classmates, and leading up to their real-life rivalry. Together, Misawa and Kawada put on state-of-the-art, revolutionary matches that are considered the Japanese equivalent of the Flair-Steamboat series of the '80s.

Misawa's proficiency in the ring cannot be understated. Neither can his influence.

If Jumbo Tsuruta can be credited with pioneering Japanese wrestling by introducing a more advanced and punishing style, then it can be said that Misawa took it to another level. He used the rings of All Japan Pro Wrestling as his personal stage to put on one memorable performance after another against wrestlers of the highest caliber.

After Tsuruta was diagnosed with Hepatitis B in 1992, it was Misawa who became the flag-bearer for All Japan. He went on to lead the company through the most profitable business period in its history, including an incredible string

Misawa in his classic tights, AJPW, January, 1991.

of sellouts at Tokyo's Budokan Hall, the company's home base, that lasted seven years and pulled in several $1 million gates a year.

Born on June 18, 1962, Misawa was a national high school wrestling champion in Japan in 1980. He joined All Japan's training camp and made his debut against Shiro Koshinaka on August 21, 1981. Misawa was sent to Mexico in 1984 to learn Lucha Libre. He returned to Japan a few months later and debuted as the second Tiger Mask, based on the original masked character made famous by Satoru Sayama.

In an attempt to capitalize on the success New Japan had with the gimmick from 1981 to 1983, All Japan pushed Misawa as its top junior heavyweight. They programmed him in a feud against Kuniaki Kobayashi, one of Sayama's big rivals in New Japan. On August 31, 1985, Misawa defeated Kobayashi in Tokyo for the NWA International Junior Heavyweight title.

He vacated the title in March 29, 1986, when he decided to move to the heavyweight division. He received his first major singles push as a heavyweight when he faced Tsuruta on March 9, 1988.

Misawa won the All Asia Tag titles with Kenta Kobashi on April 9th, 1990. A month later, he ordered his partner to remove his mask during a match, in one of the most memorable angles of the '90s. Two days later, Misawa began wrestling without the mask, using his real name.

A month earlier Genichiro Tenryu, the number two man in the company, left All Japan for Super World Sports, leaving a gaping hole in All Japan's main event roster. Giant

Baba, realizing he had to elevate his young talent to create new main event stars, chose Misawa as the heir apparent and programmed him in a feud with Tsuruta. In one of the most memorable scenes in Japanese wrestling history, Misawa pinned Tsuruta on June 8, 1990 at Tokyo's Budokan Hall, in a bout widely considered the match of the decade for its compelling storyline and psychology. The surprise result not only reduced many of the 14,800 fans in attendance to tears, but it instantly made Misawa a star.

The match ignited an incredible business run, as All Japan went on to enjoy a string of over 200 consecutive sellouts in Tokyo over several years.

Three days prior to the Misawa-Tsuruta match, Tsuruta dropped the Triple Crown to Terry Gordy. It was a calculated move by Baba who, after deciding to elevate Misawa by finally having him go over Tsuruta, didn't want it to be for the Triple Crown.

The story of All Japan in the '90s is directly tied to the rise of Misawa, as fans anxiously waited for him to win the title. The groundwork was laid when he upset Tsuruta. For the next two years, the legendary Misawa vs. Tsuruta feud set All Japan on fire with an incredible series of singles main events and six-man tag matches. With Misawa generally regarded as the top wrestler in the world, All Japan became renowned for staging wrestling's best main event matches.

Misawa teamed with Kawada from 1990 to 1992, winning the Unified World Tag titles on two occasions and the Real World Tag League tournament in 1992. In 1993, Misawa began partnering with Kobashi, picking up where he and Kawada left off as the best tag team in the world and winning the Real World Tag League tournament from 1993 to 1995.

After losing to Hansen on January 19, 1991, and Tsuruta on January 29, 1992 in two of the greatest Triple Crown Title matches of the '90s, Misawa finally won the title on August 22, 1992, from Hansen. Misawa's title victory was the culmination of a perfectly executed storyline by Baba that paid great attention to detail and progressed at a slow, methodical pace – taking All Japan fans on an emotional ride. When Misawa finally won the Triple Crown, the symbolic torch had been passed, and he became the promotion's undisputed marquee star. From there, Misawa went on to hold the title for close to two years.

Misawa would go on to win the title four more times by 1999, in monumental matches against Kawada, Hansen, Vader, Kobashi, and Akira Taue. He also appeared in the

Mitsuharu Misawa against Masa Chono.

finals of the Champion Carnival Tournament five times, winning in 1995 and 1998.

By 1999, All Japan was in chaos in the wake of Giant Baba's death. Misawa was named All Japan President and booker but found himself constantly at odds with Baba's widow Motoko over the direction of the promotion.

Business continued to slide as the result of Baba's failure to create any new main event stars before he passed away. Misawa dropped the Triple Crown title for the last time to Vader on October 30, 1999. The situation with Motoko soon reached its boiling point as Misawa became fed up with her conservative booking and business views.

In June 2000, more than a year after Baba's death, Misawa left All Japan and announced the formation of Pro Wrestling NOAH. With the backing of NTV – which had kicked All Japan off its network after a 28-year relationship – Misawa took the majority of All Japan's top talent with him. The move decimated the once proud company, leaving it crippled and on the brink of extinction.

NOAH debuted on August 5, 2000, and with stars like Vader, Kobashi, and Jun Akiyama, it instantly supplanted All Japan as the number two promotion in the country.

21

Verne Gagne

One of the most influential and powerful promoters of all time in the U.S., Verne Gagne *was* the American Wrestling Association.

Gagne wore many hats during his storied career in the Midwest-based AWA: he was the president, owner, promoter, and main-event star. He was also a trainer, taking many future stars under his wing, including Ric Flair, Ricky Steamboat, and Curt Hennig. But the role Gagne seemed most comfortable with was that of champion, holding the AWA World Heavyweight title ten times between 1960 and 1981. Over his ten title reigns, Gagne held the AWA championship for a cumulative period of over ten years.

Ten time AWA Title Champ, Verne Gagne.

Gagne's legendary world title matches and feuds against The Crusher, Mad Dog Vachon, Dick The Bruiser, Fritz Von Erich, Harley Race, Nick Bockwinkel, and Billy Robinson helped the AWA become one of the hottest, most profitable territories in the United States in the '60s and '70s. Gagne's superior knowledge of maneuvers, counter-maneuvers, and ring psychology enabled him to become one of the best in-ring workers in the world during his prime.

Born in 1926, Verne grew up in rural Minnesota before leaving home at age 14. He entered Robbinsdale High School where he became a local star in football, baseball, and wrestling. Gagne won the district, regional, and state championships in high school wrestling and was selected to play on the All-State football team. In 1943 he was recruited by the University of Minnesota, and became a member of the All-Conference team that same year.

While at the University of Minnesota, Gagne established himself as one of the top amateur wrestlers in the country by winning several prestigious honors, including two NCAA wrestling championships in 1948 and 1949, four Big Ten wrestling championships in 1944, 1947, 1948 and 1949 and an AAU championship in 1949. Gagne was also an alternate for the U.S. Freestyle wrestling team at the 1948 Olympics in London.

After graduating from university, Gagne had a brief playing career with the Green Bay Packers. At this time, the late Tony Stecher, a wrestling promoter based in Minneapolis, encouraged Gagne to try pro wrestling. In 1949 Gagne made his debut, defeating Abe "King Kong" Kashey (with former world heavyweight boxing champion Jack Dempsey as the referee). He became a successful light heavyweight, winning the NWA Junior Heavyweight title on November 13, 1950.

Then he received his first big break, appearing on the old Dumont Network's weekly Saturday evening wrestling show out of Chicago. Thanks to the national exposure network television granted him, Gagne, with his good looks and taut physique, quickly became a matinee idol and a household name. He also became one of the highest paid wrestlers in the '50s, reportedly earning $100,000 a year.

Throughout the '50s, Gagne was a main event star all across the U.S., particularly in the Midwest, where he was a huge box-office draw. On September 3, 1953, Gagne was awarded the NWA Chicago version of the U.S. title, which he would defend for close to three years before losing to Wilber Snyder on April 7, 1956. Gagne regained the title on April 12, 1958, when he defeated Dick the Bruiser. The same year, he also won the Omaha version of the NWA world title.

Two years later, the AWA was formed. At first, they recognized then-NWA Heavyweight Champion Pat O'Connor as the first AWA World Heavyweight Champion. Gagne, who had bought interest in the AWA, was awarded the World Heavyweight title on August 18, 1960, after O'Conner failed defend it within the mandatory 90-day period. The AWA title gained further legitimacy as a world championship on September 7, 1963, when Gagne, the reigning AWA World Champion, defeated Omaha World Champion Fritz Von Erich to unify the two titles.

Between 1960 and 1968 Gagne held the AWA World title nine times, exchanging the strap with Gene Kiniski, Bill Miller, The Crusher, Fritz Von Erich, Mad Dog Vachon, Dick the Bruiser, and Dr. X (Dick Beyer under a mask). His most famous title reign was his ninth when he held the title from August 31, 1968, to November 8, 1975. During this time he wrestled in countless classic matches against Nick Bockwinkel and Billy Robinson.

Gagne won his tenth and final AWA World title on July 18, 1980, at Chicago's Comiskey Park, defeating long time archrival Nick Bockwinkel. Gagne held the strap until May 19, 1981, when he retired from active wrestling. Gagne received widespread criticism from within the industry for his decision to simply relinquish the title without having anybody beat him for it before he retired.

Although he came out of retirement a few times to make several ill-fated appearances in the ring, Gagne spent the bulk of the '80s focusing on expanding his empire, becoming one of the biggest and most powerful promoters in the U.S. He helped develop stars such as Jesse "The Body" Ventura and "Mean" Gene Okerlund, and helped to launch "Hulkamania" in the '80s long before the McMahon-Hogan relationship first formed in 1984.

Hulk Hogan first became a phenomenon as a main event star and top babyface for the AWA in 1982, chasing heel AWA World Champion Nick Bockwinkel for the belt. The feud culminated on April 24, 1983, as Hogan pinned Bockwinkel for the World title. However, the result was overturned because Hogan had thrown Bockwinkel over the top rope earlier in the match. The frequent use of this tactic, referred to as the "Dusty Finish," infuriated AWA fans, who wanted to see Hogan win the title.

The WWF's expansion from 1983 to 1984 saw Vince McMahon deplete the AWA's talent roster, most notably taking Hogan, Dr. D. David Shultz, Ventura, and announcer Okerlund. McMahon's raiding of the AWA sabotaged

AWA Kingpin Verne Gagne.

months of house shows and storylines that Gagne had planned out.

To combat Vince McMahon's national expansion, Gagne teamed with NWA promoter Jim Crockett Jr. to form the promotional umbrella of Pro Wrestling USA. Together, Gagne and Crockett put on a series of mega-cards and inter-promotional dream shows in McMahon's backyard, at the Meadowlands in New Jersey. The relationship eventually disintegrated.

Gagne continued to operate the AWA, but could not compete with the expanding WWF. To make matters worse, the NWA now had national TV exposure on Ted Turner's TBS cable superstation. Even though he secured a TV deal with ESPN, Gagne remained stuck in a promotional rut, failing to adapt to the times and presenting the same old product. His business began to taper off drastically as the decade wore on. By 1990, the company was hanging on by a thread. One year later the AWA finally folded.

22

Jumbo Tsuruta

A world-class caliber wrestler, Jumbo Tsuruta was a main event star from 1973 to 1992 in All Japan Pro Wrestling, and is considered on par with the likes of Jack Brisco, Dory Funk Jr. and the legendary World Champions of the '70s.

A three-time Triple Crown Heavyweight Champion, Tsuruta – more than any other heavyweight of his era – embodied pro wrestling in Japan. He was a pioneer inside the ring, ushering in a more advanced, physically demanding style in front of the most critical, discerning fans on the planet.

His legendary matches against The Funks, Harley Race, Ric Flair, Abdullah the Butcher, Jack Brisco, Mil Mascaras, Stan Hansen, Genichiro Tenryu, and countless others established him as the cornerstone of Giant Baba's promotion during its glory years. Tsuruta helped All Japan earn the reputation of having the best main events in the industry, while at the same time trailblazing a path with his groundbreaking style for future Japanese stars like Mitsuharu Misawa.

An amazing worker in the ring, Tsuruta was renowned for putting together intricate matches that seamlessly weaved a complex and punishing set of moves. He was a brilliant ring psychologist who could tell a story within the confines of a match better than any of his contemporaries.

Born Tomomi Tsuruta on March 25, 1951, Jumbo was a star basketball player, swimmer, and sumo wrestler in high school before attending Chuo University, in Tokyo. Tsuruta picked up the sport immediately and became a star, winning the All Japan Amateur Wrestling Championship in freestyle and Greco-Roman competitions in 1971 and 1972. After only

Tsuruta applies the Abdominal stretch.

18 months he qualified for Japan's Olympic team and represented his country in the 1972 Olympics in Greco-Roman wrestling, finishing in seventh place.

Because of his size and natural ability, he was heavily sought after by wrestling promoters when he returned from the Olympics. Giant Baba won the sweepstakes and signed Tsuruta to a contract on October 31, 1972 – a mere ten days after forming All Japan Pro Wrestling.

After training for four months in Japan, he was sent to the U.S. to train under then-NWA World Champion Dory Funk Jr. On March 24, 1973 he had his first pro match in Amarillo.

At the time, most promoters in the U.S. portrayed Japanese wrestlers as salt-throwing, sneaky heels who vowed allegiance to the Emperor.

Tsuruta was the exception.

"He was the only Japanese wrestler that I knew that was really well accepted as a good guy here in America," states Funk. "All the fans really liked him…He worked for me in Amarillo and when I was booking in Florida and when I was in Mid-Atlantic, he was accepted very well in each place as a babyface. That's at a time when all the Japanese were working as heels over here."

Just as he did with the amateur style, Tsuruta picked up pro wrestling with stunning ease. Tsuruta wrestled Funk for the NWA World title a mere eight weeks after making his pro debut, losing the match in 56 minutes.

He returned to Japan in October and began teaming with Giant Baba. In their second match the duo wrestled the Funks to a 60-minute draw on live network television.

The match not only made him into a household name in Japan, but also established Tsuruta and Baba as the country's top babyface duo. After being given the nickname "Jumbo" in an NTV sponsored contest, Tsuruta and Baba feuded with the Funks over the International Tag Team titles for the next few years.

By the early '80s, Tsuruta had become a singles star, and Baba began to build the company around him. He won the Champion Carnival tournament in 1980 and spent the following years in heated feuds with Stan Hansen and Bruiser Brody. Tsuruta also challenged Ric Flair for the NWA World title, resulting in a legendary best two-out-of-three falls match on June 8, 1983.

On February 23, 1984, Tsuruta pinned Nick Bockwinkel in Tokyo to win the AWA World Title, before dropping the strap to Rick Martel on May 13.

His career then went into a holding pattern from 1985 to 1987, when Riki Choshu and his army set All Japan on fire. Tsuruta began to coast on his legend, refusing to adapt to the fast-paced style that Choshu introduced when he jumped to All Japan. However, by the time Choshu returned to New Japan in 1987, Tsuruta had raised the level of his performance and was back on top, feuding with Tenryu in a headline program.

By 1989, Baba had grown increasingly frustrated with the Crocketts after they pulled Flair from several advertised All Japan tours. He decided to alleviate the problem by creating his own world title. On April 18, 1989, Baba's dream was realized as Jumbo Tsuruta (then All Japan International champion) defeated Hansen (the PWF and United National champion) to create All Japan's Triple Crown.

But perhaps more than winning the Triple Crown title, and more than being the cornerstone of All Japan, Tsuruta is best remembered for a June 8th, 1990, loss to Misawa at Tokyo's Budokan Hall.

Tenryu left the promotion in 1990 for Super World Sports, leaving a gaping hole in All Japan's main event roster. Baba, realizing he had to make his young talent into main event stars, turned to Tsuruta.

Tsuruta could see the writing on the wall. He knew the match was to be a symbolic passing of the torch from the old to the new. He could have put up a fuss and made life difficult for Baba. Instead, he gave the performance of his life, reducing the 14,800 fans in attendance to tears in one of the most memorable matches of the '90s.

Tsuruta didn't just "job" to Misawa that night, he put

Seventies Tsuruta with United National belt.

him "over." He made Misawa's career in that one match, sending him down a path that led him to becoming the wrestler of the '90s. The win made Misawa an instant star, and the Misawa vs. Tsuruta feud set All Japan on fire for the next two years with an incredible set of matches.

Then, just as he was at the apex of his career, Tsuruta was diagnosed with Hepatitis B in 1992, ending his run as a serious main event star and top-caliber performer. He wrestled a reduced schedule, mostly in mid-card comedy matches with Baba, but the ravages of the disease slowed down his work inside the ring and he quickly became a shell of his former self. He retired from wrestling on March 6, 1999, bringing to an end a storied 26-year career.

After retiring, Tsuruta moved to the U.S. By the end of the year his condition took a turn for the worse, and he returned to Japan for treatment.

Cancer in his kidney had spread to his liver and he checked himself into a hospital in Gifu for treatment. Because of the complication of internal organ transplant laws in Japan, he flew to Australia in hopes of finding a suitable donor. After finding a donor in the Philippines, he flew to Manila, where he underwent transplant surgery. Post-operative complications ensued and he suffered from heavy internal bleeding.

As it turned out, it was too much of an obstacle to overcome. One of the great ring warriors of Japanese wrestling was gone, as Tsuruta died on May 13, 2000. He was 49.

23

Terry Funk

Whether as the NWA World Champion, the "middle-aged and crazy" Texan, the king of hardcore, or the icon of All Japan Pro Wrestling, Terry Funk carved out a spellbinding career as one of the greatest all-around performers.

Following in the footsteps of his father Dory Funk Sr., a former NWA Junior Heavyweight Champion and legendary promoter, Terry Funk was a star in both the U.S. and Japan. Perhaps more than any other wrestler of his time, Terry Funk *believed* in the wrestling business. Over five decades, his unmatched work ethic compelled him to give a 100 percent effort every time he stepped into the ring.

His monumental matches with the likes of Abdullah The Butcher, The Sheik, Dusty Rhodes, Stan Hansen, Giant Baba, Ric Flair, Harley Race, Jack Brisco, and many others rank among the greatest of all time. Both as a singles wrestler and teaming with brother Dory (an NWA World Champion himself from 1969 to 1973), Funk was one of the world's biggest stars during the '70s and '80s.

The mesmerizing wrestling career of Terry Funk began in his hometown of Amarillo, Texas, where he made his pro debut on December 9, 1965, against Sputnik Monroe. Funk made a name for himself wrestling in his father's Amarillo-based promotion in the late '60s.

Funk competed on his first tour of Japan in the summer of 1970, teaming with brother Dory against Giant Baba and Antonio Inoki in a series of high-profile matches in the Japanese Pro Wrestling Alliance.

In 1972, Giant Baba left the JWA and – with the help of the Funks – formed All Japan Pro Wrestling. The Funks

The Wildest NWA World Champ ever!

were the backbone of All Japan during the '70s, both as headliners and as bookers in charge of bringing in foreign workers. The Funks developed a strong working relationship with All Japan that saw Baba send aspiring Japanese stars – including Jumbo Tsuruta and Genichiro Tenryu – to Amarillo to train with the Funks.

On December 10, 1975, Funk captured the NWA World title, defeating Jack Brisco in Miami.

Funk's 14-month title reign was a new chapter in the storied history of the NWA World Championship. When Funk was world champion, NWA promoters became more prone towards finishes that were anything but conclusive. As a result, the NWA World title, bit by bit, became diluted. By the time the '80s rolled around, screw-job endings had become the norm rather than the exception.

Funk dropped the title to Harley Race on February 6, 1977, in Toronto and returned to focus his attention on his Amarillo promotion and on touring for All Japan. On December 15, 1977, he teamed with Dory against Abdullah the Butcher and The Sheik in the Real World Tag League Tournament. In the bloody aftermath, the Funks emerged as the heroes and top babyfaces in the promotion, forever changing the long-held notion that American wrestlers had to be pushed as heels in Japan.

Terry and Dory continued to headline in Japan as the top foreign tag team, winning the Real World Tag League Tournament three times between 1977 and 1982. Their only singles match against each another came on April 30, 1981, when Dory defended the NWA International Heavyweight.

Terry Funk against Bret Hart at Funk's Amarillo retirement show, 1997.

In 1983, Terry announced that he was quitting the business, and embarked on a heavily publicized retirement tour in All Japan. His "final" match was on August 31 in Tokyo, where he teamed with Dory against Stan Hansen and Terry Gordy. In one of the most memorable scenes ever in a wrestling ring, a teary-eyed Funk delivered a gut-wrenching speech after the match, reducing much of the crowd at Tokyo's Sumo Hall to tears.

However, like many retirements, it didn't last. He returned to All Japan in November of 1984, infuriating fans, who felt betrayed. After a run in the WWF from 1985 to 1986, he began to dabble in acting, appearing in several Hollywood films and TV programs.

Then, just as the sun appeared to be setting on his legendary career, Terry Funk was reborn in 1989.

He embarked on a seminal feud with Ric Flair, attacking him after he had won the NWA World title back from Ricky Steamboat. Funk and Flair feuded for five months in a series of main event matches that set the promotion on fire. The timeless Flair-Funk series ended on November 15, 1989, with their epic "I Quit" match. Considered one of the greatest matches of the '80s, the 18-minute brawl was a brilliant exhibition of storytelling, psychology, and scripted violence.

The '90s saw a new Terry Funk emerge: the hardcore icon. Whether it was in ECW (where he had notable matches with Mick Foley and Sabu) or in FMW (where he became a main event star feuding with Atsuhi Onita in a series of exploding ring death matches), Funk continued to punish his broken-down body. However, wrestling in the garbage promotions of Japan took its toll on Funk: his knees grew worse with each passing day as he continued to ignore the advice of doctors who told him to retire.

In 1997, he wrestled then-WWF World Champ Bret Hart – a man he helped train in the '70s – in a match that was billed as his Amarillo retirement. However, like so many times before, Funk did not make good on his retirement. He chose instead to ignore the messages sent to him by his aging body, and continued to wrestle at a torrid pace. With stints in the WWF and WCW, Funk wrestled into the new millennium, defying all the nay-sayers and continuing an amazing career that now spanned five different decades.

24

Mil Mascaras

Nicknamed "The Man of 1,000 Masks," Mil Mascaras was one of the biggest stars in the world during the '60s and '70s and is arguably the greatest masked wrestler of all time.

Known for his trademark barrel-chested physique and colorful array of masks, Mascaras stood 5'11" and weighed 230 pounds; yet, he moved around the ring with the agility and speed of a junior heavyweight, brilliantly combining high-flying moves with a vast display of mat wrestling maneuvers.

Mascaras is credited with popularizing many of the trademark moves of Lucha Libre, including the *plancha*, the *tope*, and the suicide dive. He was a trendsetter in the field of aerial wrestling who influenced many future high-fliers, including the original Tiger Mask. Mascaras was a tremendous box-office draw and a hugely popular babyface not only in Mexico, but in Southern California, Texas, and Japan, as well. He dazzled fans and promoters with a fast-paced, high-flying style that was years ahead of its time, and formed a legendary tag-team with his brother, Dos Caras.

Mascaras, like El Santo before him, was also a huge movie star during the '60s. Mascaras starred in 17 action pictures over his film career, starting with the self-titled *Mil Mascaras* in 1966 and ending with *La Llave Morta* (The Deadly Wrestling Hold) in 1990. He co-starred in several films with Santo and Blue Demon, including *Las Momias de Guanajuato* (The Mummies of Guanajuato) in 1970, the highest-grossing Mexican wrestler film of all time; and the epic *Misterio En Las Bermudas* (Mystery in Bermuda) in 1978.

Mascaras, born Aaron Rodriguez in 1938 in San Luis

Mascaras in 1972.

Potosi, Mexico, grew up like millions of other Mexican children, idolizing El Santo. An accomplished amateur wrestler, bodybuilder, and judo expert in his youth, Mascaras made his pro wrestling debut in April 1964 under the name Ricardo Durán.

Rodriguez was given the Mil Mascaras character by magazine mogul Valente Pérez, who was looking for a sculpted, high-flier who would wear a different mask in every match. He first wrestled as Mil Mascaras on July 16, 1965, partnering with Black Shadow. They defeated René Guajardo and Karloff Lagarde, Mexico's most famous heel team in history, in the finals of a tag team tournament.

Mascaras would go on to regularly team with Black Shadow and his idol, El Santo. After receiving rave reviews from both the media and his colleagues in the locker room, he became a main-event star in Mexico. Mascaras won his first title on June 12, 1967, defeating the original Espanto for the Mexican National Light Heavyweight strap in Mexico City. As he defended the title and became a headliner in Mexico, word of his reputation crossed the border into California, where promoters were eager to bring him in.

Mascaras left Mexico in May 1968 for Gene LeBell's Los Angeles territory. Mascaras became a household name in Southern California thanks to his feuds with the likes of The Sheik, John Tolos, and Black Gordman. In late 1969, he defeated Gordman and Bull Ramos in "mask vs. hair" matches, winning the scalps of the two hated heels and cementing his status as a hero to Los Angeles' Hispanic community.

Mascaras won the prestigious NWA Americas title three times between 1968 and 1971. During this period, he became one of the most popular stars in the promotion, and paved the way for other Mexican stars to come to Los Angeles.

Mascaras first toured Japan in February 1971 for the old Japan Pro Wrestling Alliance, defeating Kantaro Hoshino in his Tokyo debut. After the JWA folded, Mascaras joined Giant Baba's All Japan Pro Wrestling, where he feuded against The Destroyer, the U.S.'s greatest masked wrestler. He became one of the country's top foreign stars and an idol to young children, who were enamored with his colorful masks and ring attire. By introducing Lucha Libre to Japanese fans, he established a new market for Mexican wrestlers in the country and challenged the concept that foreign stars in Japan had to be pushed as heels.

By now his status as a drawing card extended to the northeastern part of the U.S., as well, where he had begun to appear on cards for WWWF promoter Vince McMahon Sr.

On December 18, 1972, Mascaras made his debut in Madison Square Garden, becoming the first masked man to compete at the venerable building. The New York State Athletic Commission had imposed a longstanding ban on masked wrestlers; for years, New York promoters tried to bring him in but Mascaras turned down their offers because he did not want to appear without his mask. Ironically, Mascaras defeated The Spoiler, who had himself been previously denied the right to wrestle with his mask on at the Garden.

In 1975, U.S. promoter Eddie Einhorn created the International Wrestling Association and recognized Mascaras as its world champion. Mascaras defended the IWA Heavyweight title several times in major territories across the U.S. (including a July 10, 1975, match against Ivan Koloff that drew 27,000 fans in New Jersey); but, after Einhorn pulled his funding, the promotion was taken over by Johnny Powers, and folded the following year. Despite this, Mascaras kept the belt and continued to defend the title into the 21st century.

On December 19, 1977, and January 23, 1978, Mascaras challenged "Superstar" Billy Graham for the WWWF World Title. Both matches were such huge draws that they sold out not only Madison Square Garden, but also the adjacent Felt Forum, where several thousand fans watched the match on closed-circuit television. Mascaras, believing a little too much in his own star power, refused to lose cleanly to Graham in the second match (which Graham won by

Mascaras in an outdoor IWA title defense against Ernie Ladd.

disqualification) after he had won the first bout when the ref stopped the match due to blood.

Age began to catch up with Mascaras as he competed on his last All Japan tour in 1987. He returned to North America and split his time between the U.S. and Mexico, developing a notorious reputation for refusing to job to anybody or sell his opponents' offense. As a new generation of stars emerged and wrestling hit an all-time boom period in Mexico in the early '90s, Mascaras began to be phased out; he accepted more independent dates in the U.S., Central America, and Japan.

Mascaras continued to wrestle throughout the '90s and into the new century. He returned to All Japan for the first time in 14 years on January 28, 2001, for Stan Hansen's retirement show, teaming with El Hijo del Santo to defeat Blue Panther and Arkangel de la Muerte.

Even though Mascaras infuriated promoters with his uncompromising stance in his later years, his rightful place in wrestling history cannot be questioned.

"There are very few wrestlers that can claim unarguable legendary status in Mexico, the United States, and Japan, but Mascaras is one of them," states Lucha Libre historian Jose Luis Fernandez. "His unique and spectacular style got him over as a solid main event star everywhere he went and his great work and flamboyant personality made him a big money draw right from the start."

25

Bret Hart

A second-generation star and five-time WWF World Heavyweight Champion, Bret Hart was one of the most popular stars in the '90s and is arguably the greatest Canadian wrestler in history.

The son of legendary promoter Stu Hart, Bret was a brilliant mat technician and a master ring psychologist over a 24-year career that saw him advance the style of wrestling in the WWF.

Bret Hart transformed the WWF from an organization dominated by hulking steroid freaks into a company that featured smaller, talented wrestlers and a more athletically-progressive product. Hart's most memorable in-ring exploits

Multi-World title Champion, Bret "Hitman" Hart.

stem from his early days as one half of the Hart Foundation tag team in the WWF, with brother-in-law Jim Neidhart, and later for his epic battles against Ric Flair, Curt Hennig, Jerry Lawler, Shawn Michaels, brother Owen, and Davey Boy Smith as WWF World Champion.

And yet, for all his classic matches, Hart will forever be remembered as the victim of the "Montreal screw-job" on November 7, 1997 – the most famous double-cross in the modern era of pro wrestling.

Born July 2, 1957, Hart seemed destined to become a wrestler. At age six, he worked for his dad helping to set up the ring and selling programs. While still a teenager, he became a referee. Trained by the Funks, Hart turned pro in 1978.

Hart was Stampede's top babyface between 1978 and 1984, feuding with the Dynamite Kid and Bad News Allen, and winning the North American title six times. In between Stampede runs he toured with New Japan Pro Wrestling,

feuding with Tiger Mask and becoming an integral part of its emerging junior heavyweight division.

In August 1984, Stampede closed down when Stu Hart sold the territory to Vince McMahon Jr., during the WWF's national expansion. As part of the buyout, Hart landed in the WWF where he began as an opening card jobber in late 1984. He eventually worked his way up the ladder as part of the Hart Foundation, feuding with the British Bulldogs and winning the World Tag Team titles on January 26, 1987. They teamed together for the next three years before breaking up in 1991.

After the breakup, Bret pursued a singles career and quickly established himself as one of the top workers in North America, embarking on a classic feud with Curt Hennig that ended with him winning the Intercontinental title on August 26, 1991. A year later, he wrestled brother-in-law Davey Boy Smith before 78,927 fans at London's Wembley Stadium, dropping the title in one of the greatest matches in WWF history.

By 1992, the WWF was mired in sex and steroid scandals, and as a result, the company was wallowing in a down period of business. The introduction of stringent drug testing prevented the WWF from pushing steroid monsters as its top stars, forcing McMahon to elevate a clean-cut, smaller wrestler around whom the company could plan its future.

Bret Hart turned out to be the choice. He defeated Ric Flair for his first WWF World Title on October 12, 1992, in Saskatoon, Saskatchewan, Canada. Between 1992 and 1997, Hart would go on to hold the strap five times. Although he wasn't a great domestic draw during his title reigns, Hart was a tremendous draw in foreign markets, where the WWF often toured when business in the U.S. was slow. As the company's champion and most popular star during the scandal-plagued '90s, Hart was the glue that held the company together when it appeared it would crack under the constant scrutiny of the government and media.

In 1996 he walked away from the WWF to pursue an acting career and Shawn Michaels was tabbed as the next leader of the company. He dropped the title to Michaels in a memorable 60-minute marathon match in the main event of WrestleMania XII on March 31. Later that year, he was the subject of the biggest bidding war in wrestling history between the WWF and WCW. He turned down a larger guaranteed contract and a reduced schedule from WCW to return as the top star to the promotion that made him famous, signing a 20-year deal that he thought would allow him to end his career in the WWF with dignity.

If he had only known.

After winning his fourth WWF world title on February 16, 1997, he was turned heel at WrestleMania XIII during an epic match against Steve Austin. The angle not only established Austin as the lead babyface in the company but also set him on his way to becoming the dominant star in wrestling during the '90s. In the aftermath, Hart became a full fledged-heel as part of the memorable Canada vs. U.S.A. feud that marked the beginning of the WWF's incredible turnaround.

On August 3, Hart beat the Undertaker to win his fifth and final WWF world title. By this point McMahon, who regretted signing him to the deal told Hart that he was going to breach his contract, and encouraged him to negotiate with WCW. Hart signed with Eric Bischoff and WCW in November – a three-year deal worth $2.5 million per year – and gave his notice to the WWF. By then, Hart had already been booked into the main event of Survivor Series with Michaels.

Hart, who had creative control of his character for the final 60 days in the WWF, as stipulated in his contract, and not wanting to lose in Canada, refused to put Michaels over for the title at Survivor Series in Montreal. Hart gave several other options to McMahon, including losing to Michaels on a future episode of RAW or at the next WWF pay-per-view. McMahon, knowing that the word of Hart's arrival on WCW would be announced on Nitro the next day hatched a double-cross scheme to take the title off of Hart, despite the fact that Hart had offered to call Bischoff and

get WCW to delay the announcement. Ever the master revisionist, McMahon managed to rewrite the history behind his dealings with Hart for the public record, saying he had no choice but to double-cross Hart (ignoring the fact he told Hart it wouldn't be necessary to call Bischoff to delay the announcement in the first place), and that Bret had flat out refused to ever drop the title (when, in fact, he only refused to drop it in Montreal and the next night on RAW in Ottawa). Prior to the match, McMahon appeared to yield to Hart's wishes, agreeing to a finish that would allow him to win via DQ. Little did Hart know that he was about to become the victim of the most notorious double-cross in wrestling history.

When Michaels secured Hart in a sharpshooter, referee Earl Hebner rang the bell, signaling that Hart had submitted, even though he was about to reverse the hold. In the aftermath, McMahon became the top heel in the company, and a rival for Austin. The McMahon-Austin storyline turned the company's fortunes around, and the WWF went on to enjoy the most incredible run of business in wrestling history. The entire Hart vs. McMahon saga was the subject of a critically acclaimed 1998 documentary by filmmaker Paul Jay entitled *Wrestling with Shadows*.

Hart debuted in WCW two months later as the hottest babyface in the world, thanks to the double-cross. However, Hart never really made it in WCW, as injuries, backstage politics, and a booking committee that didn't know how to push him properly marred his stint there.

Bret's misfortunes continued, when he had to bury younger brother Owen, who tragically plummeted to his death from the ceiling of the Kemper Arena in Kansas City on May 23, 1999, during the WWF's *Over the Edge* pay-per-view. The tragedy only served to fuel the flames of resentment that Bret harbored for McMahon, as he went on to slam him in media interviews for not only contributing to the death of Owen but also for continuing on with the show after the tragedy had occurred. Martha Hart, Owen's widow, filed a wrongful death lawsuit against the WWF that was settled out of court in November 2000 for $18 million.

He won the WCW world title on November 16, 1999, but a month later, in the main event of Starrcade, suffered a serious concussion when Goldberg accidentally booted him in the head. He wrestled a few more matches, further aggravating his head trauma, and was sidelined. As a result, WCW released him from his contract on October 19, 2000.

One week later, Bret Hart announced his retirement.

Famous Holds and Finishers

top: Tiger Mask delivers a reverse karate kick, stunning his opponent. *bottom:* Edouard Carpentier delivers his Savate-Kick finisher to Bobby Shane, 1973.

clockwise from top left: Bret Hart applies his sharpshooter move to Hulk Hogan; Hiroshi Hase tosses Pegasus Kid (Chris Benoit); Terry Funk Pile Drives Ric Flair; Akira Nogami subdues Jushin Liger with a figure-four leg lock; Dory Funk Jr uses his famous Toe-Hold against Harley Race.

clockwise from top left: Billy "Man of 1000 moves" Robinson uses his own toe-hold to keep Nick Bockwinkel pinned to the mat; Chris Jericho, Steve Austin, and Kurt Angle display the headlock train made famous by Santo Sr; Terry Funk puts a tight headlock on Eddie Gilbert; Dara Singh endures a Half Nelson before turning the match around and defeating Sam Betts in front of a crowd of roughly 75,000 spectators, Bombay, 1967.

clockwise from top left: Tatsumi Fujinami being held by Vader's Rack; Terry Funk prepares to hammerlock Chavo Guerrero in a World Title defense; Mil Mascaras overpowers Ivan Koloff in a test of strength; Sting gets the better of Ric Flair with an armbar; Perro Aguayo Surfboards Bulldog KT.

26

Dory Funk Jr.

NWA **World Champion** from 1969 to 1973, Dory Funk Jr. was one of the greatest world champions of all time.

Funk was well respected within the industry for his superior wrestling skills, impeccable work ethic, and professionalism in the ring. He was also an accomplished trainer, responsible for training Bret Hart, Ted DiBiase, Stan Hansen, Bob Backlund, Kurt Angle, Jumbo Tsuruta, and Genichiro Tenryu.

A football standout at West Texas State University, Dory followed in the footsteps of his father, Dory Funk Sr., a former NWA Junior Heavyweight Champion and legendary promoter. He quickly became one of the top workers of his era, winning the NWA World title from Gene Kiniski on February 11, 1969. As champion, Funk faced the top stars in every major territory. He became an instant sensation in Japan after wrestling Antonio Inoki to a one-hour draw in 1969, marking the first time the NWA title had been defended in Japan in 12 years.

However, it was his epic feud in the early '70s against Jack Brisco that permanently cemented Funk's legend. For years, Brisco, the young up-and-comer and top babyface in the country, chased the veteran Funk all across North America in one of the greatest feuds of all time. The two engaged in a series of brilliant scientific matches that became the archetype of the "world title chase" program that promoters have copied ever since.

The Funk-Brisco feud was the equivalent of the Flair-Steamboat series of the '80s. It was a huge gate attraction, drawing packed houses all across the country (especially in Florida), and it was so memorable that longtime fans can

Classy Dory Funk Jr.

still recall and recite the entire progression of their legendary matches, move for move.

"I wrestled Jack over 300 times in my career," recalled Funk, "and everywhere we went, from St. Louis, Florida, Texas and Japan, it always sold out."

Funk dropped the title to Harley Race on May 24, 1973, but would go on to achieve great fame in Japan as a main-event star, booker, and foreign talent liaison for All Japan during the '70s and early-'80s. Funk also played a key role in the secret negotiations between Stan Hansen and Giant Baba that saw Hansen leave New Japan for All Japan in 1981.

As booker, he was the architect behind some of the biggest bouts in Japanese history. He was also responsible for training several of All Japan's top domestic stars, most notably Tsuruta, who traveled to Amarillo to train under Funk and work in his father's promotion.

He teamed with brother Terry on December 15, 1977, against Abdullah the Butcher and The Sheik in the Real World Tag League Tournament. It proved to be one of the most important matches in Japanese history: in the aftermath, the Funks emerged as top babyfaces and huge icons in Japan, forever changing the concept that American wrestlers had to be heels.

On April 30, 1981, Funk was awarded the vacant NWA International Heavyweight title when Bruiser Brody was unable to wrestle in the tournament finals due to injury. Instead of wrestling Brody, Dory had his first title defense against Terry that evening, in their only singles match with each other.

Dory Funk Jr. battles Chief Peter Maivia, The Rock's grandfather.

27

Tiger Mask

The greatest and most influential junior heavyweight wrestler in history, the original Tiger Mask took the wrestling world by storm and captivated audiences with his exhilarating, ground-breaking style.

At a mere 5'5" and 160 pounds, Tiger Mask changed the landscape of Japanese pro wrestling with his legendary series of matches against the Dynamite Kid from 1981 to 1983. Combining shoot, Lucha Libre, and traditional Japanese wrestling into a hybrid style that was years ahead of its time, Tiger Mask became a huge star for New Japan at the height of its boom period in the early-'80s, while shattering the proverbial glass ceiling in wrestling that kept junior heavyweights from advancing past mid-card status.

By taking the junior heavyweight style to new levels of popularity and acceptance, Tiger Mask flung open a door that had forever been closed to men of his size in Japan. His influence can be directly seen in the work of Jushin "Thunder" Liger, Ultimo Dragon, The Great Sasuke, Rey Misterio Jr., and virtually every major high-flying junior heavyweight that followed him.

Born Satoru Sayama on November 24, 1957, Tiger Mask was an accomplished amateur wrestler and judo expert in his youth. He dropped out of high school in 1975 to train at the New Japan dojo, where he made a name for himself as an accomplished shooter and kick-boxer.

Sayama made his pro debut on May 28, 1976, at the age of 19, under his real name, losing to future New Japan referee Shoji Kai in Tokyo. Because of his size, New Japan shipped him off to EMLL in Mexico in 1978 where he

Tiger Mask at Madison Square Garden in New York.

learned Lucha Libre. He quickly picked up the style and won the NWA Middleweight title in 1979, following up with a memorable series of matches against El Satanico. Despite wrestling in EMLL for less than two years, he attained legendary status in Mexico, and to this day is still regarded as one of the greatest wrestlers, either domestic or foreign, to ever wrestle in that country.

In between tours of Mexico, he wrestled in England as a "kick-boxer." Wrestling as Sammy Lee (billed as Bruce Lee's cousin), Sayama became an overnight sensation thanks to his feud with Mark "Rollerball" Rocco – who would himself go on to greater fame in New Japan as the masked Black Tiger.

Sayama debuted the Tiger Mask character (based on a popular comic book and children's television cartoon in Japan) on April 23, 1981, at Tokyo's old Sumo Hall, against the Dynamite Kid. The character was the creation of New Japan President and booker Hisahi Shinma, who wanted to create a popular children's star to combat the success All Japan was having at the time with the masked Mil Mascaras. Dressed up in a cartoonish costume complete with a flowing blue cape and a tiger mask with whiskers, Sayama was marketed towards small children as the real-life version of the popular cartoon.

Sayama brought the cartoon character to life in his debut match – putting on a dizzying and dazzling display of aerial moves and maneuvers the likes of which fans had never seen before – in a bout that many insiders consider the match of the '80s. From that point on, Tiger Mask and the Dynamite Kid engaged in a landmark feud that

facing page: Tiger Mask does a back flip over El Solitario.

produced countless classic matches and captured the imagination of Japanese fans. Tiger Mask and the Dynamite Kid set a new standard of ring excellence with their blinding quickness and flawless execution of innovative moves. Their careers, much like Ric Flair and Ricky Steamboat, became inextricably tied together.

Although it was a hit with the young kids, Tiger Mask was a flop at first with New Japan's base of hardcore fans, who didn't appreciate his unique style and thought he was too small. Eventually, Tiger Mask won them over with his mat classics against the Dynamite Kid, while at the same time turning heads with his equally brilliant matches against a young Bret Hart, Black Tiger, and the slew of Mexican stars that regularly toured for New Japan. These matches, along with the Ishingun vs. Seikigun feud, led New Japan through one of the most financially successful house show runs in the history of the industry.

Due to Sayama's rising popularity, junior heavyweight star Tatsumi Fujinami was moved to the heavyweight division. Tiger Mask was now the seminal figure in New Japan's burgeoning junior heavyweight division. On January 1, 1982, he defeated the Dynamite Kid for the vacant New Japan/WWF Junior Heavyweight Title.

He vacated the title following a match against Black Tiger on April 21, after sustaining an injury. He quickly returned to action and became a double champion, winning the NWA Junior Heavyweight title on May 25 from Les Thorton and the New Japan/WWF Junior Heavyweight title on May 26 from Black Tiger. By having him capture both the NWA and WWF World Junior titles – a huge deal in an era when titles still meant something in wrestling – New Japan attempted to establish Tiger Mask as the greatest junior heavyweight of all time.

Tiger Mask defended both titles simultaneously in Japan, Mexico, and in the U.S, including an epic August 30, 1982, match against the Dynamite Kid at Madison Square Garden that received rave reviews and critical praise from insiders and fans in the U.S. and Japan. Tiger Mask eventually vacated the titles in April of 1983 after sustaining another serious injury. He regained the NWA Junior Heavyweight title a second time and the New Japan/WWF Junior Heavyweight title for a third time in separate bouts less than two weeks apart in June 1983.

Seemingly on top of the wrestling world, Sayama shocked the entire industry on August 12, 1983, when he announced his retirement at age 25. Feeling he was under-paid, he attempted a coup to grab more power and more money. When it failed, Shinma was fired and Sayama found himself on the outs with the company. Less than a year later, Tiger Mask resurfaced in the original Universal Wrestling Federation, a worked shoot style pro wrestling promotion formed by Shinma that featured Akira Maeda as its top star. Sayama made his return to the ring as "The Tiger" on July 24, 1984, in the UWF, defeating Mach Hayato at Tokyo's Korakuen Hall. He later changed his ring name to "Super Tiger."

The company eventually fell from grace and by the end of 1985 it was unable to draw outside of Tokyo. With tensions in the locker room at an all-time high, and knowing the promotion was about to go under, Sayama shot on Maeda during a match on September 11, throwing several intentional kicks into his groin. A month later the promotion folded.

In retirement, Sayama caused quite a stir in Japan with the release of his book *Kay Fabe*, a scathing record of his thoughts on the wrestling industry that exposed the many "secrets" of the business, including the "revelation" that pro wrestling was a work.

After forming Shooting, a 100% shoot promotion featuring real fights blending catch-as-catch-can wrestling, Thai boxing, sambo, judo, and ju jitsu, Sayama came out of retirement to wrestle a series of matches between 1995 and 1996. In 1998, he helped Antonio Inoki launch UFO (Universal Fighting-arts Organization).

28

Blue Demon

Despite living in the shadow of El Santo his entire career, Blue Demon is one of the biggest stars in Mexican wrestling history and is among the most famous masked wrestlers of all time.

Blue Demon was a cultural icon in Mexico both as a main-event performer and as a matinee movie idol, starring in several B-movies in the '60s and '70s. He was a huge gate attraction during an amazing career that spanned over 40 years, with his trademark blue and white mask becoming one of the most revered symbols in all of Lucha Libre. As a welterweight, Demon was among the best mat wrestlers in Mexico. Trained by the legendary Rolando Vera, Demon was considered one of the toughest shooters, pound for pound, ever to come out of Mexico.

Wrestling great and movie star, Blue Demon.

Demon made his pro debut in 1948 as a *rudo*, becoming a top star in his hometown of Monterrey before going to Mexico City and becoming a *technico* in 1952 while feuding with El Santo. His best years were during the '50s – the "golden era" of Mexican wrestling – when he first became a main-event star and a legitimate box-office draw. He held the NWA World Welterweight title from 1953 to 1958, after defeating El Santo for the strap in one of the most important matches in Mexican wrestling history, setting off a bitter, real-life feud in the process.

Demon harbored animosity towards Santo his entire career, resenting the fact that, although he was hardly an accomplished wrestler, it was Santo who was a nationally revered hero. The Santo vs. Demon feud was so big that it became the subject of "Los Luchadores," a popular song that is played regularly in Mexico to this day. His bitterness towards El Santo grew in the '60s when they first co-starred

in several films. From the late '50s through to the '70s, Santo popularized the Lucha Libre film genre in Mexico, starring as a masked pro wrestler who fought crime with the help of Demon and Mil Mascaras as his partners. Despite Demon being in his physical prime (while Santo's best days were clearly behind him), it was Santo who always received the top billing.

As Santo became a huge movie star, he turned *technico* in 1962. Promoters tried in vain to partner Demon and Santo after Santo's turn, but Demon refused. He eventually relented in 1968, and the two finally teamed up, amid heavy fanfare and media coverage.

From 1961 to 1978, Demon starred in 28 movies, including his most famous film, *Las Momias de Guanajuato* (The Mummies of Guanajuato) in 1970. After helping to instruct several young wrestlers at Arena Mexico's training gym, Demon opened his own gym in the mid-'70s and went on to become a respected wrestling trainer.

In 1989, while in his sixties, Blue Demon decided to call it quits. His retirement tour included a series of high profile matches in Mexico City, Tijuana, and several other major cities. On July 30, 1989, he defeated Rayo de Jalisco, one of the biggest stars in Mexico from the '60s and 70s, in a mask vs. mask match. A month later he wrestled in his last match ever in Monterrey, unmasking the hooded El Matematico.

Blue Demon, born Alejandro Muñoz Moreno, died on December 16, 2000, after suffering a heart attack. He was 78. Adhering to Mexican wrestling tradition, he was buried in his casket with his mask on.

29

Perro Aguayo

One of the most popular Mexican stars ever to wrestle without a mask, Perro Aguayo was a gifted brawler who secured a spot in the hearts of Mexican wrestling fans with his hard work and famous feuds with Fishman, Gran Hamada, Cien Caras, and Konnan.

Aguayo began his career as a *rudo*, but turned *technico* in the early-'90s, quickly winning the adulation of Mexican fans. Between 1994 and 1996 it was Aguayo – not Hulk Hogan, Bret Hart, Shawn Michaels, or Sting – who was the top-drawing babyface in North America, as fans would regularly pack outdoor soccer stadiums and bullrings to watch him wrestle. He generated a run of house-show business that would prove to be one of the most profitable of the '90s, worldwide.

During his over thirty years in wrestling, Aguayo was not only a top star in Mexico, but also in Southern California, Japan, and Central America. He collected several important titles in different weight classes, including three NWA World Middleweight titles, six WWF World Light Heavyweight titles, the UWA World Light Heavyweight title, and the National Heavyweight title.

A grizzled veteran noted for his toughness, Aguayo was Mexico's answer to former NWA World Champion Harley Race. Aguayo will also be remembered as perhaps the best bleeder in the business. The gruesome spectacles of Aguayo's matches often surpassed even those of blood-letters like Abdullah the Butcher and The Sheik.

Born Pedro Aguayo Damián on January 18, 1946, in Nochistlán, Zacatecas, Aguayo was trained by legendary Lucha Libre trainer Diablo Velasco before making his pro

Perro seen before the battle.

debut on May 10, 1970. In the '70s, he became a top star in the UWA after engaging in lengthy feuds with Rey Mendoza, Gran Hamada, and his greatest rival, the masked Fishman.

During the early-'80s, Aguayo was a regular for New Japan Pro Wrestling, competing in their Junior Heavyweight division with the likes of Dynamite Kid, Tatsumi Fujinami, and the original Tiger Mask. He also bounced between the EMLL and UWA promotions in Mexico, establishing his reputation as one of the top stars in the country.

On March 22, 1991, Aguayo defeated Konnan at Mexico City's Arena Mexico (the Mexican equivalent of Madison Square Garden) in a mask vs. hair match, forcing the young bruiser to unmask. Konnan would get his revenge six months later, when he defeated Aguayo and Cien Caras in a triangle match, forcing Aguayo to have his head shaved. In May 1992, Aguayo jumped to Antonio Pena's AAA promotion and became one of the group's top babyface stars. On April 30, 1993, as part of the co-main event for the promotion's TripleMania show, Aguayo took the mask of archrival Mascara Ano Dos Mil in another mask vs. hair match. The bloody brawl sent the 48,000 fans in attendance into a state of bedlam.

He then engaged in a bloody feud with Konnan, after being turned on by his former partner (who would later go on to join the *Los Gringos Locos* faction). The feud culminated on November 6, 1994, when Aguayo defeated Konnan in a steel-cage match at the *When Worlds Collide* pay-per-view.

But perhaps the most enduring image Mexican fans will have of Aguayo will be from a match on April 30, 1995.

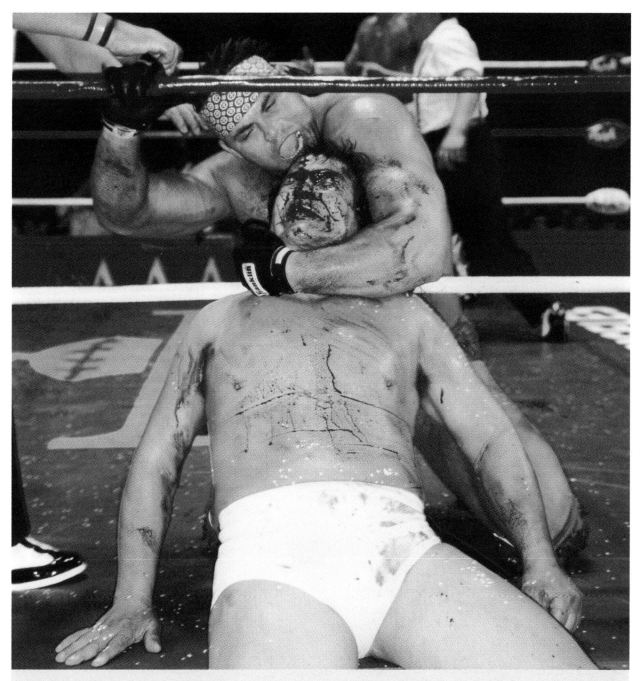

Konnan bloodies Perro in a heated grudge match.

Aguayo was facing Konnan and Cien Caras in a three-way match at the Rio Nilo Cup show in Guadalajara when rival Mascara Ano Dos Mil jumped him from behind and broke a full Corona beer bottle over his head, turning his face into a crimson mask. It turned out to be one of the most legendary angles in Lucha Libre history, setting the stage for an incredible stretch of business for AAA.

His legacy took a brow-beating as he went on several "retirement" tours while in his fifties, reneging each time on his promise to quit wrestling. After returning to EMLL and wrestling on several pay-per-view main events in Mex-ico, Aguayo finally retired in 2001 after suffering a career-ending neck injury. Still, Aguayo's reluctance to leave the ring long past his prime cannot overshadow the stardom of his earlier days.

"As a wrestler he never was anything special, although he was a very good brawler in the early-'80s," states Lucha Libre historian Jose Luis Fernandez. "[He] showed a lot of fire and passion in his matches, always worked hard, had a hard-hitting style, and took a lot of punishment. He was also blessed with incredible charisma."

30

Nick Bockwinkel

A four-time American Wrestling Association World Champion between 1975 and 1987, Nick Bockwinkel will forever be remembered for his classic rivalry with Verne Gagne.

Bockwinkel was highly respected by his peers in the business, having earned a reputation as one of the best scientific wrestlers of his era. Renowned for his professionalism, Bockwinkel was a brilliant ring psychologist whose matches against Gagne, Billy Robinson, Ric Flair, Bob Backlund, and Harley Race were legendary.

Bockwinkel taunts the crowd.

In a business where his colleagues yelled and screamed at the top of their lungs during promos, Bockwinkel distinguished himself with his mild-mannered, soft-spoken, and articulate interview style. He was also a master technician in the ring, able to carry even the most helpless opponent to a good match. In the late-'70s, Bockwinkel carried Andre the Giant (who, because of his size and girth, made it nearly impossible for opponents to work with at times) to an entertaining 60-minute draw. He earned accolades for the match, and was heralded for his amazing caliber of performance.

What's more, Bockwinkel got better with age, having his best years in the business after he turned 40. Unlike contemporaries such as Gagne and The Sheik, who were able to stay on top because they ran their own territories, Bockwinkel, due to his extraordinary conditioning and his ability to consistently produce solid matches, was a legitimate main-event star into his fifties. There is no better proof of this than when, at age 51, he wrestled Curt Hennig to a fantastic 60-minute draw. The match, airing as a taped special on ESPN on New Year's Eve in 1986, drew huge

ratings on the cable network and won Bockwinkel widespread acclaim for his working ability from those within the industry.

Born on December 6, 1934, Bockwinkel first entered pro wrestling in the mid-'50s, teaming with his father, Warren, who was a regional star in the '40s. After bouncing around between several territories across the U.S., he won his first major title in 1970, defeating Assassin #1 on April 17 in Atlanta for the Georgia Heavyweight title (which was considered one of the top regional belts in wrestling at the time).

From there, Bockwinkel settled in the AWA and began his classic feud with Verne Gagne. Bockwinkel also teamed with Ray "The Crippler" Stevens in the early '70s, winning the AWA World Tag Team titles on three occasions between 1972 and 1975. Together, the deadly duo, managed by Bobby "The Brain" Heenan, were one of the most dominant tag teams ever, having several memorable feuds with Gagne and Robinson, Dick the Bruiser and The Crusher, and Mad Dog and Butcher Vachon.

He won his first of four AWA World Heavyweight titles on November 8, 1975, defeating Gagne in St. Paul, Minnesota, ending Gagne's seven-year reign as champion. After winning the title, Bockwinkel became the focal point of the promotion and began feuding with Gagne, Billy Robinson, and Mad Dog Vachon. On March 25, 1979, Bockwinkel was involved in the first-ever AWA vs. WWWF world title unification match, battling then-WWWF World Champion Bob Backlund to double count-out in Toronto.

Bockwinkel's first reign ended after five years when he dropped the title to Gagne on July 19, 1980, at Chicago's

Bockwinkel ties up arch rival Billy Robinson.

Comiskey Park. He was then re-awarded the title on May 19, 1981, after Gagne, in a widely criticized move, retired from wrestling as world champion. Bockwinkel's second reign lasted until August 8, 1982, when he was defeated by Austrian star Otto Wanz. He regained the title two months later and for the next year-and-a-half he feuded with Jerry Lawler, Jim Brunzell, and, most importantly, Hulk Hogan.

Hogan first became a star for the AWA chasing Bockwinkel for the world title as the "Hulkamania" phenomenon was born. The feud went on for months with Bockwinkel always retaining his title via a DQ or a "screwjob" ending. The feud climaxed on April 24, 1983, in St. Paul (dubbed "Super Sunday" by promoter Verne Gagne), with Bockwinkel defending the title against Hogan in a match where he would lose the title if disqualified. Hogan ended up pinning Bockwinkel for the belt, only to have the result reversed because he had thrown Bockwinkel over the top rope earlier in the match. The feud died in late-1983, when Hogan secretly jumped to the WWF.

Bockwinkel's third title reign ended on February 22, 1984, in Tokyo, when he lost the belt to All Japan star Jumbo Tsuruta. His fourth and final world title run started on June 29, 1986, in Denver, after world champion Stan Hansen walked out of the arena with the title after refusing to put over Bockwinkel. At age 51, Bockwinkel was once again champion; however, by this time, the AWA was losing the promotional war with the WWF and had begun its slide into extinction. After feuding with several of the AWA's top young stars, Bockwinkel lost the world title for the final time to Curt Hennig on May 2, 1987, in San Francisco.

Bockwinkel retired in 1987 to take a job as a road agent for the WWF. In 1994, he was given a prominent on-air role in WCW as commissioner, before leaving the company in 1995. Today, he is the vice-president of the Cauliflower Alley, an organization that holds annual reunion celebrations to honor wrestling's rich history and to help out former stars in need of financial assistance.

31

Dusty Rhodes

A three-time NWA World Champion between 1979 and 1986, "The American Dream" Dusty Rhodes was one of
wrestling's top babyfaces and most
charismatic wrestlers. He was an unbe-
lievably magnetic performer and one of
the industry's biggest stars, particularly
in Florida and Georgia, where he was a
huge box-office draw during his prime.
At 6'1" and 302 pounds, Rhodes was not
the most gifted of wrestlers, and had to
rely heavily on a stationary working style
where he basically juked and jived in the
middle of the ring while his opponent
worked around him. However, in spite of
his girth and limited wrestling skills,
Rhodes combined his abundance of

Dusty Rhodes and the Road Warriors in
Miami, 1987.

charisma in the ring with a promo style based on the fran-
tic interviews of Muhammad Ali to become one of the
most popular stars in the sport.

Rhodes is best remembered for his feuds against the
top heels in the business, including Ric Flair, the Funks,
Abdullah the Butcher, Jos LeDuc, Pak Song, Harley Race,
Ole Anderson, and Tully Blanchard. From 1983 to 1988,
Rhodes was also one of the most powerful men behind the
scenes in wrestling, as booker for Jim Crockett Promotions,
and was a central figure in the national wrestling wars
between the WWF and the NWA in the mid-'80s. Rhodes is
also credited with "killing" the Mid-Atlantic area and several
other major markets with his repetitive, ego-driven book-
ing-style, wherein he pushed himself as the company's top
star while simultaneously diluting the NWA World Championship, and its holder, Ric Flair. Rhodes is best known for
his famous "Dusty Finish," an ending to a match that was
repeated so often during his tenure as booker that it killed

off business in numerous cities.

There were innumerable variations
and twists on the Dusty Finish, but the
basic premise was to send fans home
from the arenas thinking they had seen
an important title switch hands. The
kicker came when fans tuned into TV
the next week and found out that the
decision had been reversed after the
defending champion was disqualified
for an infraction earlier in the match.

A native of Austin, Texas, Dusty
Rhodes was born Virgil Runnels Jr. on
October 12, 1945. He played college football at West Texas State – the same school
that produced Stan Hansen, the Funks,
Ted DiBiase, Bruiser Brody, and Bobby
Duncum – before entering pro wrestling in 1969. Rhodes
first gained fame as a heel, partnering with Dick Murdoch
in a tag team dubbed The Texas Outlaws. The duo eventually split up and Rhodes pursued a singles career, wrestling
in several big territories before winding up in Florida.

A member of Gary Hart's heel stable and tagging with
Pak Song upon arriving in Florida, Rhodes became a babyface in 1975 after turning on Song during a tag match
against Eddie and Mike Graham. Rhodes was given "The
American Dream" moniker by booker Bill Watts and feuded with Song, Jos LeDuc, and Hart's stable before weekly
sold-out crowds in cities all over the territory. Rhodes
became the top-drawing star in the Sunshine State, winning the Florida Heavyweight title ten times between 1974
and 1980. He eventually became booker of the territory and
kept Florida as his home base, maintaining its status as one
of the hottest territories in the business while working programs in other NWA offices.

During the late-'70s, Rhodes became a huge star in the Atlanta territory while feuding with Ole Anderson. He also worked a headlining program at Madison Square Garden against wwwf Champion "Superstar" Billy Graham. Their title match on October 4, 1977, drew a sellout crowd of 22,092 and an additional 4,000 fans who watched on closed circuit tv in the adjacent Felt Forum.

Despite being one of the top drawing cards in wrestling, the nwa never considered making Rhodes its long-term world champion due to his flabby physique, limited in-ring ability, and the nwa's longstanding policy of keeping the belt on someone who could actually wrestle. Instead, Rhodes was given short title runs and was used as a transitional champion. He won his first nwa world title on August 2, 1979, when he defeated Harley Race in Tampa, Florida. Five days later in Orlando, he dropped the title back to Race. He won his second nwa World title from Race on June 21, 1981, in Atlanta, but dropped the belt to Ric Flair on September 17 in Kansas City, ushering in the "Ric Flair Era" of the nwa world title.

In 1983, Rhodes left Florida for Jim Crockett's Charlotte-based Mid-Atlantic territory, where he served as booker until 1988. It was there that Rhodes became one of the most influential men in wrestling as the architect behind the territory's major storylines and events, including the Starrcade concept, a major televised production that was used to blow off all the year's major feuds and programs.

He was a key figure in the promotional wars between Crockett and Vince McMahon Jr. in the mid-'80s, as both companies expanded from regional territories to national entities. From 1984 to 1986, Rhodes led the company to an incredible run of house show business, writing and booking critically acclaimed wrestling shows that aired nationally on tbs. As the promotion's top babyface, Rhodes collected all the major titles in the company along the way. He was the focal point of the promotion in his memorable feuds against Flair for the nwa world title, Tully Blanchard for the World tv and U.S. title, and later as the leading babyface against The Four Horsemen heel clique. He won his third and final nwa world title on July 26, 1986, when he defeated Flair in a cage match in Greensboro, North Carolina. On August 7, Rhodes dropped the title back to Flair in St. Louis.

By 1987, Crockett's business began to suffer at the gate due to Rhodes repetitive booking and having world champion Flair constantly lose by dq. Rhodes and Crockett, looking to save the company's dwindling fortunes and

Rhodes squares off with Dory Funk Jr. with the late Jerry Monti refereeing.

prospects, booked Starrcade on pay-per-view, the company's first venture into that market.

Crockett took a financial bath. The wwf staged its first-ever Survivor Series head-to-head with Starrcade on pay-per-view. McMahon successfully strong-armed the majority of cable operators by threatening that any cable system that carried Starrcade would not be allowed to carry future wwf shows. Coming off the tremendous success of WrestleMania III months earlier, most cable operators, seeing bigger pay-days ahead, bended to McMahon's will. As a result, Starrcade was a financial disaster that plunged Crockett further into debt. By the end of 1988 he sold the company to Ted Turner, who wanted to keep wrestling on tbs.

In the fallout, Rhodes was declared *persona non grata* and left the promotion. He returned to Florida and worked for Mike Graham's Florida Championship Wrestling territory before debuting in the wwf in the summer of 1989. Rhodes filmed several embarrassing, campy skits in the wwf – posing as a plumber and pizza deliveryman – that were meant to get him over as a working-class-hero character. Rhodes retired in 1991 and assumed the booker's position in wcw.

Once again, Rhodes was in charge of booking and running a national wrestling company and, just like he had done before, he ran into the same traps and repeated the same mistakes that bedeviled his previous booking stint. In 1994, Rhodes was let go as booker, but maintained a position in the company as a color commentator.

Rhodes left wcw in late 1999 and formed his own wrestling promotion, Turnbuckle Championship Wrestling, in Georgia, and came out of retirement on a few occasions to wrestle on ecw pay-per-view events.

32

Johnny Valentine

A main-event star and box-office draw in every territory he appeared in, Johnny Valentine was reputedly one of the toughest men in wrestling over a brilliant 28-year career that was tragically cut short by a 1975 plane crash.

Valentine was one of the top-five workers in the business at his peak in the '60s and '70s. Although respected and feared alike by fans, he was much more of a legend among his wrestling brethren for his toughness in and out of the ring. He wrestled every major star in the U.S., but is remembered most for his feud against Wahoo McDaniel, which featured long and brutally stiff matches.

Father of Greg "The Hammer" Valentine, Johnny, perhaps more than any other wrestler during his era, was committed to putting on matches that looked as real as possible. He was an influential performer with incredible presence and charisma, and believed in the legitimacy of the business, always striving to get fans to suspend their disbelief while watching his matches. Valentine's style proved successful: his feud with McDaniel turned sleepy territories like Texas in the late-'60s and the Carolinas in the mid-'70s into box-office cash cows.

Valentine gave as good as he got. Renowned for his insatiable pursuit of realism, Valentine told his opponents to lay into him as hard as they could every time he stepped into the ring. The results were matches that became orgies of twisted flesh, broken bones, bloody brows, and sweat-soaked torsos.

"He was as tough as any man could be. He was almost masochistic…he almost liked it," says Tim Woods, a frequent opponent of Valentine's in the Carolinas. "Valentine

Tough Johnny Valentine.

would take a hold and just grind the guy right down to nothing with it."

Born John Wisniski on September 22, 1928, Valentine grew up in Hobart, Washington, where he trained to be a boxer as a teenager before getting into pro wrestling. After starting his career in South America, he bounced around between Florida, Texas, California, Minneapolis, and Ohio, collecting regional titles in every territory before winding up in New York for Vince McMahon Sr. in 1958.

He became a top star for McMahon, wrestling in Madison Square Garden both in singles and tag team main events between 1959 and 1965. During the '60s, he wrestled NWA World Champions Lou Thesz, Buddy Rogers, Gene Kiniski, and Dory Funk Jr., and worked in several territories in the U.S. and Canada.

In 1966, he completed his first tour of Japan while holding the Toronto version of the U.S. Heavyweight title and had a series of famous matches against a then 23-year old Antonio Inoki in the short-lived Tokyo Pro Wrestling promotion. On October 12 at Tokyo's Sumo Hall, Inoki beat Valentine in 32 minutes via countout. They followed that up with a 60-minute draw on October 25 and an Inoki two-out-of-three falls win on November 19. Because of his reputation as one of the top workers in the U.S., Valentine put Inoki's career on the map. After Tokyo Pro Wrestling folded and he returned to the JWA, Inoki, on the strength of beating Valentine, assumed the number two position in the company (below Giant Baba) and went on to become a cultural icon in Japan.

In 1969, Valentine worked for Fritz Von Erich in Texas. His feud with McDaniel revitalized the stagnant promotion, turning it into one of the strongest territories in the country. They would continue to tear up the circuit with their legendary stiff matches until Valentine suffered a heart attack on March 15, 1973.

After recovering from the heart attack, he worked a program with The Sheik in Detroit. Mid-Atlantic booker George Scott then brought him to the Carolinas, a territory he had never wrestled in previously. Because Mid-Atlantic was a tag team promotion that featured mostly fast-paced matches with high spots, Valentine, with his deliberate and realistic style, wasn't an instant hit. But Scott remained patient and as the fans became educated and appreciative of his matches, Valentine turned the territory around. His feud with McDaniel was renewed and Mid-Atlantic became one of the hottest promotions in the country. Their ground-breaking program not only was a box-office success, but also established a more physical and athletic style in the territory, paving the way for Ric Flair and Ricky Steamboat to flourish in later years.

Flair first teamed and traveled with Valentine in 1975 in Mid-Atlantic. As someone who had only been wrestling since 1972, Flair recalls how different Valentine's in-ring approach was for that era.

"It was hard to understand his style of work being a guy who was just getting started myself but everybody who ever worked with him or was around him had huge respect for him. He had an unbelievable work ethic and he liked to work long, hard matches. He had a real unique style. He was the only one that ever worked that way but it really worked for him."

In 1975, the United States Heavyweight title was created for Valentine as he continued to feud with McDaniel and Woods. Even at age 47, Valentine appeared in several territories and was still considered one of the top workers in the world.

And then, in an instant, his career was over.

On October 4, 1975, a Cessna 310 plane carrying Valentine, Flair, Woods, Bob Bruggers, and promoter David Crockett crashed in Wilmington, North Carolina, when the tank ran out of gas. Although all six were admitted to New Hanover County Hospital in Wilmington, it was Valentine who suffered the worst fate as he broke his back and was paralyzed for life. He never wrestled again.

Crockett kept him on the payroll for 18 months after the

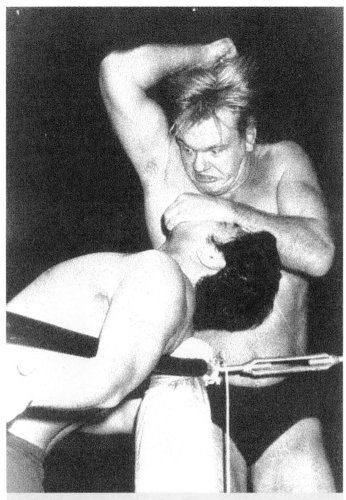

Valentine elbow smashes Wahoo McDaniel.

crash but the well eventually dried up. Although he saved his money during his career, the cost of medical care depleted his savings, leaving him destitute.

For the next 25 years, Valentine lived off social security disability income and was totally ignored and forgotten by the industry he had given his life to. As his pain and the cost of his care began to increase, his condition grew steadily worse. In the summer of 2000, he fell off his porch, fracturing his back and twisting his colon in the process. He was hospitalized for several months and sustained a litany of further health problems that became too overwhelming for his weak heart to bear.

Johnny Valentine, the epitome of toughness, passed away on April 24, 2001. He was 72.

33

Freddie Blassie

Renowned for his violent feuds with John Tolos, The Sheik, The Destroyer, and Japanese legend Rikidozan, "Classy" Freddie Blassie was the single biggest star of the Los Angeles-based World Wrestling Association during the '50s, '60s, and '70s.

Blassie (born Fred Blassman) was the archetypal wrestling villain. Smug and brash, Blassie was one of the best talkers in the business, perfecting a heel interview style that would influence countless future superstars. He also coined one of the all-time great catch phrases in wrestling history, referring to opponents and fans as "pencil-neck geeks."

Blassie is synonymous with the word "heat." He elevated the portrayal of the heel to an art form, striking terror into the hearts of the audience and often inciting them to riot. He was nicknamed "The Vampire," due to his penchant for filing his teeth during interviews and biting his opponents during wild and bloody matches. Blassie became so hated at Los Angeles' Olympic Auditorium that the building had to hire uniformed Los Angeles police officers to escort him to and from the ring, to prevent him from being attacked by fans. Legend has it that, after one show, a mob of angry fans turned over Blassie's brand new Cadillac and set it on fire.

"Freddie taught me a lot in terms of ring psychology," remembered Dick Beyer, one of Blassie's most famous Los Angeles opponents, who wrestled as the masked Destroyer. "The way you could excite a crowd – bring 'em up and sit 'em down – without having to walk out of the ring and fear for your life. Inside the ring he had control of everything. He could get more heat than anybody without doing anything."

Freddie Blassie as a manager.

Blassie was a four-time holder of the WWA World Heavyweight title, having defeated Edouard Carpentier twice, Rikidozan and The Destroyer. He was a huge money draw in southern California, as droves of rabid wrestling fans routinely packed into the old Olympic Auditorium in Los Angeles to root against him.

On March 28, 1962, Blassie lost the WWA World Title to Japanese legend Rikidozan, dropping the only fall in a two-out-of-three falls match that went past the time limit. Blassie followed Rikidozan to Japan and lost the rematch on April 23. It was a wild, brutal affair that saw Blassie cut open Rikidozan with his trademark biting. Ringside fans were horrified, and TV viewers had heart attacks (and some even died) watching Blassie's carnivorous bloodletting of the Japanese hero. The match is still talked about today among Japanese fans, cementing Blassie's reputation as one of Japan's all-time great foreign heels.

By the early '70s, Blassie was receiving so many cheers from the fans that promoters turned him into a babyface. Originating the "kick-ass good-guy" role that Steve Austin would make famous in the late '90s, Blassie was booked against the top heels: The Sheik, Don Carson, Kinji Shibuya, and Goliath.

Blassie's famous feud with John Tolos began in 1971. In one of the most enduring angles of the '70s, Tolos blinded Blassie by throwing powder in his eyes while he was receiving a wrestler of the year award. Blassie, in the unfamiliar role of chasing the heel, embarked on a legendary series of matches with Tolos, culminating at the Los Angeles Colise-

The first historic match between John Tolos and Freddie Blassie.

um in front of a crowd of 25,847 and bringing in a gate of $142,158.50, both California records at the time.

Blassie retired in 1974, after 30 years as an active wrestler, because of a California law at the time that prohibited licensing of anyone past the age of 55. He remained involved in wrestling as a manager for Vince McMahon Sr. and later for Vince McMahon Jr. in the WWF, until he left the sport in 1986.

34

Vader

Vader is considered the greatest super-heavyweight in wrestling history, having redefined the role of the monster foreign heel as one of Japan's biggest box-office draws from the late-'80s to the early-'90s.

At 6'4" and ranging in weight between 330 and 415 pounds, Vader moved around the ring with great agility and speed, setting a new standard of athleticism for wrestlers his size. He was a stiff worker who took big bumps and effectively sold his opponent's offense, and was always committed to making his matches look as real as possible.

Masked Vader during his New Japan days.

Vader (born Leon White) was a former offensive lineman at the University of Colorado. He was trained for wrestling by Brad Rheingans before turning pro in 1985, debuting in the AWA as "The Baby Bull." Later, as "Bull Power," he ventured to Otto Wanz' Catch Wrestling Association in Austria where he became a main event star. He won his first of three CWA World titles on March 22, 1987, from Wanz.

He signed with New Japan and debuted as the masked Big Van Vader on December 27, 1987, in one of the most famous angles in Japanese history. Managed by Japan's top late night TV show host, Vader defeated Antonio Inoki in under three minutes in the main event of a nationally televised show from Tokyo's Sumo Hall. The match was designed to get Vader over as a new killer heel, but the promoters did not anticipate the effect it would have. Fans in attendance, irate after watching their hero lose in a squash match to a green worker, rioted and tore the building apart.

Vader gradually improved, and did in fact become the monster heel that New Japan had originally envisioned him

as. He won the vacant IWGP title after defeating Masahiro Chono, Tatsumi Fujinami, and Shinya Hashimoto in a tournament on April 24, 1989, at New Japan's first Tokyo Dome show.

Vader won the strap a second time on August 10, 1989, from Riki Choshu and later that month traveled to Germany to defeat Wanz to regain the CWA title. Then, on November 22, 1989, he beat Canek for the UWA World title in Mexico City and became the first man in history to hold three world titles from three continents simultaneously.

Vader's relationship with New Japan slowly deteriorated as he spent more time in the U.S. He made his debut in WCW in July 1990 at the *Great American Bash*, and joined full time in 1992. He was immediately pushed as the promotion's top heel, winning the world title from Sting on July 12. By 1993, he had become the focal point of WCW's major storylines.

Vader still spent time wrestling in Japan, where he jumped to UWFI. He faced Nobuhiko Takada in a battle of world champions on December 5, drawing 46,168 fans to Jingu Baseball Stadium in Tokyo. He lost the match after submitting to Takada's cross armbreaker. Vader finished off his year by losing the WCW World title to Ric Flair at Starrcade '93 in a memorable storyline where Flair promised to retire if defeated.

Vader was pushed aside in the WCW in 1994, when Hulk Hogan entered the promotion, and was fired in 1995 following a backstage fight with Paul Orndorff. However, he remained a huge star in UWFI. With the trio of Takada, Vader, and Gary Albright on top, the promotion averaged more than 14,000 fans per show in 1994. Vader knocked out

Vader against Hashimoto (on mat) while Fujinami looks on.

Takada on August 18 to win the world title, and held it for nearly a year before finally leaving the promotion.

Vader debuted in the WWF at the 1996 Royal Rumble, and went on to feud with Shawn Michaels over the world title. Heat between him and the front office began to grow when they gave Sid Vicious a title reign that had been promised to him. The tension grew between both sides from 1997 to 1998. His weight began to balloon, and he was arrested in Kuwait while on tour for assaulting a TV announcer. The WWF let White out of his contract in late 1998.

Following his stint with the WWF, he signed with All Japan Pro Wrestling, a move that not only revitalized his career, but also provided a shot in the arm for the promotion. He reached a milestone on March 6, 1999 when he pinned Akira Taue to win the vacant Triple Crown, becoming the first man in history to have held both the Triple Crown and the IWGP Heavyweight title. He would later go on win a second Triple Crown, as well as the Champion Carnival tournament. He left All Japan in 2000 to join Mitsuharu Misawa's Pro Wrestling NOAH organization.

35

George Hackenschmidt

A bodybuilding strongman who was wrestling's biggest star at the turn of the century, George "The Russian Lion" Hackenschmidt is considered by historians to be pro wrestling's first true World Heavyweight Champion.

Born in 1877 in Dorpat, Estonia, Hackenschmidt boasted a massive, muscular physique and incredible natural strength. At first, he was a massive box-office draw in England, but soon parlayed his status as "World's Strongest Man" into worldwide celebrity, helping to popularize pro wrestling.

The Russian Lion.

Having broken several world weightlifting records while still a teenager, the 5'9", 218-pound Hackenschmidt entered pro wrestling in the late-1890's and quickly became the top wrestler in Europe. In 1901, Hackenschmidt won championship tournaments all across the continent and was recognized in Europe as the legitimate world titleholder. On May 5, 1905, in New York, Hackenschmidt defeated Tom Jenkins, the American claimant to the world title, to become the first true World Heavyweight Champion.

History records that Hackenschmidt remained undefeated until meeting Frank Gotch in 1908. Gotch beat Hackenschmidt for the World title on April 3, 1908, in Chicago in a two-and-a-half hour marathon that was reputed to be a shoot. Hackenschmidt lost the first fall when Gotch forced him to submit using an ankle lock submission. After the fall, both wrestlers went to their dressing rooms for a ten-minute break, but Hackenschmidt refused to return to the ring. Gotch was awarded the match and became the new World Champion in what would turn out to be one of the most important matches in wrestling history.

A rematch three years later at Chicago's Comiskey Park drew 28,757 fans for a gate of $87,000 (a record at that time). The match has become legendary as it is reputed to have involved one of the first double-crosses in wrestling. A few weeks before the match, Hackenschmidt tore up his knee during a training session. Historians are divided on whether the sparring partner was Ad Santel or Ben Roller, but the end result was that Hackenschmidt's knee was severely damaged. It was later revealed that either Santel or Roller had been paid off by Gotch to injure Hackenschmidt. Hackenschmidt wanted to pull out of the match, but was persuaded to go ahead with it after he was conned into believing that Gotch had injured his neck in training.

According to many historians, the two combatants agreed to work a match where Gotch would retain the title but where Hackenschmidt would win one fall, thus appearing strong in defeat. Gotch had other ideas. Once the match started he double-crossed Hackenschmidt and started to shoot on him, quickly winning two straight falls in less than half an hour. By all accounts, Hackenschmidt had no business being in the ring at all due to his knee injury and was easy prey for the conniving Gotch. The match turned out to be an over-hyped and under-athletic failure that didn't even come close to living up to their first bout.

Because Hackenschmidt couldn't move well during that match and was destroyed rather easily by Gotch, fans in attendance felt ripped off, and as a result the Chicago market was killed off for years. Hackenschmidt retired shortly after the rematch, remaining bitter about losing to Gotch and maintaining that he had been cheated in both matches.

He died in London on February 19, 1968.

Former body builder, Hackenschmidt shows off his fine form.

36

Jushin "Thunder" Liger

Jushin "Thunder" Liger is one of the most influential junior heavyweights in history, whose style of pro wrestling was copied by virtually every junior heavyweight that came after him, including Chris Jericho, Brian Pillman, Rey Misterio Jr., and Psicosis.

At 5'4" and 206 pounds, Liger combined a breathtaking aerial repertoire with lightning-quick mat skills. Bridging the gap between pioneers like Satoru Sayama and the Dynamite Kid and today's bottomless reservoir of junior heavyweight wrestlers, the one quality that defined Liger's amazing in-ring career was his ability to put on consistently great matches with so many different styles of opponents.

Jushin Liger dives onto El Samurai in New Japan action.

According to many insiders and critics, Liger was the best pound-for-pound wrestler of the '90s, setting an unmatched standard of ring excellence in his epic IWGP Junior Heavyweight title matches against Owen Hart, Chris Benoit, El Samurai, Ultimo Dragon, and Hiroshi Hase.

Born Keiichi Yamada on November 10, 1964, in Hiroshima, Japan, Liger grew up a lifelong wrestling fan. He was an amateur wrestling standout in high school, losing to future All Japan Pro Wrestling star Toshiaki Kawada in 1981 in the national high school wrestling championships in the 165-pound weight division.

After graduating, Yamada tried to get into New Japan's dojo, but was turned down because of his size. So he traveled to Mexico and learned pro wrestling there. While on tour a company official from the New Japan dojo saw him perform. Impressed with what he saw, he decided to give him another opportunity with the company. Yamada then became part of the same training camp that produced Keiji

Muto, Masahiro Chono, and Shinya Hashimoto, before making his pro debut on March 3, 1984, against Shunji Kosugi. He worked undercards for two years before winning New Japan's Young Lions Cup tournament on March 26, 1986.

New Japan sent him to England later that year to gain some seasoning with the intention of bringing him back with a renewed push. While in England, he wrestled as Flying Fuji Yamada, winning the World Heavy Middleweight title twice and feuding with British legend Mark "Rollerball" Rocco (formerly the original Black Tiger in New Japan in the early-'80s).

From England, Yamada went to Stu Hart's Stampede promotion in Calgary, before eventually returning to Japan in 1987. In the fall of 1988, a Jushin Liger cartoon debuted in Japan, becoming an instant hit with young children. With the success of the Tiger Mask gimmick seven years earlier still fresh in their minds, New Japan decided to use the Jushin Liger comic character to rejuvenate Yamada's career.

Yamada debuted as the masked Jushin "Thunder" Liger at the very first wrestling event at the Tokyo Dome on April 24, 1989, defeating Kuniaki Kobayashi, one of Tiger Mask's biggest rivals from his glory days in the early '80s.

Liger was pushed as the new top junior heavyweight star of the promotion and as the second coming of Tiger Mask, winning the IWGP Junior Heavyweight title from Hiroshi Hase on May 25, 1989. Liger would go on to dominate the title over the next decade, holding the strap on ten different occasions while having some of the greatest matches of the '80s and '90s against Wild Pegasus (Benoit), Owen Hart, El

Japan promotions collide as Jushin "Thunder" Liger takes on The Great Sasuke.

Samurai, Naoki Sano, Koji Kanemoto, Ultimo Dragon, Black Tiger (Eddie Guerrero), Great Sasuke, and Super Delfin.

By the early '90s, Liger was booking the New Japan junior heavyweight division. He became one of the most influential matchmakers of his era, importing a diverse mix of junior heavyweights from promotions in Japan, Mexico, the U.S., Canada, and Europe. Liger became renowned for his selfless booking, routinely putting over his rivals in the ring cleanly, thus creating more stars within the division.

In December 1991, Liger made his U.S. debut by defeating the late Brian Pillman for the WCW Light Heavyweight title. Together, Liger and Pillman put on the best matches in the U.S. at the time on television and at house shows, before Liger dropped the title back to Pillman on February 29, 1992, at WCW's SuperBrawl pay-per-view.

On April 16, 1994, Liger helped organize the first ever Super-J Cup, an historic, one-night tournament staged by New Japan featuring the best junior heavyweights in the world. Liger put over The Great Sasuke in a memorable, five-star semi-final match before Chris Benoit beat Sasuke in the finals to win the tournament.

In August 1996 he put together the J-Crown tournament. The one-week affair featured eight different junior heavyweight champions, from five different promotions in Japan and Mexico, in a tournament to unify the belts into one title. It took place during New Japan's annual G1 Climax tournament.

Despite organizing the tournament and being the top junior heavyweight worker in the world, Liger booked himself to lose in the first round to Ultimo Dragon, who lost to The Great Sasuke in the finals. On the last day of the G1 tournament, Liger announced to the live audience he had a brain tumor and that his career might be over.

Fortunately, the tumor turned out to be benign. After having an operation to remove it, Liger returned months later, modifying his style to include more mat wrestling and storytelling. Despite this, he still got over well with fans, and remained one of the ten best workers in the world.

Other career highlights include winning the J-Crown in 1997, three Top of the Super Junior Heavyweight Tournament championships (1992, 1994, and 2001), and two Super-J Cup championships (1995 and 2000).

37

Toshiaki Kawada

A legend in All Japan Pro Wrestling, Toshiaki Kawada was one of the top heavyweight workers of his generation.

His career is inextricably tied to that of Mitsuharu Misawa, dating back to their high school days when they were classmates and leading to their real-life rivalry both in and out of the ring. Together, Kawada and Misawa had their greatest series of matches against each other during the '90s. They were grandiose exhibitions of captivating storytelling, brilliant psychology, flawless selling, and seamless transitions, setting a standard for match quality and workmanship that may never be equaled again.

Kawada was a Japanese national high school champion in 1981, winning the 165-pound weight class by defeating Keiichi Yamada (who would later go on to fame as Jushin "Thunder" Liger) in the finals. A year later he joined All Japan Pro Wrestling.

Kawada's first big break came teaming with Misawa – then wrestling as Tiger Mask – as a solid mid-card tag team. He later went on to partner with Samson Fuyuki in 1987 in a combination named "Footloose," as members of Genichiro Tenryu's Revolution stable. Kawada played a major role in the fabled Tsuruta & Co. vs. Misawa & Co. program of 1990, feuding with Akira Taue and firmly establishing himself as a main-event star. Kawada teamed with Misawa again in the early '90s, winning the Unified World Tag titles on two occasions and the Real World Tag League tournament in 1992, on their way to establishing

Kawada, renowned for his stiff powerful kicks.

themselves as the top tag team of the decade.

Kawada won his first of four Triple Crown titles on October 22, 1994, defeating Steve Williams in Tokyo. Other career highlights include: eight reigns as Unified World Tag Team Champion, Champion Carnival tournament wins in 1994 and 1997, and three Real World Tag League championships.

Kawada was the lynch pin that held All Japan together after Misawa departed in June 2000 to form Pro Wrestling NOAH, taking the bulk of All Japan's roster with him. With its locker room depleted, All Japan would have folded had Kawada decided to leave.

That same year All Japan began working with New Japan, exchanging top talent for several big shows. On October 9, Kawada defeated IWGP Heavyweight Champion Kensuke Sasaki in a non-title match at the Tokyo Dome. Memorable for its stiff, physical spots, with both stars pushing themselves to the point of physical exhaustion, the bout was named Match of the Year in the prestigious year-end awards handed out by the Tokyo Sports newspaper.

In 2002, Kawada was back on top, winning the Triple Crown title after defeating Keiji Muto at Tokyo's Budokan Hall on February 24. By capturing the title, Kawada joined Stan Hansen as a four-time champion, trailing only Misawa, who held the title five times.

38

Keiji Muto

Keiji Muto was the backbone of New Japan Pro Wrestling during its glory years of the '90s, leading the company through one of the most successful periods of business in wrestling history.

Muto was one of the best workers of his era, possessing an innovative ring style that combined aspects of Japanese-, submission-, and American-style wrestling. Able to carry even the most clueless opponents in the ring, Muto constantly incorporated new moves into his vast palette of maneuvers, allowing him to stay on top of a fiercely competitive promotion that stressed work ethic and match quality.

A Young Keiji Muto in New Japan.

Muto wrestled like a junior heavyweight, routinely executing dizzying moves that belied his 6'2", 260-pound frame, including handspring elbows, Dragon-Screw leg whips, and power elbows. Muto was also responsible for popularizing the moonsault. He was a brilliant ring psychologist and a master of communicating subtle storylines through simple gestures and facial expressions.

After training in the New Japan dojo with classmates Shinya Hashimoto, Masahiro Chono and Jushin "Thunder" Liger, Muto debuted in 1984 and after a year went to the U.S., bouncing between Florida, Texas, and Puerto Rico. He joined WCW in 1989 as the Great Muta, gaining worldwide acclaim for his unique ring style. In 1990 he returned to New Japan, where he would headline for over a decade.

Muto was a central figure in the historic New Japan vs. UWFI feud of 1995-96, drawing crowds of 67,000 and 64,000 for title defenses against Nobuhiko Takada. He was one of the top draws in Japan during the '90s, headlining six shows that drew over 50,000 fans each.

In 1995, Muto capped off a fantastic year by being named Wrestler of the Year in the annual year-end awards sponsored by Tokyo Sports Newspaper. (He would go on to win the prestigious award again in 1999 and 2001.)

However, years of performing moonsaults had caused irreparable damage to his knees. Amazingly, Muto adjusted his style to accommodate his injuries and went on to wrestle in some of the best matches of the '90s.

Johnny Smith, a regular with All Japan since the late-'80s, was impressed by Muto's ability to work through the pain and put on matches of such a high caliber:

"What a performer...absolutely fantastic. You see him backstage and he's kind of [hobbling] around on his bad knees; but once he gets into the ring he turns it on and it's as if there's nothing wrong with him."

Perhaps his greatest honor came on December 28, 2000, when Nikkan Sports Newspaper published their "Top 20 Wrestlers of the 20th Century" list. Muto finished in 10th, ahead of such legends as Genichiro Tenryu and Tatsumi Fujinami.

As New Japan and All Japan began working together in 2001, Muto defeated Tenryu on June 8 in Tokyo to win All Japan's Triple Crown title. By virtue of his win, Muto joined Tenryu and Vader as the only men in history to have held both the IWGP and Triple Crown titles.

On January 18, 2002, Muto shocked the wrestling world when he announced he was leaving New Japan. After wrestling his final match for New Japan, he signed with All Japan in February, dropping the Triple Crown title to Toshiaki Kawada in Tokyo on February 24.

Muto as the Great Muta.

39

Jack Brisco

Jack Brisco was a two-time N W A World Heavyweight Champion between 1973 and 1975, and is regarded as one of the best pure wrestlers of all time.

A former N C A A amateur wrestling champion in 1965 and a two-time Big Eight Conference champion at 191 pounds while at Oklahoma State, Brisco is considered by many within the industry to be the greatest in-ring performer of the '70s.

His fame as an amateur wrestling champion lent credibility to the entire industry, as Brisco became renowned for his professionalism inside the ring. His execution of wrestling holds was flawless, enabling him to carry lesser opponents through incredible matches. He was also the single most popular babyface in the U.S. during the early-'70s, earning fame for his lengthy, monumental feud with Dory Funk Jr. over the N W A Heavyweight title.

Pushed as the young, handsome up-and-comer, Brisco wrestled Funk before sold-out crowds all across the U.S. during the early-'70s, perfecting the world title chase program that became a standard booking pattern that promoters have been following ever since.

But perhaps more than his two N W A titles or his feud with Funk, Brisco is best remembered for changing the course of wrestling history in 1984 when he and brother Jerry sold their controlling interest in Georgia Championship Wrestling, Inc. to Vince McMahon.

McMahon had visions of taking the W W F, a regional promotion based in the Northeast that he had purchased from his father, to a national level. After buying out the Briscos, McMahon closed down Georgia Championship

NWA World Champion, Jack Brisco.

Wrestling and assumed the company's T V contract, bringing the W W F to Ted Turner's T B S. The time slot on T B S allowed McMahon to get a leg up on the competition in the early days of the national wrestling wars, and helped him set the W W F on course to becoming the most dominant wrestling promotion in history.

Coming off his N C A A championship, Brisco turned to pro wrestling amid heavy fanfare and mainstream media attention after graduating from college in 1965.

"I always wanted to be a pro wrestler," confessed Brisco. "I wrestled amateur in high school and everyone always asked me what I wanted to do in the future; I said I wanted to be a wrestler. We got T V from Oklahoma City and I always read the wrestling magazines. Lou Thesz and Danny Hodge were my idols. I won a scholarship to Oklahoma State and I let it be known that I wanted to be a professional wrestler. Leroy McGuirk was the promoter in Oklahoma. He sent some of his men over to ask me if I wanted to be a pro wrestler. I said yes. That's how I got started."

After a spell with McGuirk in his Oklahoma-based territory, the Sunshine State became his adoptive home as Brisco became the top babyface in Eddie Graham's Florida territory. He held the N W A Southern title three times between 1969 and 1971 and the Florida Heavyweight title another three times from 1970 to 1972.

As his popularity grew, Brisco was being touted as a future N W A World Champion and began his legendary program with Funk. Funk and Brisco toured the country and put on their masterful matches – many of them 60-minute

Jack and Jerry Brisco.

marathons – before packed audiences in every major NWA territory. Together, they took the NWA title to a new level of prestige, putting on athletically credible matches that left fans wondering whether or not what they had just seen was real.

Brisco never got the chance to defeat Funk for the heavyweight title. He was scheduled to finally defeat Funk as a finale to their legendary feud, but Funk suffered a serious shoulder injury that forced him to miss the match. Instead, it was Harley Race who Brisco defeated to win his first NWA title on July 20, 1973, in Houston, Texas.

After defeating Race for the strap, Brisco defended the title all across the U.S. and Canada against the likes of "Superstar" Billy Graham, Paul Jones, Ivan Koloff, Pat Patterson, Ox Baker, and Bob Roop. As all NWA champions did in the '70s when touring All Japan, Brisco dropped the title to Giant Baba on December 2, 1974, only to regain it a week later as the tour concluded.

Brisco's second title reign ended on December 10, 1975, when he lost to Terry Funk in Miami. Brisco continued on as a main event star and collected several major regional titles, including two Missouri State Heavyweight titles and five Mid-Atlantic Heavyweight titles.

He went on to form one of the greatest tag teams in history with brother Jerry in the late-'70s, dominating tag team wrestling in Florida. In the early-'80s, the brother tandem jumped to Jim Crockett's Mid-Atlantic territory and became heels, feuding with Ricky Steamboat and Jay Youngblood and winning the NWA World Tag Team titles three times from 1983 to 1984. Brisco retired shortly after.

Even in retirement, the accolades and honors never stopped. On June 16, 2001, Brisco was inducted into the International Wrestling Institute and Museum's Professional Wrestling Hall of Fame in Newton, Iowa.

40

Harley Race

An eight-time NWA World Heavyweight Champion between 1973 and 1984, Harley Race was one of the toughest men in wrestling during his prime and was considered one of the best workers of his era. For over 10 years, Race dominated the NWA World title, feuding with such stars as Dusty Rhodes, the Funks, Ric Flair, and Jack Brisco. While not the most charismatic wrestler in history, Race's straightforward approach as world champion elevated the NWA title to new levels of prestige, earning the respect of fans everywhere.

World champion Harley Race, 1977.

Born on April 11, 1943, in Quitman, Missouri, Race was trained by Hobby Graham and Ray Gordon before beginning his wrestling career in 1959 – while still a teenager – under the tutelage of NWA promoter Gus Karras. Shortly after making his debut, he was involved in a serious car accident and doctors at the time told him that he would never wrestle again. However, Race recuperated and went on to become one of the biggest stars in the Central States territories of the NWA and a local celebrity in his home base of Kansas City.

Race's first big break came in 1964 when he began teaming with Larry Hennig in the American Wrestling Association. The rugged duo established themselves as one of the most successful teams of the '60s, feuding with Dick the Bruiser and The Crusher and holding the AWA World Tag Team titles three times between 1965 and 1967.

Race's greatest moment came on May 23, 1973, when he defeated Dory Funk Jr. for his first NWA world title in Kansas City. Race was merely a transitional champion though, as he dropped the title to Jack Brisco two months later in Houston. However, Race bounced back, winning

his second world title on February 6, 1977, from Terry Funk at Toronto's Maple Leaf Gardens. His victory over Funk ushered in a new era in the NWA, with Race as its flagship wrestler and long-term champion. Race would go on to become one of the most dominant and respected NWA world champions in history, defending the title all across North America, Japan, Australia, and Mexico.

Race's second reign was highlighted by two NWA vs. WWWF world title unification matches. On January 25, 1978, Race battled "Superstar" Billy Graham to a bloody one-hour draw at the Orange Bowl in Miami. A month later, he wrestled newly crowned WWWF champion Bob Backlund in Jacksonville, Florida. Race lost the NWA strap to Dusty Rhodes on August 21, 1979, in Tampa, Florida but regained it five days later in Orlando. Like former NWA world champion Jack Brisco before him, Race dropped the belt to Giant Baba on October 31, 1979 while on tour for All Japan, only to regain the title a week later. The stunt would be repeated again in September 1980.

After losing the belt to Tommy Rich and Dusty Rhodes in 1981, Race won the title for the seventh time on June 10, 1983, from Ric Flair in St. Louis. His classic feud with Flair was a perfectly executed, highly profitable program that lasted for months, with the young, brash Flair chasing Race all over the Mid-Atlantic territory for the world title.

Their legendary program climaxed at the first Starrcade event on Thanksgiving Day, November 24, 1983, which saw Flair regain the title in a steel cage match with former NWA World Champion Gene Kiniski as the special referee. The match, which drew a sold-out crowd of 18,000 fans to the

Long time rivals Ric Flair and Harley Race during one of their many NWA World Title matches.

Greensboro Coliseum, was beamed via satellite to several closed-circuit locations around the Mid-Atlantic region. In total, over 54,000 fans watched the event live.

Race won the title for the eighth and final time on March 21, 1984, defeating Flair in Wellington, New Zealand, while on tour for NWA promoter Steve Rickard. He lost the title back to Flair two days later in Kallang, Singapore. Referred to as the "South Pacific quickies," neither title switch was recognized on American television or in magazines at the time.

As his NWA career slowly wound down, Race signed with the World Wrestling Federation in 1986. Dubbed "The King" and managed by Bobby Heenan, Race feuded with "Hacksaw" Jim Duggan, Hulk Hogan, and The Junkyard Dog (whom he wrestled as part of the undercard at WrestleMania III).

He left the WWF in 1988 and continued wrestling for a few more years before retiring from active competition to become a manager in WCW in 1991. Race went on to manage several big stars, including former WCW World Champions Lex Luger and Vader, before he was sidelined by another serious auto accident in 1995, which forced him to retire from wrestling.

41

El Hijo del Santo

The son of the legendary El Santo, arguably the most beloved wrestler in history, El Hijo del Santo became a second-generation star in his own right, and was the best in-ring performer in Mexico from the early-'80s through to the 21st century.

Although not as big a star as his father, El Hijo del Santo (born Jorge Guzman) was a far superior worker, renowned for his dizzying arsenal of aerial moves, solid mat skills, sublime ring psychology, and unmatched work ethic. He was a pioneer inside the ring, bridging the gap between the era of Mil Mascaras and the generation of daredevil luchadors that emerged in the early-'90s. He paved the way for wrestlers like Rey Misterio Jr., Psicosis, and Juventud Guerrera.

Because he was the prodigy of El Santo, El Hijo del Santo was seen as the bearer of his father's name and legacy. His matches where his mask was at stake became huge events, as he was protecting not only his own honor by holding on to the mask, but also his father's.

From 1984 to 1989 he was the single biggest box-office draw in Mexico. His feud against long-time rival Negro Casas began in 1984 over the UWA Lightweight title, sparking a brilliant program that continued off and on for the better part of 17 years. The Santo-Casas feud, featuring main event matches both in Mexico and Los Angeles over several welterweight titles – and with a few mask vs. hair matches thrown in for good measure – set a new standard of in-ring excellence in Mexican wrestling.

After starring in several films like his famous father before him, El Hijo del Santo debuted as Korak in February of 1982. Eight months later he donned the illustrious silver

Mexican legend El Hijo del Santo.

mask made famous by his father, and took the name El Hijo del Santo (The Son of the Saint). He split his formative years between Mexico's big promotions, winning titles and collecting the masks and scalps of some of Mexico's top stars along the way.

In 1993, he formed a tag team with Octagon, embarking on a feud against Eddie Guerrero and "Love Machine" Art Barr over the AAA World Tag titles. The legendary feud culminated in a double mask vs. hair match at AAA's *When Worlds Collide* pay-per-view in Los Angeles on November 6, 1994. Considered by many fans as one of the best bouts of the '90s, it capped off a remarkable program that produced many incredible matches.

"I'll always remember the feud Art Barr and I had against Octagon and El Hijo del Santo," stated Eddie Guerrero in 2001. "That was great…we stretched it out for two years. I'll always remember that program; it's embedded in my memory for life."

Despite approaching middle-age in the late '90s – when Mexican wrestling became dominated by twenty-something luchadors with high-flying, suicidal styles – El Hijo del Santo remained head and shoulders above his young contemporaries. His perfect balance of smooth mat wrestling, breathtaking aerial moves, and gripping storytelling kept him on top of the game as Mexico's best wrestler.

Art Barr and El Hijo del Santo during their groundbreaking feud in the '90s.

42

Tatsumi Fujinami

Forever living in the shadow of his mentor Antonio Inoki, Tatsumi Fujinami was among the top-five workers in the world during his prime in the '80s, before a severe back injury nearly cost him his career.

Fujinami, a six-time IWGP Heavyweight Champion and former UWA World Heavyweight Champion, put the junior heavyweight division on the map in the late '70s. His innovative ring work elevated the credibility of the junior heavyweight division, paving the way for the revolution that took New Japan Pro Wrestling by storm in the early '80s, led by the original Tiger Mask and The Dynamite Kid.

His matches as WWF Junior Heavyweight and NWA International Junior Heavyweight Champion against Bret Hart, Canek, El Solitario, Steve Keirn, Dynamite Kid, and Chavo Guerrero earned him praise from fans and critics as one of the best in-ring wrestlers in Japan. That reputation was solidified when he graduated to the heavyweight division and had a series of legendary matches against Riki Choshu, Antonio Inoki, Akira Maeda, and Vader.

His feud against Riki Choshu between 1982 and 1983 ushered in a new era of Japanese wrestling, changing the long established booking tradition in Japan that main-event programs had to feature Japanese vs. foreign wrestlers. Perhaps even more important than that, his decision to stay with New Japan while being heavily courted by All Japan and the UWF in 1984 ensured the company's survival and prevented it from being closed down in the aftermath of Choshu and several top performers' jump to All Japan.

Fujinami wins both NWA and IWGP World title belts in unification.

Born December 28, 1953, in Oita, Fujinami was trained by Inoki before making his pro debut in the Japanese Pro Wrestling Alliance as a 17-year-old. He went with Inoki when he formed New Japan Pro Wrestling a year later and in 1975 was sent to the U.S. and Mexico to gain experience. He captured his first title on January 23, 1978, defeating Jose Estrada for the WWF Junior Heavyweight title in Madison Square Garden.

He returned to Japan and became a top star, with Inoki and Hisashi Shinma building the junior heavyweight division around him. Fujinami was one of the best overall workers in the company and helped establish the credibility of the junior division among Japanese fans. In 1981, New Japan moved him to the heavyweight division to make room for the original Tiger Mask.

During a six-man tag match on October 8, 1982, Choshu turned on Fujinami. The angle was the birth of the famous Ishingun vs. Seikigun feud that set New Japan on fire for two years and led the company through one of the biggest boom periods in its history.

After Choshu left for All Japan in 1984, New Japan was on the brink of disaster. TV-Asahi, the network that kept New Japan in the black during the Inoki embezzlement scandal, was about to shut the company down when they found out that both All Japan and the UWF were pursuing Fujinami. However, Fujinami turned down their offers and decided to stay with New Japan, going on to become one of the top stars in the company. At the same time he formed a legendary duo with Kengo Kimura, as the dynamic pair won the IWGP tag titles three times between 1985 and 1988.

Fujinami against Ric Flair, rematch for the World Tille in Tampa Bay, Florida, 1991.

Then, in 1989, while considered alongside Ric Flair as the top worker in the world, Fujinami was stricken by major back injuries – the culmination of the grueling schedules and vicious poundings he had been subjected to over the years. Foolishly, he ignored the pain and continued to wrestle. However, his injuries soon caught up with him, and he was sidelined.

He eventually returned to the ring and although still a good worker, he was never the same world-class caliber worker he once was. Nevertheless, he was pushed as a head-liner and won his first IWGP Heavyweight title on May 8, 1988, from Big Van Vader in Tokyo. Over the next few years he feuded with Choshu and Vader, winning the IWGP two more times before wrestling in the biggest match of his career.

On March 21, 1991, Fujinami met Ric Flair for the WCW World title in the Tokyo Dome in front of 64,500 fans. Although a great match, the ending was marred by the infamous "Dusty Finish." (Not so coincidentally, Dusty Rhodes was the WCW booker at the time.) Fujinami pinned Flair and was recognized as the new champion in Japan, but Flair returned to the U.S. with the belt after WCW reversed the decision (due to Fujinami being disqualified for an infraction during the match). The return match was set up two months later at the *SuperBrawl* pay-per-view in Tampa, Florida, with Flair going over clean.

As the '90s progressed, Fujinami began to slow down in the ring but continued to be pushed, winning the 1993 G1 Climax tournament and picking up three more IWGP Heavyweight Titles by 1998. He began to cut back his schedule after being named president of New Japan in 1999, and despite a looming retirement, remained active into the new century.

43

Danny Hodge

One of the greatest amateur wrestlers the United States ever produced, Danny Hodge was a brilliant mat technician and a trailblazing performer as the perennial National Wrestling Alliance World Junior Heavyweight Champion from 1960 to 1976.

Through his epic battles with Hiro Matsuda, Angelo Savoldi, and Sputnik Monroe, Hodge, a former Olympian and NCAA champion, established himself as the foremost junior heavyweight in the world during the '60s and '70s.

His Olympic and collegiate career lent instant credibility to the NWA title and to the industry as a whole. At 5'10" and a mere 220 pounds, Hodge was considered, pound for pound, the best pure wrestler of the modern era. Graced with a wiry, muscular build, lightning-quickness, and a vice-like grip, he was universally recognized as the toughest wrestler in the business. Throughout his 16-year career, the credo, "You don't mess with Hodge," became common in wrestling locker rooms everywhere.

"I was smaller than everybody," admits Hodge, "but God gave me a lot of strength, a lot of stamina, a lot of conditioning. I had knowledge of holds, I could wrestle, and I could fight; so really, you had five strikes against you when you stepped in the ring with me."

Hodge first gained national recognition wrestling on his high school team in Perry, Oklahoma, by going undefeated his entire time there – helping to turn the school into a wrestling powerhouse. As a nineteen-year-old, Hodge represented the U.S. at the 1952 Olympics in Helsinki, placing fifth in the freestyle competition.

As a 177-pounder, Hodge found a spot on the wrestling

Danny Hodge perennial NWA Junior Champ.

squad at the University of Oklahoma, where he went on to win three NCAA national titles from 1955 to 1957. Ineligible to compete in his freshman year, Hodge went undefeated in his remaining three years at Oklahoma, winning all 46 of matches – 36 by pinfall. Amazingly, he was never taken down to the mat from a standing position.

In 1956, he represented the U.S. in the Olympics in Australia, winning the silver medal in the freestyle competition after losing a controversial match to Nikola Stanchev of Bulgaria in the final. Hodge was winning the match on points by a score of 8-1 when he rolled through on a move, and wasn't even touched by the Bulgarian when they called a fall on him. The decision was widely considered to be the most unjust in amateur wrestling history. However, even the loss couldn't dim Hodge's rising star as he graced the cover of the April 1st, 1957, issue of Sports Illustrated.

After his collegiate wrestling career, Danny Hodge won national Golden Gloves and National AAU championships in boxing, becoming the first athlete in more than 50 years to win national titles in boxing and amateur wrestling. He had a brief career as pro boxer before turning to pro wrestling in 1959.

It was in Leroy McGuirk's NWA-affiliated office that Hodge had his greatest fame. While the New York and Los Angeles territories at the time featured heavyweights, McGuirk's sleepy circuit based out of Oklahoma and Arkansas focused on the junior heavyweights. McGuirk, a former NWA junior heavyweight himself, liked what he saw in Hodge and decided to build his promotion around him.

Within nine months of his pro debut, Hodge defeated

Danny Hodge with former Olympic wrestling champ Kosrow "Iron Sheik" Vaziri, Louisiana, 1972.

Angelo Savoldi to win his first of seven NWA World Junior Heavyweight titles. From 1960 to 1976, Hodge traveled all over the world, squaring off against the top wrestlers in all of the NWA's territories. He often wrestled outside of his weight class, taking on some of the biggest stars of the era, including Jack Brisco, Terry and Dory Funk Jr., Verne Gagne, and Bobo Brazil. Hodge single-handedly carried the junior heavyweight division during his storied career. Incredibly, he worked main events 85 percent of the time and was the last Junior Heavyweight Champion to do so,

establishing a niche for today's cruiserweights.

Sadly, it was an auto accident, and not an opponent, that finally put him down for the count. On March 15, 1976, Hodge suffered a broken neck in a car accident that nearly took his life. Hodge was lucky to be alive. Doctors told him that if he took one more serious bump on his neck that he would be paralyzed for life. Amazingly, Hodge came back and wrestled in several matches, before finally retiring in 1983.

In 1976, Hodge received a tremendous honor, when he was inducted into the U.S. Amateur Wrestling Hall of Fame.

44

Akira Maeda

Trained by the legendary Karl Gotch, Akira Maeda is among the most influential and revolutionary wrestlers in history, and is responsible for changing the landscape of Japanese wrestling in the '80s.

As the top star of his own UWF promotion from 1988-1990, Maeda was one of the hottest box-office draws in the world. By promoting realistic-looking worked shoot matches, Maeda's UWF paved the way for today's UFC, Vale Tudo, K-1, and mixed-martial arts promotions. Maeda is credited with amending booking patterns in Japan, placing more emphasis on strong submissions and clean finishes, and creating a work environment where even main event stars were not immune from jobbing.

A former karate fighter, Maeda made his pro debut for New Japan Pro Wrestling in 1978. He worked as a jobber for several years before heading to England, where he won the European Title in 1981 under the name Kwik-Kik Lee.

He returned to New Japan in 1982, where he built a solid reputation for himself as an in-ring worker. Maeda was seen as the next Antonio Inoki, and New Japan pegged him as the promotion's leader when Inoki eventually retired. But that day never came: Inoki refused to put over any of New Japan's young, emerging talent and held on to his top spot long after his best days were behind him.

Maeda developed a reputation among American wrestlers as being difficult to work with in the ring, balking whenever he was asked to do a job. He was becoming increasingly disenfranchised with the "phoniness" and showmanship of American wrestlers and worked pro wrestling matches in general. Ironically, as a worker himself, Maeda was always capable of carrying opponents

Shoot kick king Akira Maeda.

through fantastic, entertaining matches.

He joined Hisashi Shinma and Satoru Sayama's UWF in 1984, and was pushed as the top star in the worked "shoot-style" pro wrestling promotion. By 1985, the UWF was in dire financial trouble due to mismanagement. Knowing the promotion was about to go under, Sayama shot on Maeda during a match in September, throwing several intentional kicks into his groin. A month later the promotion folded.

Nevertheless, the UWF had introduced a concept that was several years ahead of its time. By the time Maeda returned to New Japan in 1985, he had become a big star on TV, getting himself over as a maverick shooter and laying the foundation for future shoot and mixed-martial arts promotions.

For the next few years he would become more well-known for his antics outside the ring than for his performance in it. First, he became involved in a real-life feud with Antonio Inoki, refusing to work with the veteran in what could have potentially been a huge moneymaking program. Then, in April of 1986, his match against Andre the Giant quickly lost all spirit of co-operation as the bout deteriorated into one of wrestling's most notorious shoots.

The most infamous moment in his career, however, came during a six-man tag match on November 19, 1987. At one point in the match, Riki Choshu's arms were tied up as he locked Osamu Kido in a Scorpion Deathlock. Fully aware of the compromising position Choshu was in, Maeda delivered a vicious shoot kick to Choshu's eye, breaking his orbital bone and knocking him out cold. The resulting injury would sideline Choshu for six weeks.

Predating Vince McMahon's infamous screw-job of Bret

A master of submission holds and strong-style wrestling, Akira Maeda grinds his opponent into the mat.

Hart at the 1997 Survivor Series in Montreal by a decade, "the shoot kick" was the most talked about double-cross in history and one of the biggest news items in the industry. Word of the incident spread around the wrestling world. Maeda was suspended, and later fired, by New Japan. Ironically, though, much like McMahon did in the aftermath of Montreal, Maeda was the one that ultimately benefited from his act of cowardice. He became an instant celebrity as a rebel shooter and was hailed as a mainstream sports star by the Japanese media. As a result, he became the single greatest box-office draw in wrestling, with every UWF house show selling out in one to two hours – a staggering accomplishment considering that the promotion did not even have its own television program.

He banked on his newfound stardom and opened the new Universal Wrestling Federation in 1988 along with Nobuhiko Takada and Yoshiaki Fujiwara. Thanks to Maeda's fame, the latest incarnation of the UWF would become the most successful wrestling promotion in the world from 1988 to 1989.

On November 10, 1988, Maeda did a clean KO job for Takada in the main event of a UWF house show, redeeming him in the eyes of the public and forever changing the concept that the top wrestlers had to be protected from doing clean jobs. As a result of UWF's policy of having every match end in a clean knockout or submission, New Japan and All Japan fans grew increasingly hostile over main event matches that ended in DQS or double count outs. Maeda forced both

of the big promotions to change their booking philosophies towards more traditional and clean finishes, changing the way they had been doing business for decades.

Maeda was so big at the box-office that less than two years after its formation the UWF became the first promotion to sell out the Tokyo Dome. On November 29, 1989, 60,000 fans packed into the Dome to watch Maeda defeat Willie Wilhelm in the main event. In 1991, a year after the UWF folded, Maeda formed RINGS. It was a groundbreaking promotion that progressed from worked matches to an all-shoot format in late 1999.

Maeda retired on February 21, 1999, losing his final match to three-time Olympic Greco-Roman Gold medallist Alexander Kareline at Yokohama Arena. The match gained widespread media coverage, including mentions in the New York Times and Sports Illustrated, and drew an amazing gate of $2.5 million.

Famous for his short temper, Maeda was always a magnet for trouble and was known for punching reporters and fans who grilled him about the legitimacy of the UWF. In 1986, during his second stint in New Japan, he was involved in several legitimate scraps away from the ring, including a bar fight with Keiji Muto. Later in his career he was the victim of a surprise attack at a UFC event from Yoji Anjoh, resulting in criminal charges.

In late 2001, Maeda held a press conference, announcing that RINGS was folding due to financial difficulties and the growing popularity of the PRIDE promotion.

45

Chigusa Nagayo

A cultural icon in her native Japan who inspired a generation of young Japanese girls to get into pro wrestling, Chigusa Nagayo is arguably the most influential women's wrestler of all time.

As one half of the famous Crush Gals tag team with Lioness Asuka in the All Japan Women's promotion, Nagayo took women's wrestling to dizzying heights of popularity and an entirely new level of mainstream recognition in the mid-'80s. Nagayo and Asuka became the most successful female tag team, changing the face of women's wrestling with their historic feuds against Dump Matsumoto and Bull Nakano, and the Jumping Bomb Angels.

Woman's wrestling innovator Chigusa Nagayo.

The Crush Gals became pop idols to millions of Japanese schoolgirls who swarmed to arenas to watch their matches and fervently cheer them on. During the height of the Crush Gals phenomenon, their matches on AJW's weekly Saturday afternoon program on Fuji TV drew ratings comparable to the NFL's audience in the United States.

The Crush Gals were huge crossover stars, becoming a marketing marvel long before Vince McMahon Jr. turned Hulk Hogan into a merchandising jackpot. Their popularity knew no bounds: Nagayo and Asuka recorded several top-10 pop singles, had their faces plastered on magazine covers and posters, and were the focus of major print media stories, including an article in the Wall Street Journal.

Amazingly, Nagayo made her pro debut at age 15 on August 8th, 1980, in Tokyo against Yukari Omori and won her first title, the AJW Junior title, on May 15th, 1982. In 1983, at the age of 18, Nagayo formed the Crush Gals with Asuka. Success came their way quickly: they won their first All Japan Women's Tag Team titles on August 25, 1984, from the Dynamite Girls. They lost the belts on February 25, 1985, to Dump Matsumoto and Crane Yu, but would go on to enjoy two more reigns.

In 1985, Nagayo had an unforgettable singles feud with Dump Matsumoto. Together, Nagayo (playing the cute-young-girl underdog) and Matsumoto (the hardened, monstrous heel) created magic in the ring and at the box office. On August 25, 1985, over 13,000 fans packed Tokyo's Budokan Hall, drawing a gate of $250,000 (an unheard-of number in those days) to watch Matsumoto defeat Nagayo in an unforgettable hair vs. hair match. Nagayo would get her revenge on November 7, 1986, defeating Matsumoto in another hair vs. hair match in Osaka.

Nagayo and Asuka's battle over the tag belts with Matsumoto and Bull Nakano would turn out to be the greatest women's tag team feud in the history of wrestling; but in 1986 the Crush Gals fad all but died, and the team split up. Nagayo went on to win the WWWA Heavyweight title on October 20, 1987, and began feuding with Asuka, her former partner. Producing several match-of-the-decade candidates, the Nagayo vs. Asuka feud set a new standard of quality in women's wrestling and laid the foundation for Manami Toyota, who would lead the next boom in women's wrestling in the early '90s.

Nagayo remained champion until August 25, 1988, when she was forced to vacate the title due to injury. She left wrestling in May 1989 but came out of retirement in 1993, ironically, as the monster heel that beat up the new crop of cute, young underdogs in the promotion. She formed the Gaea promotion in 1995, and was the subject of *Gaea Girls*, a documentary film that looked at her methods as a wrestling trainer.

Chigusa Nagayo prepares to send her opponent crashing down onto the canvas.

46

Ricky Steamboat

A former NWA World Heavyweight
Champion remembered for his classic
matches against Ric Flair and Randy Savage, Ricky Steamboat was one of the top
stars in the business during his 18-year
career.

Steamboat (born Richard Blood) is
generally recognized within the industry
as one of the best workers of the '80s. A
career babyface, Steamboat was the epitome of professionalism and class both in
and out of the ring. With his great workrate and athleticism, he could carry even
the most helpless opponent to a decent
match.

Former NWA World Champ.

Steamboat was one of the biggest stars during '80s
thanks to his high profile stints in Jim Crockett's Mid-Atlantic territory and the WWF. He was trained by Verne
Gagne before making his pro debut in 1976. Mid-Atlantic
booker George Scott brought him to the Carolinas after
seeing him on television in Atlanta.

"He caught on like wildfire," Scott recalled for journalist
Mike Mooneyham. "I immediately recognized his potential.
The kid had something special."

Steamboat is best known for his milestone matches
against Flair in 1989 that saw both superstars tax their
bodies to the point of exhaustion. Together, the two created
pure magic inside the ring, pushing the envelope and setting the standard of excellence that all future matches
would be measured against. His first feud with Flair,
between 1977-1980 over the Mid-Atlantic TV and U.S titles,
set off one of wrestling's all-time greatest feuds that would
rage, off and on, for the better part of 17 years.

In 1979, Steamboat formed what would become one of
the greatest tag teams of the '80s, with Jay Youngblood.

Between 1979 and 1983, Steamboat and
Youngblood won the NWA Tag Team
titles five times. In late-1984, after a
memorable series of tag team matches
against the Brisco Brothers, Steamboat
announced his retirement.

However, Steamboat came out of
retirement in 1985 and joined the WWF,
where he went on to become a household name. He won the Intercontinental
title from Randy Savage at WrestleMania
III in 1987 in what many consider one of
the greatest matches in modern WWF
history, upstaging the historic Hulk
Hogan vs. Andre the Giant main event
that followed.

He returned to the NWA in 1989 and began a landmark
feud with Flair that produced no less than three match of
the decade candidates: February 20 in Chicago, in the main
event of the *Chi-Town Rumble* pay-per-view, when he won
the NWA title in a 23-minute barnburner; April 2 in New
Orleans, as part of a Clash of the Champions live special on
TBS, when Steamboat won the two-out-of-three falls match
in a 55-minute mat classic; and May 7 in Nashville, where
Flair regained the title in a 31-match that many critics consider the best of the decade.

Shockingly, after close to 20 years in the business, and
with only three months left on his contract, Steamboat was
fired in 1994 by WCW after suffering a back injury during a
match with Steve Austin during a Clash of the Champions
special.

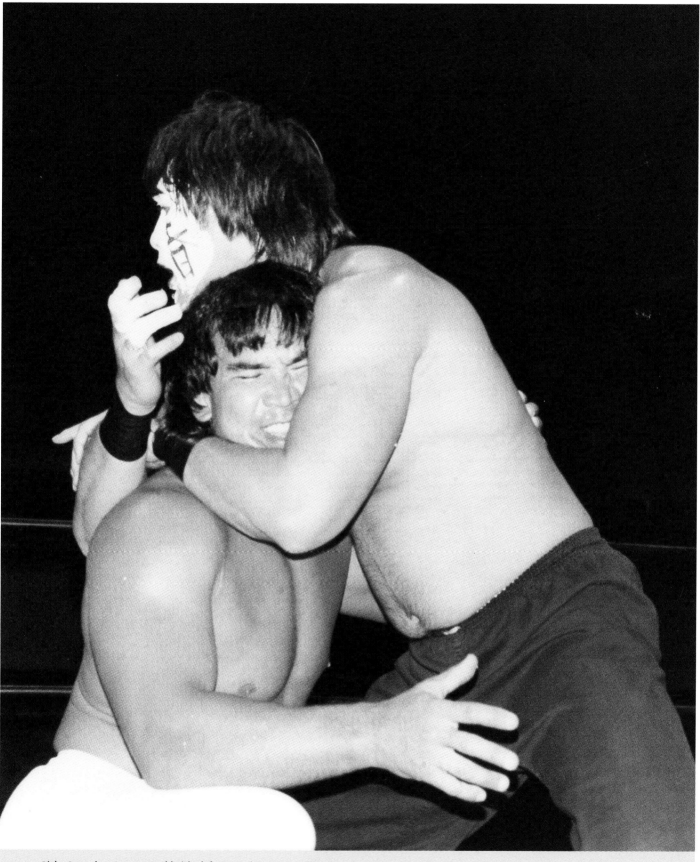

Ricky Steamboat's NWA World Title defence against Muta, 1989.

47

Shawn Michaels

A three-time WWF World Heavy-weight Champion, Shawn Michaels was arguably the greatest in-ring worker in North America from 1993 to 1997.

Nicknamed "the Heartbreak Kid," he was a charismatic performer and one of the biggest stars of his era.

Michaels came into prominence as a singles star in the WWF during the early-'90s when the WWF was mired in a series of steroid scandals. The introduction of stringent drug testing made it impossible for Vince McMahon to continue to push steroid-enhanced monsters, forcing the company to build around Michaels and Bret Hart.

Young Shawn Michaels in Japan, 1990.

With the plodding, hulking monsters out of the picture, Michaels helped introduce a quicker and more athletic ring style into the WWF, elevating the quality of the overall product while becoming a main event star. His matches against Bret and Owen Hart, Razor Ramon, and Steve Austin cemented his status as a world-class caliber worker and one of the premier wrestlers of his era, while inspiring a whole new generation of fans to get into pro wrestling.

Born Michael Hickenbottom on July 22, 1965, Michaels was trained by Jose Lothario before making his pro debut at the age of 19 in Bill Watts' Mid-South territory in 1984. After six months in Mid-South, Shawn moved on to Bob Geigel's Central States territory in Kansas City and later returned to his hometown of San Antonio where he worked for Texas All-Star Wrestling.

In 1986, Michaels found himself back in Central States where he met Marty Jannetty and formed the Midnight Rockers, a pretty-boy tag team that appealed to squealing teenaged girls. At the end of 1986, the Rockers jumped to

the AWA, where Verne Gagne gave them a major push. While at first they were viewed as a lame rip-off of the Rock 'n' Roll Express, they eventually got over due to their overwhelming in-ring skill before jumping to the WWF in early 1988.

Billed as the Rockers, Michaels and Jannetty established themselves as one of the top tag teams in the promotion, winning widespread acclaim in 1989 for their house show feud with Tully Blanchard and Arn Anderson.

The duo split up in January 1992 following an angle where Michaels turned heel after attacking Jannetty. Now competing as a singles wrestler, Michaels' career began to take off, and he quickly became one of the best workers in the WWF. On October 27, 1992, he defeated Davey Boy Smith to win the Intercontinental strap. While enjoying his second Intercontinental reign, Michaels briefly quit the promotion in September 1993 over contractual problems. Because of his departure he was stripped of the title without dropping it inside the ring, establishing a reputation that he would later become notorious for.

Michaels returned in November and began feuding with Razor Ramon, who had won the Intercontinental title in his absence. The two embarked on a lengthy feud, climaxing with their epic five-star ladder match at WrestleMania X in Madison Square Garden, considered the greatest match in the modern era of the WWF.

He won his third and final Intercontinental title on July 23, 1995 from Jeff Jarrett but was stripped of the title on October 22 at a WWF *In Your House* pay-per-view. Nine days earlier, Michaels was attacked outside a Syracuse bar by a gang of servicemen. Although people knew that he was

Midnight Rockers in Japan, Shawn Michaels against Naoki Sano.

legitimately hurt and would not be able to work the show, Michaels' reputation took a beating for once again failing to lose belt inside the ring.

At WrestleMania XII on March 31, 1996, Michaels defeated Bret Hart in a one-hour marathon match to capture his first WWF World Title. Over the next few months, he feuded with Vader, Diesel, and Davey Boy Smith before dropping the title to Sid Vicious at Survivor Series. Less than two months later, Michaels regained the title in January, 1997 at the Royal Rumble in San Antonio. His title reign was short-lived: on a live broadcast of RAW on February 13, he forfeited the title due to a knee injury, claiming that he had "lost his smile." While he was banged up, it was widely believed Michaels gave up the title not only because he had been asked to lose the strap to Sid that evening, but also because the plan for that year's WrestleMania was for him to drop the title back to Bret Hart. Again, Michaels had somehow managed to drop the title without losing it.

Michaels returned to action months later and began feuding with Bret Hart in a program that mirrored their real-life animosity towards each other. Things came to a boil on June 9 when Hart, angry because he felt Michaels

stepped over the line when making "shoot" comments about him on TV, attacked Michaels backstage at a RAW taping. Michaels briefly left the company, but returned in July, although the tension between him and Hart still existed. Michaels formed Degeneration X, a cheap NWO rip off, with Hunter Hearst Helmsley, Chyna, and Rick Rude. The clique feuded with Hart and his faction, which included brother Owen, Davey Boy Smith, and Jim Neidhart.

Michaels then chased Hart for the WWF title, leading to their infamous match on November 9, 1997, at Survivor Series in Montreal.

From there, Shawn began feuding with the Undertaker, but Shawn suffered injuries to his knee and back that would eventually end his career. While ailing, he returned for one last match at WrestleMania, fighting through the pain to put on a spectacular match in dropping the title to Steve Austin. After seeing the doctor, it was discovered that the discs in his back were ruptured. His in-ring career was over.

After undergoing back surgery on January 12, 1999, Michaels periodically returned to the WWF in various on-air roles.

48

Shinya Hashimoto

One of the greatest heavyweight
workers of his generation, Shinya
Hashimoto was the top box-office draw
in Japan during the '90s, remarkably
headlining eight shows that drew over
50,000 fans each.

Alongside Keiji Muto and Masahiro
Chono, Hashimoto was the backbone
of New Japan Pro Wrestling, leading the
company in its glory years of the '90s.
Hashimoto was a master of ring psychology – his realistic looking matches and
extraordinary skills as a storyteller made
him a main-event star. He entered New
Japan's training dojo on April 21, 1984,
with fellow "classmates" Muto and
Chono, and made his pro debut on
September 1 against Tatsutoshi Goto in Tokyo.

New Japan's box-office sensation
Shinya Hashimoto.

Hashimoto was a mid-carder in Japan for years before
being sent to North America to gain some seasoning. He
shuffled around between Calgary, Puerto Rico, and Tennessee, before returning on April 24, 1989, as part of New
Japan's tournament to crown a new IWGP champion. The
one-night tournament, as part of the first pro wrestling
show at the Tokyo Dome, saw Hashimoto elevated to main-
event status, scoring "upset" victories over Riki Choshu and
Russian star Victor Zangiev, before losing to Big Van Vader
in the finals.

He won his first IWGP title in 1993 by defeating Muto
and would win the title again from Tatsumi Fujinami in
1994, and from Nobuhiko Takada in 1996 (in the climax of
the historic New Japan-UWFI feud). In 1994, Hashimoto
was named Wrestler of the Year in Tokyo Sports Newspaper's annual year-end awards.

In 1997, Hashimoto lost a non-title, mixed martial arts

bout in front of 60,000 fans at the Tokyo
Dome to Naoya Ogawa, a former
Olympic silver medalist in judo who was
making his wrestling debut. A rematch
one month later sold out the first-ever
show at the Osaka Dome. Hashimoto
won the match via submission. A third
match on January 4, 1999, at the Tokyo
Dome ended in a no-contest when
Ogawa "shot" on Hashimoto to further
fuel the angle, with Hashimoto elevating
Ogawa into superstardom in the process.

The Hashimoto-Ogawa feud was very
successful, headlining four major-dome
shows during what is generally considered a dead period in Japanese wrestling.
Their April 7, 2000, match at the Tokyo
Dome was the most-watched wrestling match on live TV in
over a decade, drawing over 34 million viewers as
Hashimoto lost and retired.

However, Hashimoto came back in October, defeating
Fujinami in the opening match of a show at the Tokyo
Dome. A month later, New Japan released Hashimoto and
he created his own promotion, Zero-One.

In December 2000, Hashimoto was ranked 17th on
Nikkan Sports Newspaper's "Top 20 Wrestlers of the 20th
Century" list, one place ahead of Fujinami. On December
15, 2001, Hashimoto defeated Gary Steele and Steve Corino
in a triangle round-robin tournament held in McKeepsport,
Pennsylvania, to capture the NWA World Heavyweight title.
He held the title until March 9, 2002, when he dropped the
belt to Dan Severn at Tokyo's fabled Korakuen Hall.

Hashimoto and rival Vader prepare to square off.

49

Ray Stevens

The most famous wrestler ever in Roy Shire's San Francisco territory, Ray "The Crippler" Stevens was considered by many to be the best worker in the business during the '60s.

Stevens was one of the biggest box-office hits in northern California from the '60s to the early-'70s. He won the NWA U.S. Heavyweight title nine times between 1960 and 1970, and drew sold-out crowds for his legendary feuds at the historic Cow Palace against Pepper Gomez, Wilbur Snyder, Bearcat Wright, King Curtis Iaukea, and Kinji Shibuya.

In a business where big, muscular men thrived, Stevens, at 5'8" and weighing a stout 230 pounds, would have to overcome his small size. He managed to do so by revolutionizing a unique, hard-bumping ring style that was years ahead of its time. His unparalleled ability to have great matches with a wide variety of opponents made him the premier worker of his generation, long before Ric Flair became heralded for the exact same reason in the '80s.

He was the best-selling heel of his era, respected by those within the industry for his workmanlike attitude in the ring and the great pride he took in his craft. While others shied away from working with green and inexperienced wrestlers when promoters asked them to do so, Stevens thrived on the challenge, always confident that he could pull out a decent match with any opponent, regardless of his skill level. He was also one half of two of the greatest tag teams in wrestling history, first, with Pat Patterson in San Francisco in the '60s as the Blond Bombers, and then in the '70s with Nick Bockwinkel in the AWA.

Carl Raymond Stevens was born on September 5, 1935, in Point Pleasant, West Virginia. He made his pro wrestling

Stevens at a Cauliflower Alley reunion.

debut in 1950 at the age of 15 and was a main-event star by the time he was 17, feuding with Gorgeous George at the height of the "Golden Era" of wrestling when it was broadcast on network television. Roy Shires brought Stevens to San Francisco in 1960. Stevens immediately became a main-event star in the territory, averaging crowds of 12,000 fans for the biweekly shows at the Cow Palace from 1961-1962. His landmark feud against Pepper Gomez established him as one of the top heels in the business, following a famous angle in 1962.

Gomez, a former bodybuilder, challenged anybody in the territory to jump off a ladder onto his rock-hard stomach. With Gomez lying prone on the mat, Stevens came crashing down off the top of the ladder, dropping his knee into Gomez' throat. As a result, Gomez was left for dead, coughing up blood, and Stevens' "Bombs Away" became the most feared maneuver on the west coast. After sitting out for several weeks, Gomez returned, setting the stage for a feud that set the territory on fire. More than 17,000 fans jammed into the Cow Palace for the grudge match, with several thousand more turned away at the door. The event broke the attendance record at the building set by Elvis Presley and took in over $65,000 in gate receipts, a record for northern California that stood for close to two decades.

Shires wanted to hold the rematch at Candlestick Park, the home of the NFL's San Francisco 49ers, as he had ambitions of breaking the all-time wrestling attendance record set one year earlier by the Pat O'Connor vs. Buddy Rogers World title match, which drew 38,622 fans to Chicago's Comiskey Park. It was not to be, however, as Stevens broke

Ray Stevens pinning Harley Race at San Francisco's Cow Palace, 1974.

his ankle in a go-cart race and was sidelined for eight months. However, the Stevens-Gomez ladder angle was so strong that they feuded for the next five years.

He began teaming with Pat Patterson, and the duo soon became the best tag team in the business, winning the San Francisco version of the NWA World Tag Team titles twice between 1965 and 1967. They split up in 1969 when Stevens turned babyface. A match was set that would see the two battle over the U.S. title, but history repeated itself: Stevens fractured his cheekbone prior to the August 9 match, and they were forced to postpone their feud. Patterson won the title in a tournament that evening and feuded with Stevens when he returned to action. The two Blond Bombers thrilled fans in a series of violent, bloody brawls, climaxing in an unforgettable Texas Death match on July 11, 1970, where Stevens won the U.S. title for the final time.

Stevens left San Francisco in 1971 for the greener pastures of Verne Gagne's AWA in Minneapolis. He earned the nickname "The Crippler" after he used his Bombs Away to "snap" Dick Beyer's leg in half (allowing the masked Destroyer to leave the territory and tour Japan). Entering what was mostly a tag team territory at the time, Stevens thrived in the AWA, teaming with Bockwinkel to form what

would become one of the greatest tag teams of the decade. Together the duo, later managed by Bobby Heenan, won the AWA World Tag Team titles three times between 1972 and 1974, feuding with the likes of The Crusher and Dick the Bruiser, and Gagne and Billy Robinson.

The duo split up in 1975, with Bockwinkel going on to become a singles star and win the AWA World title. Stevens turned babyface and often challenged Bockwinkel for the title, while bouncing around between the AWA, Jim Crockett's Mid-Atlantic territory and the WWF in the early-'80s. While in New York, he had a marquee feud with Jimmy Snuka. The Stevens-Snuka series sold out buildings all along the east coast and established Snuka as one of the top babyfaces in the country.

Stevens slowly faded from the spotlight at the onset of the steroid era of the mid-'80s, gradually cutting back on his schedule before finally retiring in 1992. In total, Stevens wrestled for 42 years in a career that spanned five separate decades, countless territories and a slew of changes to the business.

Stevens died from heart failure on May 3, 1996, at his home in Fremont, California. He was 60 years old.

50

Randy Savage

A two-time WWF World Heavyweight Champion between 1988 and 1992, Randy Savage was one of the biggest stars in wrestling during the '80s and helped Vince McMahon expand the WWF from a regional-based promotion into a global power.

Accompanied to the ring by his fetching wife, Miss Elizabeth, and nicknamed the "Macho Man" for his flamboyant ring persona, Savage was a charismatic star who will long be remembered for his epic battles in the WWF against Hulk Hogan and Ricky Steamboat.

Savage was a gifted yet inconsistent worker during his prime, possessing excellent ring psychology and the ability to deliver some of the most entertaining promos in the business. At 6'1" and weighing 237 pounds, Savage moved around the ring with startling quickness. His flying elbow drop off the top rope became one of the signature wrestling moves of the '80s.

Savage was born Randy Poffo on November 15, 1952. After a brief career as a minor league baseball player he entered pro wrestling in the late-'70s, following in the footsteps of father Angelo and brother Lanny. Savage was a top star in International Championship Wrestling, a regional promotion based in Lexington, Kentucky, which was owned by his father. After wrestling under a mask as The Spider, Savage began billing himself as the heel "Macho Man," and went on to hold the ICW World title three times between 1979 and 1983.

By the end of 1983, the ICW was on its last legs. Before closing it down, Angelo Poffo worked out a deal with Memphis promoter Jerry Jarrett to arrange an inter-promotional

Classic Randy "Macho Man" Savage.

feud between the two groups with a Savage vs. Jerry Lawler program as the focal point. The feud, over Savage's Southern Heavyweight Title, became very hot just as Poffo's promotion was forced to shut down. After another year in Memphis, where he was a top star while feuding with Lawler, Savage jumped to the WWF.

Savage's career skyrocketed after winning the Intercontinental title on February 8, 1986, from Tito Santana in Boston. He was immediately pushed as a main-event star and became one of the focal points of the promotion, primed to feud with Hulk Hogan over the world title. His classic match against Ricky Steamboat at WrestleMania III on March 29, 1987, where he lost the Intercontinental Title, garnered match of the year honors and is considered one of the greatest matches in the modern era of the WWF.

After turning babyface, Savage won his first WWF World title on April 1, 1988, at WrestleMania IV, defeating Ted DiBiase in the final of a tournament to crown a new world champion. During his reign he partnered with Hulk Hogan to form the Mega Powers tag team; the duo later split up following a high profile angle on a live, prime-time special that aired on NBC on February 3, 1989.

Savage, once again a heel, dropped the title to Hogan at WrestleMania V on April 2, 1989. His next big feud was with the Ultimate Warrior, climaxing with their loser-leave-town bout at WrestleMania VII on March 24, 1991. Savage lost the match but returned to the ring a few months later. He won his second WWF World title on April 5, 1992, from Ric Flair at WrestleMania VIII, the culmination of a heated feud that had been built up over several months. He dropped the title

Savage whipped the crowd into a frenzy when he joined the hated NWO in WCW.

back to Flair on September 1, 1992 in Hershey, Pennsylvania.

In late 1994, Savage jumped to WCW and became one of the promotion's top stars. He renewed his feud with Ric Flair in a program that sparked the turnaround of the company, and which came to full fruition under the NWO regime in 1996.

Savage would win the WCW World title four times from 1995 to 1999. After marquee feuds with Hogan, Flair, Sting, and Diamond Dallas Page (and a forgettable run as a member of the NWO), he was sidelined in 1999 with a serious knee injury. He made only one more appearance in WCW before it was sold to McMahon in 2001.

Gene Kiniski shows how he got one of his nicknames, the Canadian Avalanche, as he dives onto former football teammate and frequent ring foe Wilbur Snyder.

51

Gene Kiniski

One of the greatest Canadian wrestlers of all time, Gene Kiniski reigned as NWA World Heavyweight Champion from 1966 to 1969 and was considered one of the top workers of his era.

All through his career, Kiniski was a top draw and headlining star in every territory he appeared in. He was famous for his sarcasm and originality in his interviews, always managing to incense fans by referring to himself as Canada's greatest athlete.

Born in Alberta, Kiniski played pro football for the Edmonton Eskimos of the Canadian Football League before a serious knee injury in 1953 forced him to retire from the game. He entered pro wrestling shortly after.

Kiniski rose to the top of the wrestling world quickly, and on July 11, 1961, he defeated Verne Gagne for the AWA world title. On August 21, 1965, he added another world title to his resume, defeating Dick the Bruiser for the WWA title in Indianapolis. Kiniski's biggest career achievement, though, came on January 7, 1966, when he defeated Lou Thesz for the NWA World Heavyweight title in St. Louis, becoming the only man to hold both the NWA and AWA world titles.

Although "Big Thunder" Kiniski was primarily known for his hard-nosed style on the gridiron and his 6'4", 272-pound frame, he managed to develop into one of the better mat wrestlers of his day. He became one of wrestling's more proficient technical wrestlers, earning the respect of many of his peers, including Lou Thesz, who admired his eagerness to improve in the ring.

"Gene was not a wrestler, but he was always wanting to learn more wrestling. He had a keen competitive spirit and

was a crowd pleaser. I was delighted when he took the title from me, because he respected it and wore it proudly. His love of the sport is what the history of wrestling should be about."

His three-year reign as NWA champion, highlighted by spectacular title defenses against Thesz, "Whipper" Billy Watson, and Don Leo Jonathan, came to an end on February 11, 1969, when he lost to Dory Funk Jr. in Tampa, Florida.

After losing the title, Kiniski maintained a hectic schedule, wrestling in promotions all over Canada and the U.S., including Sam Muchnick's St. Louis outfit, where he won the prestigious Missouri State Heavyweight title after defeating Terry Funk in 1973.

52

Nobuhiko Takada

Takada, king of UWFI.

One of the top junior heavyweight workers of the '80s, Nobuhiko Takada was a pioneer who helped popularize "strong-style" wrestling in Japan.

After debuting in New Japan Pro Wrestling in 1980, Takada jumped to Hisashi Shinma's Universal Wrestling Federation, the first strong-style pro wrestling group of its kind, in 1984. He returned to New Japan a year later and engaged in a classic feud with Shiro Koshinaka, capturing the IWGP Junior Heavyweight title on May 19, 1986.

He left New Japan for a second time in 1988 to join the resurrected UWF. With its emphasis on clean finishes by either knockout or submission and worked bouts composed of punches, kicks, and suplexes, the UWF became the hottest promotion in Japan among Japanese teenagers starved for legitimate "shoot" matches.

This last incarnation of the UWF disbanded in early-1991, but not before Takada established UWF International (UWFI) in February, setting himself up as the group's top star and world champion while feuding with Vader and Gary Albright. The high point of his reign as champion in UWFI came on December 5, 1993, when he defeated then-WCW World Champion Vader via submission before 46,168 fans at Tokyo's Jingu Baseball Stadium.

Takada was a key figure in the landmark New Japan vs. UWFI program of 1995-1996, which was the biggest money-making feud in wrestling history at the time. His October 9, 1995, match against IWGP Champion Keiji Muto drew 67,000 fans to the Tokyo Dome, setting the record for the largest pro wrestling crowd ever in Japan and breaking the all-time gate record, at more than $6.1 million.

A mere three months later, Takada won the strap in a rematch before 64,000 fans on January 4, pulling in $5.5 million at the gate. Takada dropped the belt to Shinya Hashimoto on April 29 before 65,000 fans and drawing $5.7 million at the gate, ending a historical feud that will go down in history as one of the top two biggest grossing feuds of all time.

Takada moved on to PRIDE, where he lost to Rickson Gracie on October 11, 1997, before 37,000 fans in the Tokyo Dome. Their hotly anticipated rematch a year later drew just as many fans, and put the no-holds-barred outfit on the map. Takada turned the company into the hottest promotion in Japan during the late-'90s and the beginning of the new century, helping PRIDE draw in new fans not only from the martial arts audience, but also from the much larger pro wrestling audience.

53

Mick Foley

Cactus Jack, the king of hardcore.

Wrestler. Hardcore icon. Main event superstar. Father and husband. Acclaimed author.

Whether competing as Cactus Jack, Mankind, or Dude Love, all of these labels apply to Mick Foley, one of the most beloved and revered superstars of the '90s.

His is the ultimate success story, for years barely scraping out a living on the indie circuit as a crazy bump–taker, before eventually making millions as a headliner (and three-time world champion) in the WWF.

One of the greatest brawlers of all time, Mick Foley wrestled a punishing style that endeared him to a generation of fans that appreciated his uncompromising commitment to believability and reality. He went to great, and sometimes sickening, lengths to sacrifice his body in order to put on a match (a style which would force him into an early retirement, at age 35).

Foley became an iconic figure that spawned a slew of imitators, some of whom tried to copy his hard-bumping style without a fundamental grasp of wrestling basics. Sadly, the man who dedicated so much to wrestling would prove to have an irreparable effect on the business – by popularizing the brand of "garbage wrestling" seen on the U.S. independent circuit scene and in the backyards of America's neighborhoods. Foley himself took great pride in his craft, honing a laborious and taxing style that was complemented by expert ring psychology and masterful interview skills.

Born June 7, 1965, Foley was a lifelong wrestling fan growing up in East Setauket, New York. Legendary tales of him hitchhiking to New York City as a teenager to see the Jimmy Snuka vs. Don Muraco cage match at Madison Square Garden suggest the passion he had for the industry at an early age. While attending Cortland State University

Cactus Jack demonstrates the perils of a barbed wire match.

in upstate New York, he commuted every weekend to Pittsburgh to be trained for pro wrestling by '70s star Dominic DeNucci.

He made his pro debut in 1985 as Cactus Jack Foley, and later wrestled as Cactus Jack Manson, in independent promotions around the Northeast, including the odd date as a jobber on WWF TV tapings. He spent the next few years working in Texas and Tennessee.

After a short run with WCW in 1990, Cactus returned to the independents, where he worked a legendary series of brutal matches against Eddie Gilbert. These matches quickly earned him a cult following, and WCW brought him back in 1991. During his second stint with WCW, Cactus Jack won acclaim from both fans and critics alike for his hard-bumping style in headline matches against Vader and Sting. During a match against Vader on March 16, 1994, his head got caught in the ropes; while he was trying to free himself, two-thirds of his ear was torn off.

He left WCW in the spring and was off to ECW, where he had a series of memorable matches against Terry Funk, Sabu, and Shane Douglas. He also began delivering some of the best interviews in the industry. At the same time he was a regular for the ultra-violent IWA in Japan, a garbage-wrestling outfit. He became an instant star in Japan when he defeated Terry Funk in the finals of the King of the Death Matches tournament on August 20, 1995, before 28,757 fans at Kawasaki Stadium.

He joined the WWF in 1996 as Mankind the Mutilator. After the gimmick didn't take off, he became simply Mankind, a tormented heel who put over the Undertaker and Shawn Michaels in much the same fashion he did years earlier with Sting and Vader.

He had his breakout year in 1998, working as both a heel and a babyface, while headlining pay-per-views against Steve Austin, The Undertaker, and Rocky Maiva. Although he won his first WWF World title on December 29, he gained more notoriety when he took two of the most sickening bumps in wrestling history during a cage match against the Undertaker on June 28.

In one of the most vividly horrifying scenes, Foley was thrown off the top of the cage and was sent crashing through the announcers' table before hitting the floor. Minutes later, after climbing back to the top of the cage, Foley was choke-slammed through the roof, and hit the mat with a sickening thud. Like Jimmy Snuka's leap off the top of the cage onto Bob Backlund in 1982, Foley's bump

instantly became one of wrestling's most memorable moments.

In 1999, he became a permanent babyface, fully immersed in the Dude Love gimmick. But he began to slow down in the ring due to nagging injuries from years of grueling punishment, and double-knee surgery in the summer. As a result, he changed his ring style and began to rely more on comedy, using his "Mr. Socko" sock puppet to appeal to the fans.

Although his in-ring career was beginning to wind down, Foley was beginning to penetrate into mainstream culture. His autobiography, *Have a Nice Day*, topped the New York Times Bestseller List and remained on it for 26 weeks, selling over 750,000 copies. The book won praise from critics for its humanization of the wrestling business. His follow up, *Foley Is Good: And the Real World Is Faker Than Wrestling*, debuted at number three on the New York Times Bestseller List in 2001 before eventually reaching the top spot. He was also the main subject of *Beyond the Mat*, an acclaimed documentary by Barry Blaustein.

He retired in 2000. He had dropped the comedy act and had begun wrestling as Mick Foley. He closed out his active career with two back-to-back main events on pay-per-view against Triple H that stand among his best matches ever. He came out of retirement for one more match in the main event of WrestleMania before disappearing for three months. When he returned, he became a key part of the promotion and storylines, as a figurehead commissioner, before parting ways with the company in November 2001.

All Japan legend, Genichiro Tenryu.

54

Genichiro Tenryu

Considered among the elite in-ring workers in Japanese history, Genichiro Tenryu is one of only three men to have held both the Triple Crown and IWGP Heavyweight titles.

Tenryu was a main event star during All Japan's glory years of the '80s, advancing the style of pro wrestling in Japan with his snug, realistic-looking matches. His battles against Riki Choshu, Stan Hansen, Jumbo Tsuruta, and Bruiser Brody helped All Japan earn the reputation as the promotion that put on the best main event matches in the world.

Tenryu had been one of the top sumo wrestlers in Japan and was trained by Dory Funk Jr. before making his pro wrestling debut in 1976 against Ted DiBiase. He wrestled for the Funks in their Amarillo promotion before making his Japanese debut for All Japan amid tremendous media hype. It was at the height of the historic Choshu's Army vs. All Japan feud in 1985 that he became known among the best workers in the world, playing a central role in the program and having several classic main event matches against Choshu.

He won his first Triple Crown title on June 5, 1989, defeating Jumbo Tsuruta. The contest garnered match of the year honors from the Tokyo Sports publication and is now regarded by critics as one of the greatest matches of the '80s.

In a shocking move, he left All Japan in 1990 and signed with Megane Super, the second biggest eyeglass company in Japan, becoming the top star of their Super World Sports promotion. Tenryu was criticized over the move, and All Japan founder Giant Baba publicly declared he would never hire him back.

After SWS folded in 1992, he created WAR (Wrestling And Romance), and pushed himself as the main event star while forging a working relationship with New Japan. On January 4, 1994, as part of New Japan's annual Tokyo Dome card, Tenryu pinned Antonio Inoki, becoming the first Japanese wrestler to pin both Baba and Inoki.

Tenryu captured the IWGP Heavyweight title from Keiji Muto on December 10, 1999, before returning to All Japan for the first time in ten years in July 2000. Giant Baba's widow, Motoko, hired Tenryu back after Mitsuharu Misawa depleted All Japan's talent roster in forming Pro Wrestling NOAH. Tenryu was pushed as a main event star and won his second Triple Crown title, defeating Toshiaki Kawada in the final of an eight-man tournament on October 28, 2000. He won the title for a third time on April 13, 2002 from Kawada.

Other notable honors during Tenryu's career include being named the Tokyo Sports Wrestler of the Year from 1986-88 and in 1993, winning the Real World Tag League Tournament three times (in 1984 and 1986 with Tsuruta and in 1989 with Hansen), and winning the Carnival Championship in 2001.

55

The Crusher

Crusher accepts his Cauliflower Alley Hall of Fame award.

One of wrestling's biggest stars of the '50s, '60s, and '70s, The Crusher was also one of its most colorful performers, earning the moniker "The Man Who Made Milwaukee Famous."

The Crusher (born Reggie Lisowski) began his career in 1949 and shuffled between territories for several years. He eventually settled down in Verne Gagne's Minneapolis-based AWA promotion, where he would become a top draw and main event star throughout the Midwest for 25 years.

Stocky and powerful with a low center of gravity, The Crusher was an effective brawler who made every move meaningful inside the ring. At 5'11" and 250 pounds, The Crusher wasn't the biggest wrestler out there, but he perfected his character of a cigar-chomping, beer-swilling roughneck to the delight of his legions of blue-collar fans.

Although The Crusher went on to win the AWA World Heavyweight title three times, he is best remembered for his legendary tag team partnership with Dick the Bruiser. The scuffling duo, famous for their wild, bloody matches, were arguably wrestling's most dominant and biggest-drawing tag team in the '60s and '70s, winning the AWA World Tag Team titles on five separate occasions.

Harley Race and Larry Hennig feuded with The Crusher and Dick the Bruiser in the '60s over the AWA straps. Hennig recalled how their series of matches set the promotion on fire: "They were classic matches. The tag team championship went back and forth between us and everywhere we wrestled we sold out in the AWA: Winnipeg, Minneapolis, Wisconsin, Chicago. It was quite a conflict…we drew a lot of money with them."

Famous partners, The Crusher (left) and Dick the Bruiser.

56

Dick the Bruiser

Dick the Bruiser prepares for a tag team match with The Crusher.

Dick the Bruiser was one of the biggest drawing cards for over 30 years throughout the Midwest, and is one of the most colorful characters in wrestling history.

Richard Afflis suited up for the Green Bay Packers from 1952 to 1954 before becoming one of wrestling's top stars in the post-World War II boom era by playing a beer-guzzling, cigar-chomping, gravel-voiced roughneck. Afflis was the archetypal brawler – a tough guy who seemed impervious to his opponent's offense. At 5'10" and a muscular 250 pounds, Afflis became renowned for his wild and violent matches.

Afflis had a one-week run as AWA World Heavyweight Champion in 1966, but his greatest success came teaming with The Crusher. Together, Dick the Bruiser and The Crusher dominated tag team wrestling in the '60s and '70s, winning the AWA World Tag Team titles three times and the Indianapolis-based World Wrestling Association titles six times, and were huge draws in the Midwest.

Dick the Bruiser is best remembered for a November 19, 1957, main event match in Madison Square Garden that saw him partnered with Dr. Jerry Graham against Argentina Rocca and Edouard Carpentier. The action in the ring spilt to the floor and became so heated that fans started a riot. As a result, the New York State Athletic Commission fined all four wrestlers and cancelled the following card at the Garden, threatening to ban wrestling in the state altogether.

Bruiser was also a successful promoter, operating the WWA (where he pushed himself on top as a ten-time heavyweight champion) for over twenty years before retiring from wrestling in 1985.

He died from a heart attack on November 10, 1991. He was 62.

Perennial UWA World Champ.

57

Canek

One of the most famous masked wrestlers of all time in his native Mexico, Canek was the top heavyweight in that country and a massive box-office attraction in the Universal Wrestling Alliance from the mid-'70s to early-'90s.

Canek was the perennial "tweener" UWA World Heavyweight Champion, holding the title 14 times before joining AAA on a part-time basis (after the UWA died in the late-'90s). As the promotion's top star, Canek played a central role in helping the UWA become one of the hottest territories in North America.

During its heyday, the UWA's booking approach was formulaic: have Canek defend the world title against a crop of rotating foreign heels who "invaded" the territory. Teaming in six-man tag matches against foreign wrestlers with fellow Mexicans who were normally his "enemies," Canek helped to popularize the "Mexico vs. The Rest of the World" booking concept that became prevalent in AAA in the '90s.

This booking philosophy paid huge dividends in the early to mid-'80s, when the UWA enjoyed an incredible run of house-show business. The promotion's home base of El Toreo De Cuatro Caminos, in Naucalpan, became the number one pro wrestling building on the planet, averaging crowds of 10,000 fans for two shows a week and pulling in approximately one million fans per year.

"Clearly the MVP of Mexican wrestling during all of the '80s, Canek was one of the first wrestlers in Mexico to blur the line between heel and babyface," states Lucha Libre historian Jose Luis Fernandez. "While he was a natural heel, he was constantly facing top foreign talent as UWA World Heavyweight Champion, which made him a big crowd favorite."

Canek debuted as El Universitario in 1972 but changed his name to Príncipe Azul a year later. He eventually settled on Canek, based on the Mayan warrior Jacinto Canek. After two years of wrestling in the Mexican independents, he joined Francisco Flores' UWA promotion in 1975. He received his first real push in 1978 when he defeated the original Dr. Wagner for the Mexican Light Heavyweight title. He was then programmed against Dos Caras for several months, igniting a marquee feud that would continue off and on well into the '80s. He won his first UWA Heavyweight title on September 27, 1978, when he defeated Lou Thesz in Mexico City.

In the late '70s, the UWA signed a deal with New Japan Pro Wrestling that would see the two promotions exchange talent over the following years. Canek would regularly tour Japan while New Japan would send fresh foreign heels for Canek to face. A steady influx of Japanese stars came to the UWA in the early-'80s, and Canek regularly exchanged the title with top heavyweights like Tiger Jeet Singh, Riki Choshu, and Tatsumi Fujinami.

Canek had some of his biggest matches in 1984, including a famous win over Andre the Giant on February 12 (where he won the match in two straight falls), a draw against WWF World Champion Hulk Hogan on September 2, and a DQ win over Stan Hansen on September 30.

The UWA continued using the "Canek vs. Foreign Challengers" formula into the '90s, feeding him a steady diet of new challengers that included Big Van Vader, Vampiro, Bad News Brown, King Haku, Bam Bam Bigelow, and Yokozuna (known as Kokina at the time). On April 29, 1991, he defeated the late Owen Hart, who was wrestling under a mask as the Blue Blazer, in a memorable mask vs. mask match that received rave reviews in the Mexican newspapers and wrestling magazines.

Due to the emergence of AAA as the dominant promotional power in Mexico, combined with a depressed Mexican economy that made it impossible to pay foreign talent a competitive wage, the UWA died a slow, lingering death, before folding in the late-'90s. On December 23, 2001, at age 49, Canek revitalized his name in Japan when he donned his famous mask once more and defeated Osamu Tachihikari in a shoot match.

The Argentine sensation.

58

Antonino "Argentina" Rocca

One of the true superstars of wrestling's "Golden Age," Antonino "Argentina" Rocca was a tremendous draw, helping to skyrocket wrestling's popularity at the outset of the television era. Along with Gorgeous George, Rocca was one of the most identifiable sports celebrities in the U.S. during the late-'40s and early-'50s.

A former acrobat in his native Argentina, Rocca (born Antonino Biasetton) displayed amazing dexterity, balance, and coordination inside the ring. Although most critics agree that he was not a good worker, Rocca had a ring style that was unique and entertaining. Up to this point, pro wrestling usually involved a series of holds and counter-holds on the mat. Rocca's repertoire of dropkicks and other aerial moves dazzled fans, and helped to change the foundation of the sport, leading the way for future aerialists like Mil Mascaras and Jimmy Snuka.

Rocca wrestled all over the U.S., but his biggest following was in the northeastern part of the country – especially New York, where he was considered a "common man" hero among the large ethnic communities in the city. Rocca first came to New York after promoter Kola Kwariani pried him away from a territory in Texas during a major program – an incident that set off a long, bitter feud between New York and Texas promoters.

Pro wrestling had been dead in New York since 1935, when drawing card Jim Londos retired, but Rocca's drawing power revitalized the territory in the late-'40s and early-'50s. A December 12, 1949, match versus Gene Stanlee drew 17,854 fans to Madison Square Garden – the first legitimate sellout at MSG since the Londos-Ray Steele main event match in 1931 – putting the fabled building on the map as the top wrestling arena in the country. This ushered

in a new era of wrestling at the Garden, with Rocca becoming one of its top stars and the focal point of a burgeoning New York territory.

After years of singles main events at the Garden against Lou Thesz, Verne Gagne and Hans Schmidt, Rocca began teaming with Puerto Rican star Miguel Perez in 1957. The Rocca-Perez duo routinely sold out the Garden for the next two and a half years on its way to becoming the biggest-drawing tag team in U.S. history.

Rocca died in 1977, at the age of 49.

59

The Sheik

Bloodthirsty heel, The Sheik.

Often imitated but rarely duplicated, The Sheik is considered the most violent, gruesome, and sadistic brawler in wrestling history and the godfather of "hard-core" wrestling.

The Sheik was the number-one heel in wrestling from the mid-'60s to the late-'70s, creating new levels of carnage wherever he wrestled. The Sheik regularly assaulted his opponents with a wide range of weapons, including metal chairs, fireballs, pencils, ice picks, and forks. To complete the image, he brought a Persian rug to the ring that he would "pray" on prior to his matches, adorned himself with a ceremonial sword and Arabian headdress, and was always accompanied to the ring by manager Abdullah Farouk.

A limited worker inside the ring, The Sheik, at 5'11" and 228 pounds, was renowned for his wild, bloody matches that usually lasted less than ten minutes and that often saw him bludgeoning opponents with one object or another. The Sheik was one of wrestling's greatest journeymen: a favorite of promoters who brought him in to pop a good crowd and rejuvenate their stagnating territories.

As a result, The Sheik wrestled in virtually every major territory across the U.S. and Canada, taking on some of the biggest names in the business. His gory, out-of-control, brawls against Dusty Rhodes, Abdullah the Butcher, Bobo Brazil, Terry Funk, Freddie Blassie, Johnny Valentine, Mark Lewin, and countless others set a new standard of violence inside the wrestling ring, decades before "hardcore" wrestling became a phenomenon in Paul Heyman's ECW and Atsushi Onita's FMW.

Born Ed Farhat in 1926, in Syria, The Sheik spent much of his youth in Michigan. He attended high school in East Lansing and then went to Michigan State University, before entering pro wrestling in the early-'50s. His unorthodox style quickly caught on with television audiences; he became a box-office sensation and one of the top-drawing heels in the business.

Although he wrestled in Los Angeles, Toronto, New York, and several other big territories, The Sheik is most closely associated with Detroit. It was there that he became a household name as the perennial U.S. Heavyweight Champion, holding the title 12 times between 1965 and 1980. As a promoter, booker, and top star, he turned Detroit into one of the hottest wrestling cities in the U.S., with his main-event matches drawing consistent sellouts at the historic Cobo Arena.

The Sheik also headlined for Frank Tunney in Toronto during the '70s, becoming the biggest gate attraction at Maple Leaf Gardens since "Whipper" Billy Watson in the '40s, '50s, and '60s. In the '70s he became one of the top foreign heels in Japan for Giant Baba, teaming with rival Abdullah the Butcher against the Funks in the Real World Tag League Tournament, resulting in one of the most memorable brawls in wrestling history.

Back home, the Detroit territory was in trouble: The Sheik was killing business in the city by pushing himself in main events long after his popularity had faded. To make matters worse, he regularly burned fans by advertising talent in big events, only to have them no-show. The territory finally shut down in 1980. Over the next two decades, The Sheik would continue to "defend" his U.S. title on the independent circuit across the U.S., Canada, and in Japan (by the end, well into his seventies). The real-life uncle of Sabu,

he was responsible for training the former ECW and current WWE star, Rob Van Dam.

After suffering a serious heart attack following a 1995 match in Japan, The Sheik became ill and scaled back his schedule. A retirement ceremony was held for him at Tokyo's Korakuen Hall on December 11, 1998. Even with a bad hip and shot knees, The Sheik rushed out to the ring with nephew Sabu and terrorized ringside photographers and fans, chasing them with fireballs and his sword in one final hurrah reminiscent of his glory days in All Japan.

60

Don Leo Jonathan

Don Leo Jonathan puts the Mormon swing on Giant Baba.

A journeyman whose career spanned over 30 years, Don Leo Jonathan wrestled in every major territory in the U.S., Canada, and around the world, from 1949 until the early '80s.

At 6'6" and weighing 300 pounds, Jonathan (born Don Heaton) was considered the best big man in the business until his retirement. Graced with unbelievable agility, Jonathan proved that not all big men were slow and plodding. He moved around the ring with deceptive speed and nimbleness, paving the way for future big men like Bruiser Brody.

"The Mormon Giant" was twice recognized as world champion of the AWA-affiliated Omaha promotion in 1961, but is best remembered for his days in Montreal. Because of his towering size, Jonathan was often pitted against other big men in the business. A May 1972 match promoted as the

"Battle of Giants" saw Jonathan battle Andre the Giant (then billed as Giant Jean Ferre) in front of a sellout crowd of over 16,000 fans in the Montreal Forum.

Jonathan and legendary heel Killer Kowalski had one of the most memorable feuds in Montreal history, wrestling all over Quebec and Northern Ontario in front of sold-out crowds. Kowalski remembered how impressed ringside fans were to see a man of Jonathan's hulking size move around the ring with such ease and quickness:

"He would come up the steps and once he was on the apron he would grab the ropes and leap over backwards and land on his feet in the ring. A complete somersault! He was good in the ring and very athletic. He could fly in the air, do somersaults and back flips. People used to say 'Boy oh boy, how can a guy that big do all these things?'"

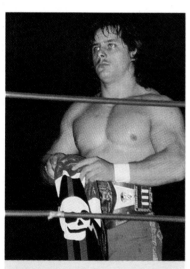
Dynamite Kid in Stampede wrestling.

61

Dynamite Kid

Famous for his legendary feud with the original Tiger Mask and as one half of the British Bulldogs, the Dynamite Kid was one of the most innovative performers of the '80s. At 5'8" and 228 pounds, the Dynamite Kid is considered one of the most influential wrestlers of his generation, having perfected a stiff working approach and a hard-bumping style that was years ahead of its time and that would inspire later stars like Mick Foley.

With his celebrated matches against Tiger Mask in New Japan Pro Wrestling, the Dynamite Kid helped to elevate the junior heavyweight division to startling new heights of popularity and acceptance, providing a blueprint to success

for virtually every light heavyweight that came after him. He was the archetypal "small" wrestler, a true pioneer whose influence can be seen directly in the work of Owen Hart, Jushin "Thunder" Liger, Brian Pillman, Chris Jericho, and, most notably, Chris Benoit.

His fame and influence came at a price, however, as the years of steroid abuse that allowed him to take those big, bruising bumps, also prematurely ended his career.

The Dynamite Kid was born Tom Billington on December 5, 1958, in Golborne, Lancashire, England. He trained at the world-famous Billy Riley's "Snake Pit" in Wigan, England – the same facility that produced Karl Gotch, Bert Assirati and Billy Robinson – before making his pro debut on the British wrestling circuit in 1975 at age 16.

After brief reigns as British and European Welterweight Champion, he left the U.K. for Canada, where he enjoyed a five-year run in Stu Hart's Stampede promotion. While in Calgary he had memorable feuds with Bret Hart and Bad News Allen, and held the British Commonwealth Mid-Heavyweight title four times between 1978 and 1982.

In between tours with Stampede, he was a regular with New Japan, where he and Tiger Mask put the company's emerging junior heavyweight division on the wrestling map. On April 23, 1981, Satoru Sayama debuted as Tiger Mask, defeating Dynamite in what many industry insiders consider to be the match of the decade. The Dynamite Kid-Tiger Mask series, the junior heavyweight equivalent of the classic Flair-Steamboat feud, would go on to dazzle fans and set a new standard of in-ring excellence.

For two years, Dynamite and Tiger Mask put on arguably the greatest series of bouts in the world. They had several match-of-the-decade candidates, including a January 1, 1982, encounter where Tiger Mask defeated Dynamite for the vacant New Japan/WWF Junior Heavyweight title. But perhaps their most famous match came on August 30, 1982, when Dynamite challenged Tiger Mask for the title at Madison Square Garden. The New York crowd, at first totally unfamiliar with both workers and their unique styles, were won over by the end of the classic encounter and gave them a standing ovation.

On February 7, 1984, Dynamite defeated The Cobra in the finals of a tournament to crown a new New Japan/WWF Junior Heavyweight champion, but vacated the title in November when he jumped to All Japan. After Vince McMahon bought out Stampede in 1984, Dynamite headed to the WWF, where he began to team with younger cousin

Davey Boy Smith. The British Bulldogs, a partnership that began when they were both in New Japan, became one of the staple tag teams of the wwf as it went from a regional promotion to a national entity. The duo feuded with the Hart Foundation, Nikolai Volkoff and the Iron Sheik, and several other teams before winning the wwf World Tag Team titles at WrestleMania 11 from Greg Valentine and Brutus Beefcake on April 7, 1986.

On December 13 in Hamilton, Ontario, Dynamite collapsed in the ring during a tag match against Don Muraco and Bob Orton Jr. After being rushed to hospital, doctors discovered that he had torn two lumbar discs in his back. Many thought that his career had ended that night; but, at the insistence of the wwf, and against all better judgment, he was soon on a flight from his home in Calgary to Tampa, Florida where the Bulldogs dropped the belts to the Hart Foundation. Although he could barely walk and had to make a super-human effort just to limp down to the ring, Dynamite was paid a paltry $25 in wages for the match. He eventually returned to action full time but the grueling wwf house show schedule began to take its toll on his body. The Bulldogs left the promotion in 1988 following the Survivor Series and split their time between Stampede (which Stu reopened in 1985) and All Japan.

Davey Boy returned to the wwf in late 1991, while Dynamite continued in All Japan, teaming with fellow British wrestler Johnny Smith. Years of backbreaking physical punishment and steroid abuse finally caught up with him, and his body could take no more. He retired on December 6, 1991 at the age of 33. He made a brief comeback in 1996 for Michinoku Pro Wrestling in Japan, wrestling in a six-man tag bout against old rival Satoru Sayama in what turned out to be his last match. Financially destitute in his home in England, his body began to deteriorate even more. He was soon unable to walk and would become confined to a wheelchair.

After years of living in seclusion, he reemerged in the wrestling world in 1999 with the release of his autobiography, *Pure Dynamite*. Detailing his in-ring career and the years of excess that took over his life, the book won critical acclaim for its brutally honest and candid portrayal of the wrestling business in the '80s, peering beyond the glitzy surface of the industry to show its seedy, dark underbelly.

facing page: Dynamite Kid dropkicks Bad News Allen.

62

The Undertaker

wwf champ The Undertaker.

The greatest character ever created by Vince McMahon, The Undertaker was a three-time wwf World Heavyweight Champion between 1991 and 1999, and was one of the promotion's most recognizable stars.

At 6'8" and 310 pounds, Undertaker is best known as the ghoulish character obsessed with death and the afterlife, wrestling the top babyfaces in the promotion throughout the '90s. Inside the ring he was an unstoppable heel impervious to pain that got over by no-selling his opponents' offense.

Born Mark Calloway, Undertaker feuded with every top star in the wwf during the '90s, helping the promotion survive through lean business periods in the wake of the steroid scandal of 1992 and Vince McMahon's subsequent federal indictment in 1994. Calloway first entered pro wrestling in the late '80s, for a while languishing in the southern territories under a wide range of gimmicks and names, such as "The Master of Pain" and "The Punisher." He won his first major regional title on April 1, 1989, when he defeated Jerry Lawler for the uswa World title in Memphis.

He landed in the nwa in 1989, where he was billed as "Mean" Mark, forming The Skyscrapers with Sid Vicious and feuding with the RoadWarriors and The Steiner Brothers. He then teamed with Danny Spivey after Vicious suffered a serious injury, before going on to wrestle in singles matches, challenging then-U.S. Heavyweight Champion Lex Luger at the 1990 Great American Bash pay-per-view.

Calloway was released from the nwa in a cost-cutting measure and debuted as The Undertaker at the wwf Survivor Series on November 22, 1990. He was a stoic figure dressed in dark clothing who moved slowly and deliberately in the ring, and initially said only a few words in interviews, as manager Paul Bearer did the bulk of the speaking for him.

One year later, at Survivor Series '91 in Detroit, he defeated Hulk Hogan for his first WWF World Heavyweight title, but dropped the title back to Hogan a week later. It would be another five years until he won his next title. Until this time, his feuds with Hogan, Randy Savage, Steve Austin, The Ultimate Warrior, Bret Hart, Shawn Michaels, and Mick Foley helped The Undertaker become one of the greatest icons in WWF history.

By the time he won his second WWF World title, he had become one of the promotion's top babyfaces. He defeated Sid Vicious on March 23, 1997, in the main event of WrestleMania 13. His third title reign came on May 23, 1999, when he defeated Steve Austin in Kansas City. Sadly, the victory was overshadowed by the tragic death of Owen Hart earlier on the card.

By this time, the Undertaker had dropped the "deadman" gimmick and managed to reinvent himself as a trash-talking biker, straddling the fence between babyface and heel, and getting over with a new generation of WWF fans.

Old Style Undertaker in battle.

63
—
El Solitario

The Man of the Golden Mask.

El Solitario (The Lonely One) is one of Mexican wrestling's greatest legends, on par with Mil Mascaras and Gori Guerrero.

Nicknamed "El Enmascarado de Oro" (The Man of the Golden Mask), Solitario is considered one of the best Mexican wrestlers of all time due to his strong work ethic, his ability to effectively communicate storylines in the ring, and the unequaled pride he took in honing his craft.

El Solitario (born Roberto González Cruz) was a kid sensation, debuting at age 14 after training in the gyms of his home state of Jalisco. For the next few years he toiled in Mexico's independent circuit, before taking the name El Solitario in 1966, which was based on the famous comic-book hero, El Llanero Solitario (The Lone Ranger).

Decked out in his trademark gold-and-black tights and golden mask, Solitario quickly became a main event star. His watershed moment came in 1968, when he defeated legendary veterans Ray Mendoza – patriarch of the Villano wrestling clan – and René Guajardo in successive mask vs. hair matches.

Solitario's popularity skyrocketed, and he became one of the top draws in Mexico – collecting the NWA Light Heavyweight and Middleweight titles along the way. He also helped rejuvenate the Mexican tradition of *trios* matches in the late-'60s as one third of the hugely successful La Ola Blanc (The White Wave) trio, with Ángel Blanco and Dr. Wagner.

"Overall [he was] a great wrestler," offered Mexican wrestling historian Jose Luis Fernandez. "He was as explosive and intense as any flyer ever in wrestling, and would be a top worker in the world if he was in his prime today."

El Solitario died on April 6, 1986, after suffering a fatal heart attack following a match. He was only 39 years old.

64

"Superstar" Billy Graham

WWWF Champ "Superstar" Billy Graham, 1977.

A former WWWF World Heavyweight Champion, "Superstar" Billy Graham was one of the top performers of the '70s and the archetype of the posing, bleached-blond bodybuilder heel that was copied by countless wrestlers that followed in his considerable footsteps. At 6'4" and boasting a chiseled 275-pound physique, Graham laid the groundwork for the muscled-up superstars that dominated the industry in the '80s, most notably Hulk Hogan and Jesse Ventura, who looked up to him as their childhood idol and who patterned their careers after him.

Admittedly a poor worker inside the ring, Graham was a charismatic heel that infuriated fans with his priming and posing prior to matches. With his long blond hair, psychedelic tie-dyed trunks, and bronzed tan, Graham was one of the best interviews in the business. He revolutionized the art of the wrestling promo in the late-'70s, coining several popular catchphrases, including his trademark line, "I am the man of the hour, the one with the power, too sweet to be sour."

With his brazen, cocky gimmick, Graham was the first major "tweener" world champion for the WWWF and was years ahead of his time, blazing a path for a heel Steve Austin to follow almost twenty years later as a popular rule-breaker who fans loved to cheer. Graham was the top box-office attraction in the U.S. in his prime, drawing more crowds in excess of 25,000 fans than any other performer during the '70s. He is also the largest-drawing heel in the history of Madison Square Garden, with his main-event matches selling out the historic building 17 out of 18 times between 1976 and 1987. He was also one of the first men to bench press 600 pounds (unofficially) and was considered one of the strongest men in the world in the late-'70s,

having competed in several network-televised World's Strongest Man contests.

Sadly, though, perhaps more than anything else, Graham is remembered for his use of steroids. While not the first to use the drug, he was the most famous star to abuse it in the '70s, giving birth to a black period of pro wrestling in the '80s dominated by the steroid-enhanced physiques of Hulk Hogan, Kerry Von Erich, The Road Warriors, and The Ultimate Warrior.

Graham was born Eldridge Wayne Coleman on September 10, 1943. Formerly a weightlifter and bodybuilder in his native Arizona, he was trained for pro wrestling by the legendary Stu Hart in Calgary, and debuted in the late-'60s as Wayne Coleman. In the summer of 1970 he met wrestler Dr. Jerry Graham and became a part of the famous Graham "wrestling family." Coleman took the name Billy Graham, partially from Dr. Jerry and partially from the famous TV evangelist, Billy Graham. He added the nickname Superstar in 1972, inspired by the rock opera, "Jesus Christ Superstar," which was a huge hit at the time.

After wrestling for promoter Roy Shire in San Francisco and Verne Gagne in Minnesota, Graham went to work in Vince McMahon Sr.'s World Wide Wrestling Federation, based in the northeast, in 1975. Graham soon began feuding with Bruno Sammartino over the WWWF World title, including two main-event matches in early 1976 that sold out Madison Square Garden. Graham eventually upended Sammartino to win the title on April 30, 1977, in Baltimore.

As a heel world champion, Graham was the hottest thing in the sport, selling out the Garden for his title defenses against Sammartino, Dusty Rhodes, Ivan Putski, Mil Mascaras, and Bob Backlund. On several occasions, the Garden wasn't big enough to house his main-event matches, so promoter Vince McMahon Sr. packed thousands of fans into the adjacent Felt Forum to watch the show via closed circuit television. Graham dropped the title to Backlund on February 20, 1978, at the Garden, but remained a top draw for McMahon, before disappearing from wrestling for several years.

He returned to the WWF in 1982 with a shaved head and a martial arts gimmick, and was thrown into a world title program with Backlund. From there Graham moved on to Florida, and then to the Mid-Atlantic territory to work for the Crocketts, before winding up back in the WWF in 1987, this time working for Vince McMahon Jr. Graham's last

"Superstar" Billy Graham in Kansas City against Mighty Angus Campbell of Ireland.

sellout main event match at the Garden came on October 16, 1987, when he defeated Butch Reed in a cage match.

By this time, Graham's health was in danger due to years of steroid abuse. Over the next 15 years, Graham would live life in a great deal of pain. A hip surgery in 1990, coupled with an operation that fused an injured ankle, took Graham off the road, ending his wrestling career. In retirement, Graham became an outspoken critic of McMahon, Hulk Hogan, and the WWF. He talked openly about his steroid abuse and embarked on a public crusade to rid the wrestling world of the drug, appearing on several national talk shows to talk about the steroid epidemic in the WWF. In 1991, Graham refuted Hogan's statement on the *Arsenio Hall Show* that he only took steroids to recover from an injury, claiming in several interviews that he helped to inject Hogan with steroids on numerous occasions.

The ravages of years of steroid abuse continued to plague Graham, as he would endure nine hip-replacement surgeries and avascular necrosis of the hip and ankle. In 2001, he was diagnosed with Hepatitis C, and was hospitalized for ten days in December for gastric bleeding and severe liver problems. Weeks later, his condition grew worse, when swelling of his liver caused four veins to burst.

Jerry "The King" Lawler in Memphis with the USWA World Title.

65

Jerry Lawler

One of the best interviews of all time, Jerry "The King" Lawler was the biggest star in the history of Memphis wrestling, achieving a level of stardom in Memphis that was second only to Elvis Presley. He was a master ring psychologist and a fantastic brawler who became famous for taking big, hard bumps in selling his opponent's offense.

As the perennial Southern Heavyweight Champion (a title he held 42 times between 1974 and 1987), Lawler established the Continental Wrestling Association as one of the premier territories in the U.S. Lawler and Memphis wrestling became an institution on WMC-Channel 5, the local NBC affiliate, where the promotion's Saturday 90-minute live program consistently drew 20+ ratings and 70+ shares, making it the highest rated local wrestling show in U.S. history.

Lawler debuted in 1970 while attending Memphis State University on an art scholarship and quickly became the top heel in the promotion. In 1974, he had a memorable feud with Jackie Fargo (the original "King of Memphis") and was passed the mantle of leadership in the company after Fargo put him over. Headlining at the Mid-South Coliseum every week, Lawler established Memphis as one of the top drawing weekly cities in the U.S. during the '70s. After recovering from a broken leg in 1981, he began a long feud with manager Jimmy Hart and his henchmen (dubbed the First Family) that would continue over the next four years.

In 1982, Lawler became embroiled in a feud with Terry Funk, which climaxed in their infamous "empty arena" match at the Mid-South Coliseum. As they brawled all over the floor and into the stands, Funk's surreal, blood-curdling screams of pain echoed throughout the empty building

after Lawler rammed a giant wooden sliver into his eye, ending the match.

Later that year, Lawler was involved in a strange program with Andy Kaufman, a comedian famous for wrestling female audience members as part of his stand-up routine during appearances on *Saturday Night Live*. He began to appear in Memphis, defending his Inter-Gender title against local female wrestlers. As Kaufman grew more belligerent and began to berate fans, Lawler, defending the integrity of pro wrestling, challenged Kaufman. The match took place on April 5 and Lawler was disqualified for using the piledriver on Kaufman, drawing widespread media coverage as reports of the comedian being "hospitalized" grabbed local and national headlines.

Kaufman, wearing a neck brace, vowed revenge on Lawler as a videotape of the match aired on *Saturday Night Live* on May 15. The feud hit an entirely new level of mainstream publicity on July 28, when both Kaufman and Lawler appeared on NBC's *Late Night with David Letterman*. The two began to trade insults, leading to Lawler slapping Kaufman in the face. Kaufman went berserk and stormed off the set in a censored verbal tirade, before returning and throwing a cup of coffee in Lawler's face.

In 1987, Lawler had a hot feud with Austin Idol and Tommy Rich, climaxing on April 27 in an unforgettable "hair vs. hair" cage match. Lawler was in control of the match when Tommy Rich emerged from under the ring and interfered, helping Idol win the Southern Heavyweight title. Idol and Rich then shaved an unconscious Lawler bald while the crowd at the Mid-South Coliseum nearly rioted.

In 1988, Memphis promoter/owner Jerry Jarrett and Verne Gagne forged a strategic alliance with one another in an attempt to boost their territories. The agreement led to Lawler winning the AWA World Heavyweight title on May 9 from Curt Hennig in Memphis. As world champion, Lawler split his time between Memphis, the AWA, and Dallas, where he feuded with World Class Champion Kerry Von Erich. The program with Von Erich culminated in a bloody title unification match at the AWA's Super Clash III pay-per-view in Chicago, which was stopped after the referee ruled Von Erich could not continue due to heavy bleeding.

Lawler was stripped of the AWA title on January 20, 1989, after Jarrett and Gagne had a falling out and the two promotions split, but Lawler continued to defend the Unified World title – the unification of the AWA and World Class World titles – for the next eight years before the Memphis promotion (by this time named the United States Wrestling Association) folded in 1997.

In 1992, Memphis struck up a working agreement with Vince McMahon, wherein Lawler became a color commentator and part-time wrestler for the WWF. At the 1993 King of the Ring pay-per-view, he attacked Bret Hart, sparking a memorable feud that was designed as pure comedy (as most in the company thought it wouldn't draw due to Lawler's lack of physique). Ironically, the program not only revitalized Hart's career, but also outdrew Yokozuna's WWF world title matches during the same time period.

On November 12, 1993, Lawler was indicted on two counts of statutory rape, two counts of sodomy, and one count of threatening a witness in Memphis involving incidents with two underage girls. Both girls later recanted their stories as Lawler and the district attorney's office reached a plea bargain on February 23, 1994. Lawler pleaded guilty to harassing a witness and, in return, the prosecutors dropped the four counts of statutory rape and sodomy. Lawler received a suspended 12-month sentence and two years of unsupervised probation for the guilty plea.

Lawler left the WWF in February 2001 after his wife Stacy Carter, a valet in the promotion at the time, was fired by the company. After splitting up with Carter, Lawler returned to the WWF in November.

Loose cannon, Roddy Piper.

66

Roddy Piper

The top heel in the U.S. during the '80s, "Rowdy" Roddy Piper was one of the most identifiable stars in wrestling during the WWF's expansion from a regional outfit based in the northeast to a national powerhouse.

Piper was the lead heel in several NWA territories from the late-'70s to the mid-'80s before jumping to the WWF. He quickly became an '80s icon, and the second biggest star in the promotion behind Hulk Hogan. Piper portrayed a wild Scotsman brawler, a loose cannon character that came to the ring wearing a kilt and playing the bagpipes. He took the art-form of the wrestling promo to a new level, delivering irreverent interviews that were renowned for their originality.

Born Roderick Toombs in Saskatoon, Saskatchewan, Canada in 1954, Piper grew up on the streets of Toronto after running away from home when he was only 12 years old. He eventually ended up in Winnipeg – a tough street kid living in youth hostels and the YMCA – when he was approached to get into pro wrestling. At age 15 he had his first pro match in Winnipeg, losing to Larry Hennig in ten seconds. He wrestled as a TV jobber for several years before receiving his first big break in 1975 in Los Angeles, wrestling as the masked Canadian. It was in Los Angeles that he first developed his arrogant, brash heel persona, feuding with local legend Chavo Guerrero in front of big crowds at the Olympic Auditorium.

Between 1976 and 1978 he held the NWA Americas title five times, while simultaneously appearing for Roy Shires in San Francisco, where he won the U.S. title in 1978. While still occasionally appearing in Los Angeles, he moved on to Portland and became a top draw and a two-time NWA Pacific Northwest Champion between 1979-1980. It was there that he forged a lasting friendship with promoter Don Owen.

Piper made his home and raised his family in Oregon, and was inextricably tied to the Owen promotion regardless of where he wrestled. Of the thousands of wrestlers who passed through Portland, Roddy Piper was the most dear to Owen. Although Piper had experience in other territories prior to coming to the Pacific Northwest, Owen was the first promoter to see potential in Piper and to give him his first big push in the business.

"Piper was one of the best talents we ever had," said son Barry, who was his father's right-hand man. "He was just an incredible personality and a great worker. He really loved my dad, and the feeling was mutual. He was like part of the family."

In 1980, Piper moved to Jim Crockett's Charlotte-based

territory and became the top heel in the company. After capturing two Mid-Atlantic titles and the TV title, he became embroiled in a lengthy feud with Ric Flair, winning the U.S. Heavyweight title on January 27, 1981. Piper then engaged in a classic feud with Greg Valentine over the belt, climaxing in their legendary dog-collar match at the first Starrcade on Thanksgiving night in 1983. Piper jumped to the WWF in January 1984 as part of the first wave of Vince McMahon's plan to go national.

Piper received critical acclaim as the host of "Piper's Pit," a groundbreaking segment on WWF television shows that saw Piper "interview" fellow wrestlers and set up his future programs. Several classic angles took place during the segment, including an attack on Jimmy Snuka (by cracking a coconut over his head) that ignited a major program between the two.

Piper became the top heel in the U.S. thanks to "Piper's Pit" and his marquee feud with Hogan, capturing the imagination of the wrestling public at the height of the "Rock 'N' Wrestling Connection." The Piper-Hogan program culminated in the "War to Settle the Score," a February 18, 1985, title match at Madison Square Garden aired live on MTV that ended when Paul Orndorff interfered and actor Mr. T rescued Hogan, setting the stage for the first Wrestle-Mania.

WrestleMania thrust Piper into the national spotlight and he became a huge crossover celebrity thanks to the media attention surrounding the event. Piper and Orndorff lost to Hogan and Mr. T in the main event, but Piper's star was clearly on the rise. His wild antics became so popular with fans that he turned babyface after being attacked by the late Adrian Adonis in 1987. He retired from wrestling following WrestleMania III on March 29, 1987, to pursue an acting career.

From 1988 to 1996 he starred in several films, most notably in director John Carpenter's *They Live*, for which he received widespread praise. In between movies, he made brief returns to the WWF, before coming back full-time in 1990. The following year he worked a program with Ric Flair when Flair was let go by WCW and signed with the WWF, rekindling their classic feud from a decade earlier.

Piper won his first title in the WWF on January 19, 1992, at the Royal Rumble, defeating Jacques Rougeau for the Intercontinental strap. Later that year, he dropped it to Bret Hart at WrestleMania VIII. He left wrestling shortly after to go back to Hollywood but would make occasional returns

Roddy Piper in action with Hulk Hogan.

to the ring in the WWF over the next few years. He signed a lucrative deal with WCW in October 1996 that allowed him to work in Hollywood and wrestle a limited schedule. He was immediately put into a program with Hogan, resulting in several main event matches, and drawing the highest grossing pay-per-views in WCW history up until that time.

Long past his prime, Piper had several forgettable matches with Hogan, Randy Savage, and others before WCW fired him in 2000 in a cost-cutting measure.

67

Ultimo Dragon

Ultimo Dragon distinguished him-
self during a brilliant 12-year career with his dazzling mat
skills and aerial wizardry. Many critics regard him as the
best wrestler of the 1990s, pound for pound.

Dragon was trained in the famous New Japan Pro
Wrestling dojo. Company officials did not offer him a
contract upon completion of his training, thinking that he
was too small to ever make it in professional wrestling.

Nevertheless, Dragon persevered, and in 1987 he
debuted in Mexico's Universal Wrestling Association under
his real name, Yoshihiro Asai. In 1990 he joined Gran
Hamada in forming the Universal Pro-wrestling Federation,
a Lucha Libre-based promotion in Japan, before moving to
EMLL, where he was given the name Ultimo Dragon (which,
translated, means the last student of "The Dragon" Bruce
Lee). Over the next few years, Asai split his time between
Mexico, WAR, and New Japan. It wasn't until he joined
WCW in 1996 that his career flourished.

Smooth and graceful in the ring, Asai combined the
ballet-like movements of Lucha Libre with the lightning
pace of the Japanese junior heavyweights to form one of
the most revolutionary working styles in the business. He
was a *renaissance* wrestler, jetting around the world and
maintaining simultaneous schedules in Japan, Mexico, and
the U.S. His work ethic inside the ring was unparalleled –
his thirst to put on great matches, insatiable.

Asai is among the most decorated champions in
wrestling history (at one time holding ten junior heavyweight titles simultaneously). He was forced to retire in
1999 after suffering nerve damage in his arm following a
botched operation in 1998. Bound by a sense of obligation

Japan's Finest Ultimo Dragon.

to pass on his knowledge to the next generation, Asai
became one of the top trainers in the world. He formed
Toryumon before retiring, which became one of the hottest
indie promotions in Japan, and a training ground for
future stars.

68

Billy Robinson

Billy Robinson in 1974.

One of the biggest stars
ever to come out of England,
Billy Robinson was a scientific marvel inside the ring
and was one of wrestling's
best hookers during his prime.

Famous for his vast array of suplexes and other offensive
moves, Robinson was respected within the industry as one
of the best mat technicians in wrestling. He went to great
lengths to ensure his matches looked like legitimate contests, using a shoot/submission style that added a touch of
realism to his bouts.

Robinson was trained at the world-famous Billy Riley's
"Snake Pit" in Wigan, England – the same gym that produced Karl Gotch, Bert Assirati, and The Dynamite Kid –
before making his pro debut in the late-'50s.

He was one of the top stars in Europe, holding the European and British heavyweight titles simultaneously for over
three years. Robinson was also a regular in Japan in the
late-'60s. He is noted there for becoming the first ever
International Wrestling Alliance World Heavyweight
Champion after defeating Japanese legend Toyonobori in

facing page: Ultimo Dragon, in Mexico's Lucha Libre Universal Group.

the finals of an 11-man round-robin tournament in 1968.

He vacated the European and British Heavyweight titles in 1970 to go to North America. Robinson's first port of call was Stu Hart's Stampede promotion, where he feuded with Abdullah the Butcher, and went on to fame as a two-time North American Heavyweight Champion.

His best days, however, were in the AWA: he was a head-liner there in the '70s, chasing Verne Gagne and Nick Bock-winkel for the AWA World Heavyweight title for several years. Robinson paired up with Gagne in 1972 to win the AWA World Tag Team titles from Bockwinkel and Ray Stevens. He also feuded with Jumbo Tsuruta and Giant Baba in All Japan, capturing the NWA United National Heavyweight and PWF Heavyweight titles.

Robinson, now living in Japan, where he instructs the next generation of shooters, was associated with the UWFI during its glory years of 1988 to 1990, and helped to train junior heavyweight standout Kazushi Sakuraba.

Ring innovator, Jaguar Yokota.

69

Jaguar Yokota

One of the greatest women's wrestlers of all time and arguably one of the top three workers in the world during her prime, Jaguar Yokota helped bridge the gap between the Beauty Pair era of the '70s and the Crush Gals phenomenon of the '80s.

Born Rimi Yokota on July 25, 1961, in Tokyo, Yokota was an innovative performer who stayed on top by continually adapting her style and updating her repertoire of moves as pro wrestling progressed and changed over the years.

Possessing tons of natural athletic ability, Yokota blew away her contemporaries with incredible matches that raised the caliber of women's wrestling.

She was the main event star for the All Japan Women's promotion, winning her first WWWA title in 1981 at the age of 19 and dominating the belt over two distinguished title reigns that lasted over two years. Yokota also gave back to the industry as an accomplished trainer, helping to launch the careers of the AJW's top stars of the early '90s.

Drawn to wrestling by AJW teen idols the Beauty Pair (Jackie Sato & Maki Ueda), Yokota was one of 600 teenage girls who took part in the promotion's rookie audition class in 1977. She made her pro debut at the age of 16 on June 28, 1977, in Tokyo vs. Mayumi Takahashi. She received a small push as one half of the Young Pair tag team with Seiko Honawa before getting her first break by becoming the first AJW Junior Champion on January 4, 1980. Yokota vacated the title in August and began teaming with Ayumi Hori, winning the WWWA World Tag titles on December 17.

Two days earlier in Tokyo, she defeated Nancy Kumi in a tournament final to become the first ever AJW Japanese Champion. Yokota's star was clearly on the rise, and she had been tagged as the future of the promotion. She vacated both belts and prepared for a run at the WWWA World title.

Yokota skyrocketed to the top of women's wrestling on February 25, 1981, by defeating AJW legend Jackie Sato to become world champion. At age 19, Yokota was the new flag-bearer of the promotion. Her win over Sato ushered in a changing of the guard in Japanese women's wrestling, effectively ending the Beauty Pair era and clearing the path for a younger generation of superstars.

Her first title reign was marked by title defenses against other Japanese wrestlers and foreign competitors like Wen-di Richter and top heel Monster Ripper. She dropped the belt to Mexican star La Galactica on May 7, 1983, in a hair vs. mask match, but regained it a month later.

Jaguar's second WWWA reign lasted two-and-a-half years, when she often defended the title against Devil Masami, the AJW's top heel. Jaguar retained the WWWA title throughout 1984, unifying it with Mexico's UWA World title when she defeated La Galactica on September 17, 1984, in Tokyo.

After embarking on a lengthy tour of Mexico in 1985, Yokota returned to Japan where she feuded with Crush Gal Lioness Asuka over the WWWA title. The Jaguar-Asuka title feud drew such interest that AJW booked Tokyo's Budokan Hall for the first time since the Beauty Pair era. Their

August 22 match aired on the Fuji TV network a few days later, drawing an amazing 15.1 rating, and proved to be one of the greatest matches of the '80s, with Yokota retaining her title.

Yokota suffered a serious shoulder injury in late 1985, forcing her to vacate the title prior to a scheduled defense against Dump Matsumoto. Devil Masami beat Matsumoto to win the vacant title and began her reign at the top. Due to her shoulder injury and growing pressure from the powers-that-be in AJW, Yokota retired in February 1986 at the age of 24, a full two years before the mandatory retirement age of 26 imposed by women's promotions in Japan.

Yokota remained attached to pro wrestling as AJW's top trainer. Over the next few years, she would be responsible for training Manami Toyota, Toshiyo Yamada, Kyoko Inoue, and several other performers who went on to become main event stars in the '90s.

Yokota occasionally stepped out of retirement in the late-'80s and early-'90s. Her matches garnered great interest, and always brought in big numbers at the box-office. She came out of retirement full-time in 1995, when she formed the JD promotion. She wrestled as the promotion's top star before retiring for good on December 26, 1998, when she faced her old partner and rival Devil Masami in her final match.

70

Lioness
Asuka

Crush Gal sensation.

A star at age 17, Lioness Asuka played a prominent role in the explosion of Japanese women's wrestling in the '80s.

Although she wasn't blessed with blinding speed or grace in the ring, Asuka was a smart worker who used her imposing size to stage hard, stiff, and believable matches. She could carry even the most inexperienced worker and was a master of selling her opponent's offense.

Born Tomoko Kitamura, Asuka was one half of the Crush Gals with Chigusa Nagayo, easily the most famous women's tag team in history. Their unforgettable matches against Dump Matsumoto's heel stable, and with the Jumping Bomb Angels in the All Japan Women's promotion, helped take women's wrestling to unforeseen heights of popularity in Japan.

The Crush Gals were huge pop icons in Japan: hordes of screaming schoolgirls packed into arenas to watch them and their matches on AJW's weekly show on Fuji TV drew consistent 12 ratings. They became major media stars, recording several top ten pop singles and selling millions of posters and magazine covers bearing their likeness. The Crush Gals became matinee idols to millions of Japanese teenagers, inspiring future superstars like Manami Toyota to get into wrestling.

Eventually the craze passed and the Crush Gals split up, beginning a memorable singles feud against each other that produced many classic matches. After chasing the WWWA title for years, Asuka won it in 1989 by defeating Nagayo. She left wrestling months later, but came out of retirement on November 20, 1994, to appear on the biggest show in women's wrestling history, in front of 42,500 fans in Tokyo. She eventually ended up in the upstart JD promotion.

Lioness Asuka (left) with Jaguar Yokota.

Lioness Asuka against Noriyo Tateno of The Jumping Bomb Angels.

71

Bobo Brazil

Bobo Brazil at the Richmond Coliseum prior to a match against the "Nature Boy" Ric Flair.

Bobo Brazil overcame the climate of bigotry and racism of 1950s America to enjoy one of the longest and most successful careers in wrestling history, remaining a main-event star and top draw for close to four decades. He was a globe-trotting trailblazer who broke down countless racial barriers and opened the door for future African-American wrestlers.

Brazil (born Houston Harris) began his career in the early-'50s after being trained by Jumping Joe Savoldi. At 6'4" and 280 pounds, Brazil was a giant of a man, and although he wasn't a great in-ring worker, he quickly became one of the most popular stars in the U.S. Because there were so few blacks in wrestling during the early part of his career, Brazil was billed as the "Negro World Heavyweight Champion," and in several promotions was only allowed to wrestle other blacks.

Brazil was a headliner in every territory he appeared in from the late-'50s to the early-'70s, but will best be remembered for his tenure in Detroit from 1961 to 1976. It was there that Brazil became the perennial U.S. Heavyweight Champion, exchanging the title back and forth with Johnny Valentine, Abdullah the Butcher, and Dick the Bruiser. His epic battle with The Sheik throughout the '70s still stands as one of the most violent and bloody feuds in history.

Brazil was also one of the top foreign draws to compete in Japan in the '60s and '70s. Over a several-year period, he was the only man to score a pinfall victory over Giant Baba, capturing the NWA International title on June 25, 1968, in Nagoya.

Brazil died on January 20, 1998, after suffering a stroke.

72

Karl Gotch

Karl Gotch twists Billy Robinson.

Considered "The God of Pro Wrestling in Japan," Karl Gotch is among the most influential wrestlers in history.

A distinguished trainer renowned for his superior technical skills, Gotch was one of the greatest shooters of all time. His realistic shoot-style matches shaped and advanced pro wrestling in Japan, and laid the foundation upon which promotions such as UWF Japan, Rings, and Pancrase were built.

Gotch first wrestled in Japan on May 1st, 1961, in a 45-minute draw against Japanese star Michiaki Yoshimura. The Japanese public became enamored with his convincing style, and he was instantly propelled into stardom. He was a seminal figure in Japan as a star for the Japanese Wrestling Association in the '60s. He is also noted for training future greats such as Antonio Inoki, Hiro Matsuda, Tatsumi Fujinami, Nobuhiko Takada, Yoshiaki Fujiwara, Satoru Sayama (the original Tiger Mask), and Akira Maeda.

Gotch, born Karl Istaz in 1924 in Hamburg, Germany, began in amateur wrestling as a schoolboy. He was a seven-time Belgium National Champion in Freestyle and Greco-Roman wrestling and represented Belgium at the 1948 Olympics in London. Gotch trained at Billy Riley's infamous "Snake Pit" gym in Wigan, England before making his pro debut in 1955 as Karl Krauser. He quickly established himself as Europe's top grappler and immigrated to the U.S. in 1959.

In 1961, he began wrestling as Karl Gotch (in honor of the legendary Frank Gotch), and won the AWA (Ohio) Heavyweight title in 1962 after defeating Don Leo Jonathon. He held the title for two years before losing it to Lou Thesz.

Gotch became embroiled in a real-life feud with then-NWA World Champion Buddy Rogers, claiming Rogers was afraid to wrestle him. Rogers, unimpressed with Gotch's "shooter" reputation, laughed off the charge. The situation escalated in August of 1962 when Gotch cornered Rogers in a locker room in Columbus, Ohio, and smashed his hand, forcing Rogers to miss several key title defenses.

Gotch was so strong that he once executed a German Suplex on Andre the Giant during a 1971 match in Japan, managing to hold the bridge in one of those magical wrestling moments that Japanese fans remember to this day.

Gotch had a brief run in Vince McMahon Sr.'s northeast territory, holding the WWWF World Tag Team titles with Rene Goulet from December 6, 1971, to February 1, 1972, before joining Inoki's newly formed New Japan office.

He played an instrumental role in helping Inoki to split from JWA in 1972 and form New Japan Pro Wrestling. Gotch was recognized as the "real" world champion, giving the promotion instant credibility. On New Japan's first show on March 6, 1972, Gotch pinned Inoki in what would become one of the most important bouts in history. The high standard of athletic credibility displayed by both competitors would set the standard for future matches, and would become a basic tenet of Japanese wrestling.

Gotch had a notorious reputation for being difficult to work with and for being uncooperative in the ring. He was constantly at odds with U.S. promoters, who felt there was no place for his "hooking" style in the realm of staged matches. Although Gotch was never a box-office draw, his place in wrestling history is unquestionable.

"Karl Gotch is the ultimate competitor," offered Lou Thesz. "Karl is as focused as anyone I ever met. History will tell the tale about Karl and his incredible ability as a wrestler. He was not willing to compromise his sport. History has to respect him for that. I do."

73

Bert Assirati

Assirati, one of the toughest hookers of all time.

Trained in the famous wrestling gyms of Wigan, England, that produced The Dynamite Kid, Billy Robinson, and Karl Gotch, Bert Assirati earned the reputation of "toughest wrestler alive" during his wrestling career, and was also considered one of the strongest men in the world.

Standing at a mere 5'6", Assirati (born Bernardo Esserati) was blessed with incredible strength, a massive frame, and powerful shoulders. At 240 pounds, he was among the heaviest men ever to complete an iron cross, a gymnastic move on the rings where the arms are fully extended to each side while the body remains vertical.

He wrestled all over Europe and India and became known for his streak of sheer, brutal viciousness in the ring – taking pure delight in injuring other wrestlers. Assirati was in disfavor with most English promoters for the bulk of his career because he often double-crossed opponents.

Despite his track record of treachery, Assirati is considered the greatest British wrestler of all time. He held the British version of the World Heavyweight title twice in the late '40s and had two lengthy reigns as British Heavyweight Champion (from 1939 to 1950 and 1955 to 1960).

Assirati was as brash and overbearing as he was tough, and had no qualms about letting people know how great he was. He took verbal jabs at many other wrestlers, including Lou Thesz, who he claimed was afraid to wrestle him. One of Assirati's favorite targets was "Big Daddy" Shirley Crabtree. According to legend, one night when Crabtree was in the ring and was announced as British Heavyweight Champion, Assirati stood up in the crowd and ridiculed him. Crabtree was so agitated that he had to leave the ring and return to the dressing room.

Assirati died on August 31, 1990, at the age of 82.

74

Salvador Gori Guerrero

Mexican pioneer, Gori Guerrero.

The patriarch of the Guerrero wrestling dynasty, Salvador Gori Guerrero was one of the biggest stars in Mexico from the '40s to the '60s.

A legend in Mexican wrestling, Guerrero was actually born in Arizona. He was trained by renowned trainer Diablo Velasco and made his pro debut in 1937 at the age of 16.

Mexico's answer to Danny Hodge, Guerrero was not only a technical marvel and brilliant mat technician, but was also a legitimate tough-man and a world-class shoot-fighter. He is credited with inventing the camel clutch and the Gori Special (a hanging backbreaker submission hold), and helped changed Lucha Libre by popularizing submission holds with the fans.

It was his pioneering ring work that changed Mexican wrestling from a series of highspots to include a more aggressive technical style, laying the groundwork for generations of mat wrestlers in Mexico that followed, including his four sons: Salvador Jr. (Chavo), Mando, Hector, and Eddie, as well as grandson Salvador III (Chavo Jr.).

Although he held the NWA World Middleweight, Welterweight, and Light Heavyweight titles on several occasions, Guerrero is best remembered for his famous tag team with El Santo in the '40s. Billed as La Pareja Atómica (The Atomic Pair), they were the most celebrated tag team in Mexican wrestling history.

According to Lucha Libre expert Jose Luis Fernandez, Guerrero also popularized bloodbath matches in Mexico.

"Blood had already been seen in Mexico from the occasional hard-away busted nose or lip, but his matches with legendary brawler Cavernario Galindo were among the first where the wrestlers intentionally bladed their foreheads."

Guerrero died on April 18, 1990. He was 69.

75

Bill Longson

St. Louis legend, Bill Longson.

Credited with inventing and popularizing the piledriver, "Wild Bill" Longson was an institution of St. Louis wrestling, and was arguably the greatest drawing card ever in that historic wrestling city.

Longson held the National Wrestling Association World title – the precursor to the National Wrestling Alliance championship – on three occasions, exchanging the belt with Yvon Robert, "Whipper" Billy Watson, and Lou Thesz.

Longson's contributions to modern-day wrestling are considerable. Loaded with charisma, he perfected the arrogant heel character in the '30s and '40s. As the first heel brawler to become a long-term world champion, Longson paved the way for future stars like The Crusher and Mad Dog Vachon.

Longson was a state amateur champion in boxing and wrestling in Utah before entering pro wrestling in 1931. His first success came in the late-'30s as the masked Purple Shadow in San Francisco.

During his reign as World Champion from 1943-1947, Longson was the top draw in St. Louis, considered by many to be the wrestling capital of the world. In 1944, he headlined 39 shows in that city, including a remarkable 16 sellouts in a row, a record from that era that remains unmatched.

Longson remained a draw in St. Louis throughout the '50s, headlining big money programs against Lou Thesz and Pat O'Connor, before retiring in 1960. He and Thesz then bought into the St. Louis promotion, retaining 15 per cent ownership of the office when it merged with promoter Sam Muchnick's outfit. Longson worked in the front office of the promotion until selling his stock in the late-'70s.

Longson died on December 10, 1982, at the age of 74.

Ring of Friendship

Whether gathering at the Cauliflower Alley's annual reunion or backstage at a WWE pay-per-view, wrestlers are able to instantly come together and reminisce about the good old days as if they were army buddies who went through hell and back together. And in many cases, they have. There is an understood, implicit bond between pro wrestlers, one that comes from spilling blood together and literally entrusting their lives in each other's hands.

top: Antonio Inoki unites with The Destroyer.
bottom from left, top row: Gene Lebell, Kenji Shibuya, Ted DiBiase, Pepper Gomez, Mike Neopardy, HB Haggerty, Lou Thesz. *bottom row;* Karl Lauer, Pat Patterson, The Destroyer.

top row: Masa Chono, Keiji Muto, Shinya Hashimoto; Pampero Firpo, Danny Hodge, The Destroyer, Kenji Shibuya; Mad Dog Vachon with Johnny Valentine; *middle row:* Tom Drake, Red Bastien, Freddie Blassie, Lou Thesz; Dan Severn, Dennis Coralluzzo, Lou Thesz, Jack Brisco; Nick Bockwinkel, Black Jack Lanza, Ray Stevens, Buddy Rogers, Verne Gagne, *bottom row:* Dory Funk Jr. with Chris Candido; Stu Hart, Killer Kowalski, Ross Hart.

top row: Roddy Piper with Chavo Guerrero; Johnny Valiant, The Fabulous Moolah, Lou Thesz, Buddy Rogers, Mick Foley, *middle row:* Killer Kowalski with Bruno Sammartino; Tiger Conway Sr., Ray Stevens; Verne Gagne headlocks Leroy McGuirk while Lou Thesz headlocks Ilio DiPaolo; Dick Hutton, Gene Kiniski; *bottom row:* Ultimo Dragon and Chris Jericho demonstrate a new angle; Chigusa Nagayo and Gary Albright shake hands while Devil Masami looks on.

top row: Nick Bockwinkel, Rocky Maivia with his father Rocky Johnson Sr., Pat Patterson; The Sheik with Killer Kowalski; *middle row:* Harley Race, Cowboy Bill Watts; Lou Thesz, Yoshihiro Asai (Ultimo Dragon), Terry Funk; Pat Patterson, Ted DiBiase, Kenji Shibuya, Ray Stevens; Bobby Heenan with John Tolos and Stan Hansen; *bottom row:* Red Bastien, Giant Baba, Lord James Blears; Don Leo Jonathon with The Destroyer and Johnny Valentine; Negro Casas with El Hijo del Santo.

The Killer's claws.

76

Killer Kowalski

One of the all-time great heels in pro wrestling, Wladek "Killer" Kowalski was a main-event star and huge draw in every territory he appeared in from the mid-'50s to the mid-'70s.

At 6'7" and 280 pounds, Kowalski was a gigantic monster who used his size to become one of the most vicious and terrifying villains in wrestling. Kowalski was not your typical, lumbering big man. He was a well-conditioned athlete who was very quick and agile in the ring, and was as adept at technical wrestling as he was at brawling.

Born in Windsor, Ontario, to Polish immigrants, Kowalski wrestled every major star in the business at one time or another, including Lou Thesz, Pat O'Connor, Bruno Sammartino, Verne Gagne, Gorgeous George, "Whipper" Billy Watson, Antonino Rocca, and Buddy Rogers.

Kowalski's greatest success came in Montreal's IWA promotion. Between 1952-1962 he won the IWA World Heavyweight title 12 times, exchanging the belt with the likes of Edouard Carpentier, Don Leo Jonathan, and Yvon Robert. His matches against Andre the Giant (wrestling as Jean Ferre) in the early '70s set the territory on fire as they wrestled before packed houses all over Quebec and Northern Ontario.

However, despite all the memorable matches and legendary opponents during his career, Kowalski is best remembered for a 1954 match against Yukon Eric at the venerable Montreal Forum, when he severed Eric's ear from his head after executing a knee-drop from the top rope. Comically, he was vilified in the Montreal newspapers the next day. When he went to visit Eric in the hospital after the match, the two combatants shared a laugh with each other over the incident. Journalists and photographers erroneously reported that Kowalski was laughing at Eric, and the headlines and photos in the papers the next morning decried Kowalski's "treacherous" conduct in the hospital.

Kowalski retired in 1977 and became a teacher, operating the Killer Kowalski Institute for Professional Wrestling in Massachusetts. In retirement, he became a respected wrestling trainer, responsible for training Triple H, Chyna, Big John Studd, Perry Saturn, and Luna Vachon.

77

Mildred Burke

Mildred Burke in her early years.

A true wrestling pioneer, Mildred Burke was the biggest female star from the late-'30s to the mid-'50s, and is credited with popularizing women's wrestling in the U.S.

With the help of her husband and promoter, Billy Wolfe, Burke changed the landscape of women's wrestling, transforming it from a novelty act staged in burlesque houses and vaudeville theatres into a major attraction in auditorium house shows. At a compact 5'2" and weighing 138 pounds, she is best remembered for her muscular physique and incredible feats of strength. She became renowned for her toughness inside the ring and was legitimately the best women's wrestler in the business.

Burke (born Mildred Bliss) began her career in 1934 at the tender age of 19, wrestling against male challengers on the carnival circuit throughout the Midwest. Legend has it that no man within 20 pounds of her weight was able to defeat her. Two years later Burke was a major drawing card, wrestling men in front of sold-out crowds in some of the

Midwest's top arenas. At the height of her career, Burke was reported to be the highest paid woman athlete of her era.

Her success as a drawing card inspired other women to take up pro wrestling. Wolfe ended up training the new prospects and eventually managing their careers, booking his stable of female grapplers around the country.

In 1937, Burke defeated Clara Mortensen for the women's title, starting a reign that would last almost two decades. She defended her title in virtually every major territory, elevating the status of women's wrestling in the process.

She split from Wolfe and his promotion in 1953, claiming that all the money she had made went directly to him and that she never saw any of it. June Byers, Wolfe's new companion, immediately laid claim to the title.

Promoters still recognized Burke as the women's champ, so Wolfe arranged a title match with Byers on August 20th, 1954, in Atlanta. The match quickly lost any spirit of cooperation and became a shoot-fight, with Byers winning the first fall. The Atlanta Athletic Commission stopped the match and awarded Byers the title, ending the only true shoot match for a world title in the U.S. in close to 40 years.

Burke died after suffering a stroke on February 14, 1989. She was 73.

Mildred Burke (right) in her later years with Marie Vagnone, one of her many protégées, who held the U.S. Ladies Championship.

78

Abdullah the Butcher

Wildman from The Sudan, Abdullah the Butcher.

Truly one of the legendary figures in pro wrestling history, Abdullah the Butcher was a star heel and a box-office draw around the world in a career that spanned five decades.

Abdullah was one of wrestling's great journeymen, appearing in every major territory in the U.S. and Canada, and was a main-event star for All Japan Pro Wrestling in the '70s. His wild, bloody feuds against Bruiser Brody, Carlos Colon, Dusty Rhodes, Bobo Brazil, Giant Baba, the Funks, The Sheik, and countless others helped establish him as wrestling's archetypal bloodthirsty brawler. His style would influence generations of brawlers that followed, including Cactus Jack, Pampiro Firpo, and "Maniac" Mark Lewin, to name a few. Abdullah took brawling to an entirely new level: his matches were gory exhibitions in bloodletting, wreaking havoc in every promotion he appeared in with his sadistic, violent style. He became famous for carving up opponents' foreheads with forks and ice picks, bloodying them beyond recognition.

Billed as the "Madman from the Sudan", Abdullah (born Larry Shreeve in 1936, in Windsor, Ontario) debuted in 1958. He toiled on the Canadian independent circuit for several years before reinventing himself as Abdullah the Butcher in the late '60s. Since his billing had him unable to speak English, he worked with several managers throughout his career, including Eddie "The Brain" Creatchman, J.J. Dillon, Gary Hart, and Bearcat Wright.

He first toured Japan in 1970, for the Japanese Wrestling Association, where he feuded with Baba over the International Heavyweight title. He would later join Baba's fledging All Japan Pro Wrestling office in 1972, and would win the Championship Carnival tournament in 1976 and 1979

on his way to becoming a worldwide star, a huge gate attraction, and one of the top heels in Japan.

His most famous feud in Japan was with The Destroyer in the mid-'70s, where the two set All Japan ablaze with their gruesome battles. At the time, The Destroyer was the host of "Uwasa no Channel," Japan's most popular live-comedy TV series. During one telecast Abdullah attacked The Destroyer, setting up one of the most memorable feuds in Japanese history. The angle was groundbreaking, as it was the first of its kind in Japan to take place outside the parameters of a regular wrestling show. The mainstream exposure to a live national audience made Abdullah a huge crossover star in Japan, and a household name overnight.

Many critics consider a match he had on December 15, 1977, where he teamed with The Sheik against Terry and Dory Funk during the Real World Tag League Tournament, to be the inspiration behind the "extreme wrestling" concept that would become hugely popular in the '90s.

In 1981, Abdullah jumped to New Japan Pro Wrestling when Antonio Inoki doubled his salary to $8,000 per week – unheard of money back then. This ignited one of the most bitter promotional wars in history, as New Japan and All Japan continually raided each other's roster over the ensuing years in a high priced game of one-upmanship.

Abdullah continued wrestling on a semi-regular basis through the late '90s and into the new century, while in his mid-60s.

The Destroyer (masked) headlocks Danny Hodge.

facing page: Abdullah the Butcher on top of The Sheik; *top:* The sensational, intelligent Destroyer, in a match with Ted DiBiase.

79

The Destroyer

The most famous masked wrestler ever to compete outside of Mexico, The Destroyer, played by Dick Beyer, was one of the biggest stars in wrestling from the '50s through to the '70s and was a main-event performer in every territory he appeared in. His trademark white mask with baby blue trim is one of the lasting symbols of pro wrestling from the '60s and '70s.

Beyer enjoyed a massively successful career both internationally and domestically, carving out a niche in the industry for future U.S. masked wrestlers. He was one of the first American wrestlers to break through in Japan as a headline star, becoming a household name in that country during his feud against Rikidozan, the father of Japanese pro wrestling, in the early '60s. He was also a main-event star in Los Angeles – his feud with Freddie Blassie over the WWA World title led him to become one of the most identifiable wrestlers in Southern California.

Beyer attended Syracuse University in upstate New York, where he played football for the Orangemen and was an amateur wrestling champion. After earning a Masters degree in Education, Beyer was trained for pro wrestling by former NWA World Champion Dick Hutton, and turned pro in 1954.

"When I graduated from Syracuse University and went back and got my Masters degree, I was recruited by Ed Don George to go into pro wrestling," Beyer told Toronto-based reporter Greg Oliver in a May 2000 interview. "I said to my family 'I'll stay in this five years, make some money, then I'll be able to afford to teach,' which is what I wanted to do. So I got into wrestling; but I didn't make the money that I envisioned I was going to make until I put a mask on as

The Destroyer out in California in '63. Then I was doing so good, I couldn't afford to quit!"

Beyer wrestled in and around the Buffalo area at the beginning of his career under his real name. He later moved on to Hawaii, where he turned heel. It was there that Blassie noticed Beyer and recommended him to promoter Jules Strongbow. He then convinced Beyer to come with him back to Los Angeles. After first putting on the mask there, his career immediately skyrocketed.

Combining his traditional wrestling skills with a unique, articulate interview style (that usually featured Beyer boasting about his college education), the Destroyer became one of the biggest stars in the U.S. As he became more famous in the wrestling world, he also became more immersed in the gimmick and went to great lengths to conceal his identity from fans, wearing the mask after he left the building and at public functions.

Beyer won his first of three WWA World Heavyweight titles on July 27, 1962, from Freddie Blassie in San Diego. He would capture the title two more times by 1964, engaging in several classic main-event matches at Los Angeles' historic Olympic Auditorium against Blassie, Rikidozan, Giant Baba, Mil Mascaras, Lou Thesz, Don Leo Jonathan, and Gorgeous George. Beyer also worked in several other territories across the U.S. and Canada, including the Pacific Northwest for Don Owen, Frank Tunney's promotion in Toronto, Roy Shire's in San Francisco, and Verne Gagne's in Minneapolis. He even had a brief run as AWA World Champion in 1968 as Dr. X, defeating Gagne for the title before dropping it back to him two weeks later.

On May 19, 1963, while on his first tour of Japan, The Destroyer defeated Rikidozan in a one-fall match with the figure-four. By handing Rikidozan his first clean singles loss on Japanese soil, The Destroyer instantly became a household name in Japan and would go on to enjoy a career as one of the top foreign stars there for the next two decades. Five days later, the two titans wrestled to a one-hour draw on live network television, garnering a staggering 67 rating (the second highest-rated program in the history of Japanese TV since 1960). Today, nearly 40 years later, the May 24 Destroyer-Rikidozan match is still ranked in the top ten and remains the most watched match in wrestling history.

After briefly going back to Los Angeles, the Destroyer returned to Japan for his second tour in December 1963, challenging Rikidozan for the NWA International title on December 2. Five days later, they found themselves on opposing sides of a six-man tag bout. The match turned out to be Rikidozan's last ever, as he was stabbed the next day in a Tokyo nightclub and died a week later.

The Destroyer returned to the States and continued to tour in Japan. In 1973, he signed a six-year deal with Giant Baba, who had formed All Japan Pro Wrestling. Beyer moved his family to Japan and from 1973 to 1979 he wrestled exclusively for Baba, becoming one of the cornerstones of All Japan and helping to put the promotion on the global wrestling map.

On the strength of his famous feud in 1963 with Rikidozan, Beyer became a huge crossover celebrity as the host of "Uwasa No Channel," Japan's number one live-comedy series from 1973 to 1977. On one show Abdullah the Butcher attacked The Destroyer, setting up one of the legendary feuds in All Japan during the '70s. The angle was truly innovative, as it was the first of its kind in Japan to cross over from a regular wrestling program into a mainstream television show. The exposure on live national television made Abdullah an instant star, and the ensuing feud featured wild, bloody brawls the likes of which Japan had never seen before.

The Destroyer returned to North America in 1979 and split his time between the Toronto and Montreal territories, before going into semi-retirement in 1984 to teach at an elementary school in Akron, New York (although he continued to wrestle in Japan in the summers). On July 29, 1993, at Budokan Hall, The Destroyer wrestled in his retirement match, teaming with Baba and his son Kurt against Masao Inoue, Haruka Eigan, and Masa Fuchi.

One of the biggest draws in history
Atsushi Onita.

80

Atsushi
Onita

One of Japan's biggest
superstars during the '90s,
Atsushi Onita took "garbage wrestling" to new heights of
popularity and mainstream acceptance in that country.

As owner and promoter of the ultra-violent Frontier
Martial-arts Wrestling outfit, Onita became one of the most
charismatic and influential stars in Japanese history, inspiring countless Japanese garbage offices as well as Paul Heyman's Extreme Championship Wrestling promotion. With
its various incarnations of exploding ring death matches,
FMW set new standards of violence and sadism in wrestling.

Onita became the single greatest box-office smash in
Japan during his prime, drawing crowds of over 40,000
fans to Kawasaki Stadium for main-event matches against
Terry Funk, Genichiro Tenryu, Wing Kanemura, and
Hayabusa on shows that lacked any kind of an undercard.
He also became a major crossover star in Japan as an actor,
and used his celebrity to get elected on July 30, 2001 as a
senator from the majority Liberal Democratic Party. In
doing so, Onita became the third pro wrestler to become a
congressman in Japanese history, following Antonio Inoki
and Hiroshi Hase.

Ironically, Onita was an accomplished wrestler earlier in
his career. On his 16th birthday he dropped out of high
school and began training for a career in pro wrestling. He
debuted on April 14, 1974, for All Japan, after which he was
immediately sent to the U.S., where he trained and worked
under Terry Funk and learned the intricacies of the business. When he returned in 1982, Tiger Mask was the top
draw in New Japan's junior heavyweight division. As a
countermove, All Japan picked Onita as the star of its own
junior heavyweight division, as NWA International Junior
Heavyweight Champion. Unfortunately, his reign was

short, as severe knee problems forced him to retire in 1984.

Onita returned to wrestling in 1989, reinventing himself
as the "master of death matches" and launching FMW – a
bloody, violent, and gory brand of pro wrestling the likes
of which Japan had never seen before. Onita became a cult
hero for his legendary brutal matches and famous ring
entrances (to the strains of a punk version of the Troggs'
classic, "Wild Thing"). A master ring psychologist, Onita
was able to rile up fans to the point of delirium with his
trademark brawling tactics and locker room interviews
(where he was often so physically spent that he would
break down and cry).

In late-1998, Onita was forced out of FMW, the organization he founded. Then, at New Japan's annual Tokyo Dome
show on January 4, 1999, he made his first of several marquee yet disastrous appearances for New Japan, getting
DQ'd for blowing fire in the face of Kensuke Sasaki. Riki
Choshu came out of retirement on July 30, 2000, to squash
Onita in less than eight minutes in a no-ropes-explosive-barbed-wire-death-match in Yokohama Arena.

Despite being such a big gate attraction for New Japan,
the relationship eventually deteriorated. Years of FMW
death matches had done so much damage to Onita's body
that his work rate started to decline dramatically. After a 17
year absence, Onita returned to All Japan for one evening
on September 28, 2001, teaming with mentor Terry Funk to
defeat Abdullah the Butcher and Giant Kimala at the Tokyo
Dome as part of Stan Hansen's retirement show.

Onita against his biggest rival Mr. Pogo.

Masked Tommy Rich belts Ted DiBiase.

The Million Dollar Man.

81

Ted
DiBiase

Best remembered as
the "Million Dollar Man"
during the WWF's glory years, Ted DiBiase was one of the
best in-ring workers of the '80s.

DiBiase was highly respected within the industry for his
professionalism and his mastery of scientific wrestling
skills, and was considered second only to Ric Flair in terms
of in-ring ability during his prime.

His heel run as the "Million Dollar Man" sparked a
series of profitable storylines, culminating in a live, prime-
time special on NBC on February 5, 1988, that still holds the
record as the most watched wrestling program in U.S. history. In a memorable angle, DiBiase bought the WWF
World title from Andre the Giant after he defeated Hulk
Hogan in the main event. The exchange was then overruled
by the WWF, and the vacated title was held up as the prize
in that year's WrestleMania.

DiBiase grew up in a wrestling family: his mother was
wrestler Helen Hild and his stepfather was the legendary
"Iron" Mike DiBiase, a former main-event star and NWA
World Junior Heavyweight Champion. "Iron Mike" died
inside the ring when Ted was 15 years old, inspiring Ted to
quit school at West Texas State in his junior year and enter
pro wrestling.

Trained by Dory Funk Jr., DiBiase started his pro career
in Funk's Amarillo promotion in 1975. He then headed off
to Bill Watts' Mid-South territory, where he became a main-
event star and top babyface. While he was there, DiBiase
caught the eye of St. Louis promoter and NWA President
Sam Muchnick. Muchnick brought him to St. Louis in 1977
and quickly pushed him into the national spotlight – as a
top contender to the NWA World Heavyweight title.

On the strength of his run in St. Louis, DiBiase was con-

sidered for a push as the longterm NWA champion in 1981.
But, despite the fact that the NWA had promised him the
title, DiBiase eventually lost out to Ric Flair, who would go
on to dominate the belt throughout the '80s. This was a
common theme during DiBiase's career, as both Bill Watts
and Vince McMahon reneged on their promises to give him
their version of the world title.

DiBiase became a heel in 1982 after turning on tag team
partner The Junkyard Dog after JYD had won the North
American title. Their feud set the Mid-South on fire, and
gave the territory its most profitable run of house shows in
its history. While he was with Mid-South, DiBiase also regularly toured with All Japan Pro Wrestling, becoming one
of its top foreign stars. In 1985, he teamed with Stan
Hansen to win the Real World Tag League Tournament.

DiBiase retired from active wrestling in 1993 due to
recurring neck injuries. After years as a manager in both
the WWF and WCW, he left the wrestling business for good
in 1999 to start his own evangelical ministry.

82

Earl
McCready

Canadian Olympian.

Recognized as one of the most skilled pro wrestlers
of the '30s and '40s, Earl McCready is the greatest amateur
wrestler Canada has ever produced.

McCready was born in Landsdowne, Ontario, in 1908
and grew up in rural Saskatchewan. He attended Oklahoma
A&M, where he became the first three-time champion in
collegiate history, winning the NCAA wrestling championships from 1928 to 1930 and remaining undefeated.
McCready served as the Canadian flag-bearer at the 1928

Olympics in Amsterdam, and two years later, after winning just about everything he was eligible for as an amateur wrestler, he turned pro.

At a lean 238 pounds, McCready used a combination of strength, superior physical conditioning, and a vast array of technical skills to earn the reputation as a pioneering mat technician. Within two years of joining the pro ranks, McCready was already wrestling stars like Dick Shikat and world champion Ed "Strangler" Lewis. He won the British Empire championship in 1933 from Jack Taylor, beginning a seven-year reign that would see him travel to England, South Africa, Australia, and New Zealand on a regular basis to defend the strap.

After dropping the title, McCready cut back on his travel schedule and wrestled for Stu Hart's Stampede Wrestling outfit in Calgary, becoming one of the promotion's top stars before retiring in 1958.

McCready was bestowed several prestigious honors after he retired, including inductions into the Canadian Sports Hall of Fame in 1967 and the U.S. Wrestling Hall of Fame in 1977.

McCready died of a heart attack in 1983, at 75.

83

Pat O'Connor

Pat O'Connor, wearing the NWA World Heavyweight Championship belt.

Enjoying a magnificent career that spanned the '50s through to the '70s, Pat O'Connor is the most famous wrestler ever to come from New Zealand. A former NWA World Champion, O'Connor was known for his mastery of scientific skills, his fluid execution of moves, and as one of the best wrestlers of his era.

Killer Kowalski feuded with O'Connor in Montreal from 1954-1955 over the AWA/IWA World title, and regards O'Connor as one of the greatest of all time.

"He was excellent. He was one of the best and was very colorful in the ring. He had new moves that he did that nobody else did. He could really show the people what he could do in that ring. He was very athletic and was an exceptionally good wrestler."

O'Connor was a huge star in St. Louis, where he won the NWA World title from Dick Hutton on January 9, 1959. During his reign as champion, O'Connor had classic matches against Lou Thesz, Buddy Rogers, Kowalski, Dick the Bruiser, and Bob Geigel.

In one of the most famous matches in wrestling history, O'Connor dropped the title to "Nature Boy" Buddy Rogers on June 30, 1961 in Chicago's Comiskey Park before 38,622 fans and taking in $148,000 in gate receipts – both U.S. records that lasted almost twenty years. Their rematch months later in Comiskey Park drew 30,000 fans, sparking an unforgettable series of matches that would go down in history as being among the greatest ever.

After going into semi-retirement, O'Connor served as a booker for the St. Louis territory during the 1970s.

O'Connor died from liver cancer on August 16, 1990, at the age of 65.

facing page: Bitter enemies Ray Stevens and Pat O'Connor, at Kiel Auditorium, St Louis, 1976.

Fritz Von Erich, master of the claw.

84

Fritz Von Erich

Although he was a main-event performer for close to thirty years, Fritz Von Erich will most likely not be remembered for being one of the industry's all-time greatest heels, but instead for suffering through heartbreaking tragedies that decimated his family during the '80s and '90s.

Von Erich had six children: Jackie Jr., David, Kerry, Kevin, Mike, and Chris. Five of them followed in Fritz's footsteps and entered pro wrestling. Only Kevin lived to see his 34th birthday. Four of them (David in 1984, Mike in 1987, Chris in 1991, and Kerry in 1993) died from either drug overdose or suicide. Fritz' wife Doris, blaming him for pushing their sons into wrestling and then ignoring their pattern of reckless behavior, brushes with the law, and drug abuse, divorced him in 1992. Yet despite the macabre, dark cloud that hovered over him and his family, Fritz Von Erich was a true legend inside the ring, both as the most famous star ever in Dallas wrestling history, and as one of the greatest foreign heels ever to compete in Japan.

Born Jack Adkisson in 1929, he became one of post-World War II America's biggest heels as Fritz Von Erich. Portraying a goose-stepping, Iron Cross-wearing Nazi that paid homage to the Fuehrer, Von Erich, at 6'4" and 275 pounds, moved around the ring like a panther, striking fear in the hearts of fans across the country with his predatory, vicious style and gruff, gravely voice. He became known as the master of the Iron Claw, thanks to his huge hands and deadly grip.

Von Erich was trained by Stu Hart in Calgary after a short stint with the Edmonton Eskimos of the Canadian Football League. He made his professional wrestling debut in the mid-'50s. He won the AWA World title on July 27,

1963, from Verne Gagne, only to lose it back two weeks later. He also held the Omaha version of the AWA World title in the summer of 1962 for a month. Although he became renowned for his world title chase programs with several NWA champions, Von Erich never won the title. As a result, he pinned his world title aspirations onto his sons, pushing them into the business at a young age and building them up as stars long before they could handle the spotlight.

Von Erich first toured Japan in November 1966, and helped to re-establish the industry there in the post-Rikidozan era. Von Erich was already a legend in Japan prior to his first visit thanks to two submission-wins over Antonio Inoki in 1965, in Texas. On December 3, 1966, he wrestled Giant Baba at Tokyo's Budokan Hall, the first ever sellout for wrestling in the venerable building. The match, which was aired live on Japanese prime-time TV, catapulted Von Erich into superstardom and established him as the number one foreign heel in the country.

Von Erich made a power play on established Dallas promoter Ed McLemore in 1965, and started his own promotion with the backing of NWA President Sam Muchnick, Dory Funk Sr., and Bob Giegel. Von Erich eventually won the promotional war with McLemore and established Dallas as the bedrock of the NWA. On June 24, 1972, Von Erich challenged Dory Funk Jr. for the NWA world title, resulting in a 60-minute draw at Texas Stadium. The match drew a crowd of 26,339 fans, setting a state record that lasted until May 6, 1984, when son Kerry defeated Ric Flair for the NWA title before 32,123 fans in the same building.

Von Erich solidified his status as one of the most powerful men in wrestling when he was named President of the NWA in 1975 after Muchnick was pushed out. By the late '70s, the Dallas territory split into several factions as Texas became a war zone between Von Erich and promoters Joe Blanchard and Paul Boesch. Fritz' Dallas promotion became one of the hottest territories in the U.S., with his sons as its main-event stars. Although the boys were portrayed as clean-cut, God-fearing Christians, the reality was somewhat different.

David, Kerry, Kevin, and Mike all had serious drug problems that the family failed to deal with (Fritz even admitted to buying Kerry steroids while he was in high school to help build him into a big track and football star). Fritz often used his influence in the community to cover up the boys' public indiscretions and arrests, or worse, made them part of the storyline, suggesting that the boys had been set up by their opponents. Finding it impossible to deal with the pressure of being Fritz' sons, and not getting the help they desperately needed, the boys spiraled further and further into drug and alcohol use.

Despite all of this, the Dallas territory (which had changed its name to World Class Championship Wrestling) was on fire. Von Erich booked his sons in a memorable feud with the Freebirds following an angle on Christmas night in 1982, where Terry Gordy slammed Kerry's head into the door of the steel cage, costing him the world title against Ric Flair. The result was spectacular. The Freebirds vs. Von Erich feud set the territory ablaze for three years and saw Kerry become one of the top babyfaces in the country. Fritz had struck gold.

But then, the ghoulish body count began. Fritz' continuing ignorance of his sons' problems, combined with the increasing pressure he put on them to perform, began to take its toll. David died from an overdose on February 10, 1984, at the age of 25 while on tour for All Japan. Although he passed away the morning of the first day of the tour, Fritz reworked the truth for public consumption, claiming that David died because he had wrestled hurt and had taken a deadly kick to his midsection. Always the opportunist, Fritz then parlayed the tragic death of his son into the David Von Erich Memorial Parade of Champions card on May 6, 1984. Fritz' family dream was fulfilled when Kerry defeated Flair for the NWA title.

After more arrests, more drugs, and a few near-death experiences, Mike was the next to pass on, killing himself with a drug overdose on April 12, 1987. He was only 23. In a move that showed little taste, Fritz added Mike's name to the billing of the annual Parade of Champions card.

With World Class at death's door in 1987, Fritz faked a heart attack and was hospitalized as part of an angle on Christmas night in Dallas after he was attacked inside the ring, playing on the emotions of local fans that had previously grieved the loss of his two sons. Yet, Fritz managed to outdo himself, hitting an all-time low when the promotion flashed updates of his condition on its weekend TV program, varying them according to what the gate looked like on the Friday house show. If the show bombed, Fritz' condition worsened, and he would plead with fans, from his hospital bed, to continue to support the promotion. Finally, with World Class on its last legs, Fritz sold his controlling interest in the company and left the wrestling business.

On September 12, 1991, Chris Von Erich committed

suicide, shooting himself in the head. He was only 21. At 5'5", Chris was too small to be a major superstar; in addition, he had severe asthma attacks which required that he take drugs to cope with the pain. When he could no longer live with the realization he would never be a star the caliber of Kerry, his idol, he decided to take his life.

After being fired from the WWF for drug problems, Kerry was found in possession of cocaine while on probation for forging drug prescriptions. Fearing a jail sentence, he shot himself in the throat on February 17, 1993. He was 33.

With the death of Kerry, the fantasy world of Fritz Von Erich exploded into the cruelest of realities. The cover-ups he orchestrated, the ignorance he pleaded when aides informed him of his sons' drug problems, the sleazy and tasteless promotional tactics he used to sell wrestling tickets – they all came back to haunt him as he buried five of his six sons.

The Von Erich dynasty ended when Fritz died from cancer on September 10, 1997, at his home in Lake Dallas, Texas. He was 68.

85

Wahoo McDaniel

McDaniel wearing his Atlantic Coast Heavyweight Championship belt backstage at the Hampton Coliseum in the early '70s.

A star linebacker with the New York Jets and Miami Dolphins during the '60s, Wahoo McDaniel is considered the greatest Native American wrestler ever to grace the sport.

The 5'11", 245-pound McDaniel began his pro wrestling

career in 1960 during the football off-season, and wrestled on a part time basis for ten years before deciding to wrestle full time in 1970. Trained by Dory Funk Sr., Wahoo (born Ed McDaniel) parlayed his notoriety from his pro football days into a successful wrestling career, becoming one of the top draws in the sport and one of the most popular stars throughout the Southeast.

Although he wrestled in virtually every territory in the U.S., Wahoo is best remembered for his stints in the Charlotte-based Mid-Atlantic promotion. It was there that he had several big-money feuds with stars such as Johnny Valentine, Ric Flair, Blackjack Mulligan, and Ivan Koloff, which set the territory on fire.

For over 20 years, McDaniel earned a reputation as one of the toughest workers in the industry. McDaniel's work inside the ring was always stiff and snug, allowing him to effectively communicate storylines to the fans and make his matches look as realistic as possible.

George Burrell Woodin wrestled as "Mr. Wrestling" Tim Woods and was a frequent tag team partner of Wahoo's in the Mid-Atlantic territory. Wahoo might not have been the greatest technical wrestler, but according to Woodin, he was one of the toughest.

"He didn't have wrestling holds so much but he was a whopper and a chopper. He could get in there, especially with [Johnny] Valentine, and they would just stand there toe to toe and just beat the hell out of each other; not so much a wrestling match as it was a 'Who can take the most?' match."

McDaniel passed away on April 19, 2002 due to complications of diabetes and renal failure. He was 63.

86

"Whipper" Billy Watson

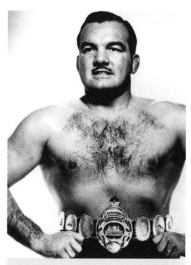

"Whipper" Billy Watson, Canadian legend and former NWA World Champ.

Toronto's top wrestling star from the '40s to the '60s, "Whipper" Billy Watson was a former National Wrestling Alliance World Heavyweight Champion in 1956.

Born just outside of Toronto, Watson (born William Potts) was a huge box-office hit at Maple Leaf Gardens for over 30 years, helping to establish Toronto as one of wrestling's hotbeds.

Watson began his wrestling career in 1936, in England, before becoming a matinee idol at the Gardens in 1940. Between 1942 and 1957, he held Toronto's British Empire title nine times, defeating the likes of Earl McCready and Yvon Robert. From 1952 to 1960, he dominated the Canadian Open Tag Team titles, winning the belts 14 times with 11 different partners, including Robert, Pat O'Connor, and Bobo Brazil.

Watson won the National Wrestling Association World title in 1947 after defeating Bill Longson in St. Louis. Two months later, he lost it to Lou Thesz. His greatest moment came on March 15, 1956, when he defeated Thesz for the National Wrestling Alliance World title by count out in Toronto. Watson held the title for eight months before dropping it back to Thesz in St. Louis.

Perhaps Watson's best-remembered match was in 1959 when he defeated Gorgeous George, forcing the gregarious star to have his head shaved. Despite the fact that wrestling was dead in most parts of North America – due to the loss of network T V coverage – their match drew a sellout crowd of over 15,000 fans to Maple Leaf Gardens.

Watson was forced to retire in 1971 following a tragic automobile accident. While standing on the side of a frozen

facing page: Wahoo McDaniel readies Johnny Valentine for a blow to the face during a match at the Richmond Coliseum, Richmond, Virginia.

road, an oncoming car slid out of control and pinned him against a stopped car, crushing his left knee and nearly slicing off his leg.

A true icon in Canadian culture, Watson was known as a humanitarian and a philanthropist as much he was a pro wrestler. For his devotion to helping disabled children for more than 40 years, as an active member of several children's groups and charities, Watson was awarded the Order of Canada in 1984, and was one of the first 20 recipients of the Order of Ontario award in 1987.

Watson died on February 4, 1990, after suffering a heart attack. He was 74.

forcing him to retire and cutting short a brilliant wrestling career. However, in the late-'50s he would gain notoriety as one of wrestling's top promoters, credited with launching the careers of Danny Hodge and former NWA World Champion Jack Brisco.

In 1958 McGuirk became the head of the Oklahoma promotion run by Sam Avey and quickly expanded the territory to include Arkansas, Texas, Mississippi, and Louisiana. The promotion had a successful 20-year run of business, with Danny Hodge and Bill Watts as its top stars.

Attendance began to wane in the late-'70s and the promotion was split in two, with Watts buying the southern portion of the territory (giving birth to Mid-South Wrestling), and McGuirk retaining control of the northern part of the promotion, renaming it Tri-State Wrestling, before retiring in 1980.

McGuirk was inducted into the Oklahoma Athletic Hall of Fame in 1977. He passed away on September 9, 1988, at the age of 78.

87

Leroy McGuirk

NWA Junior Champ and promoter.

A former NCAA champion at Oklahoma A&M in 1931, Leroy McGuirk reigned as the NWA World Junior Heavyweight Champion from 1939–1950.

A noted shooter in his day, McGuirk popularized the junior heavyweight division in the U.S., paving the way for stars like Verne Gagne, Mike DiBiase, Hiro Matsuda, Roger Kirby, and Danny Hodge.

Despite losing an eye as a child, McGuirk established himself as one the best workers in the business, taking on the top contenders from around the country. His matches with Danny McShain during the '30s over the original World Light Heavyweight title set the standard by which all junior heavyweight matches in the U.S. would be judged.

Tragically, McGuirk lost his other eye in a 1950 auto accident after being thrown through the windshield,

88

Maurice "Mad Dog" Vachon

Big time brawler, Maurice Vachon.

Maurice "Mad Dog" Vachon was one of wrestling's most vicious, hated heels during the '60s and '70s, possessing one of the all-time great monikers in history.

Vachon was considered among the best brawlers in the business, and was famous for wild matches that routinely saw him bludgeon opponents and bloody them with his trademark biting. At a mere 5'7" and 225 pounds, Vachon was one of the toughest wrestlers around during his prime, perfecting the crazed brawler gimmick that set the standard for countless imitators.

Vachon was given the "Mad Dog" nickname in the early '60s, while wrestling in Portland, Oregon. Legendary promoter Don Owen tagged him with the handle after his first night in the territory when he nearly caused a riot and began fighting with police. Ironically, though, Vachon was a well-versed technical wrestler. He was an amateur wrestling champion in his native Quebec, representing Canada at the 1948 Olympics as a middleweight, and won gold at the 1950 British Empire Games before turning pro later that year.

Although he wrestled all over Canada and the U.S., Vachon's best days were in Verne Gagne's AWA. Between 1964 and 1966, he won the AWA World Heavyweight title five times, feuding with Gagne and becoming a top draw in the Midwest.

In 1967, he won the IWA World title twice, becoming the top heel in the Montreal territory while feuding with Johnny Rougeau. In 1969, he began teaming with his brother, Paul "The Butcher" Vachon, and the two set the AWA on fire. They feuded with Dick the Bruiser and The Crusher over the World Tag titles, winning the belts on August 30 and holding on to them for 21 months.

The highlight of their title reign came on August 14, 1970, when they faced Bruiser and The Crusher in a cage match in Chicago, in front of 30,000 fans. It was one of the largest pro wrestling crowds since 1961, when Buddy Rogers and Pat O'Connor had their NWA title rematch.

As his career began to wind down in the late-'70s, Vachon turned babyface and teamed with former rival Gagne to win the AWA World Tag Team titles from Pat Patterson and Ray Stevens in 1979. They held onto the straps for over a year before dropping them to the East-West Connection of Jesse Ventura and Adrian Adonis. Vachon jumped to the WWF in 1984 when Vince McMahon went national, but he was clearly past his prime and retired shortly after.

In October 1987, he lost a leg after being hit by a car near his home in Iowa while out for some exercise. On April 28, 1996, Vachon and other old-timers were honored by the WWF at its *In Your House* pay-per-view in Omaha, Nebraska. During the main event match between Kevin Nash and WWF World Champion Shawn Michaels, Nash knocked over Vachon, who was sitting at ringside, and ripped his artificial leg from its socket, only to have Michaels grab it from him and nail him with it, helping him to score the pin.

Yvon Robert, the Pride of Quebec.

89
Yvon Robert

A former National Wrestling Association World Heavyweight Champion in 1942, Yvon Robert was one of wrestling's top stars from the mid-'30s to early-'50s, and is the most popular wrestler ever to come out of Quebec.

At 6'0" and weighing 230 pounds, Robert was a well-conditioned, muscular athlete who was also incredibly quick and nimble in the ring. Robert entered wrestling as a teenager in the early-'30s; with his natural-born skills, he quickly developed into one of the best wrestlers in the business. He was a brilliant mat technician, famous for his figure four arm scissors and for using the drop-kick (a move still relatively rare in wrestling at the time).

Robert won the AWA (Boston) World Heavyweight title on July 13, 1936, defeating Danno O'Mahoney in Montreal. He held the title for a little over a year before being stripped of it when he refused to wrestle Lou Thesz. Despite this, he was still recognized as champion in Montreal.

Robert also became a huge star in Montreal's IWA promotion, to the point where his popularity in Quebec matched that of hockey legend and Montreal Canadiens icon Maurice "Rocket" Richard. He was the top drawing card and the backbone of the territory, winning the IWA World title 16 times between 1936 and 1956. His matches against Thesz, Buddy Rogers, "Whipper" Billy Watson, Don Leo Jonathan, and Killer Kowalski set the promotion on fire, helping to establish Montreal as one of the top moneymaking territories in North America.

Although Montreal was his bread and butter, Robert traveled throughout the Northeast, to major markets such as New York, Boston, Philadelphia, and Toronto. In Toronto he was a three-time British Empire Champion between

1943 and 1950, and won the Canadian Open Tag Team titles with Watson in 1953.

Robert retired from wrestling in 1959, passing the mantle of top French-speaking star to fellow Quebecer Johnny Rougeau. He died in July 1971 at the age of 56.

90

Bronko Nagurski

NFL and wrestling legend.

Regarded as one of the best football players of all time and among the greatest athletes of the 20th century, Bronislaw "Bronko" Nagurski was one of wrestling's biggest stars during the '30s and '40s.

Standing 6'2" and weighing 230 pounds, Nagurski was a phenomenally gifted athlete who was noted for his brute strength. His success in pro wrestling helped blaze a path for future football players that followed, enabling them to get into the sport.

A member of both the U.S. College Football and NFL Halls of Fame, Nagurski was born in Rainy River, Ontario, in 1908. He attended the University of Minnesota from 1927 to 1929 on a football scholarship, and enjoyed an impressive career there. He was a near-unanimous All-American in 1928 and was the only player in U.S. college history to make All-American at two positions – fullback and defensive tackle – in 1929.

His NFL career was equally illustrious: Nagurski was chosen as a fullback on the NFL's 1930s All-Decade team. He was selected to the NFL's 75th Anniversary All-Time team in 1995 as a running back and to the 75th Anniversary All-Two-Way Team as a fullback-linebacker that same year.

He was also named by Sports Illustrated in its All-Century issue as the greatest college athlete ever to come out of Minnesota.

His football career began in 1930, when legendary Chicago Bears coach George Halas signed him to a pro contract. He went on to help the Bears win NFL championships in 1932 and 1933. An All-Pro with the Bears from 1932-1934, Nagurski wrestled during the off-season for several years. Surprisingly, in 1937, at the height of his career, he quit to wrestle full time. He had been promised the world title and was told that he could make more money as world champion than as the NFL's top player.

Nagurski first entered pro wrestling in 1933 with the help of manager Tony Stecher, and instantly became a main-event star due to his notoriety from football. Nagurski defeated Dean Detton in 1937 for promoter Joe "Toots" Mondt's version of the world title, and was a two-time National Wrestling Association World Heavyweight Champion, defeating Lou Thesz in 1939 and Ray Steele in 1941.

Despite being wrestling's biggest draw in the early-'40s, Nagurski lacked a certain charisma and didn't come across well on TV. As a result, his career outside his native Minnesota was never very strong. He wound up bouncing around between several territories before finally retiring in 1960.

Nagurski died on January 8, 1990, at the age of 81.

Legendary UWA champ, Dos Caras
(Mil Mascaras's brother).

91

Dos Caras

One of the top in-ring workers of the '70s and '80s, Dos Caras is considered the greatest heavyweight ever to come out of Mexico.

Caras, born Jose Luis Rodriguez, was famous for his sculpted physique and for teaming with his brothers, Mil Mascaras and El Sicodélico. He also played an important role in Mexican wrestling history by helping to unionize pro wrestlers in Mexico. Caras was surprisingly quick and agile considering his 5'10", 211-pound frame. He was one of the most revolutionary workers of his era, brilliantly combining mat skills and aerial moves into one of the most versatile working styles in the business.

Caras' pro debut, as an 18-year-old, on January 6, 1970, was heavily publicized due to his family connection. Rodriguez took the name Dos Caras (meaning "two faces"), and became an instant main event star in Mexico, Texas, and Southern California. He also went on over 30 tours of All Japan in the late-'70s and early-'80s, where he became one of the top Mexican stars, often teaming with his brother, Mascaras.

After several years as a main event star in EMLL, Caras left the promotion in 1975 to help promoter Francisco Flores start up the Naucalpan-based Universal Wrestling Alliance, where he went on to become a main event star. His marquee feud against perennial UWA champion El Canek changed the balance of power in Mexico, helping the UWA surpass EMLL as the number one promotion for the remainder of the '70s and into the late-'80s.

Between 1984 and 1992, he held the heavyweight title on three occasions and played a major role in turning the UWA into one of the hottest drawing promotions in the world. On May 29, 1988, he defeated legendary rudo Scorpio in a mask vs. hair match, adding his scalp to the collection of masks he had won over the previous decade.

By the '90s Caras was being phased out of the main event picture, making way for a new generation of *luchadores* that would become the new superstars in Mexico, such as Konnan. Still, as late as December 1995, when he competed in the historic Super-J Cup tournament in Tokyo, Caras, at age 44, proved that he could still be classed among the best in-ring workers in the world, when he put on magnificent performances against youngsters El Samurai and Gedo.

Despite living in the shadow of his more famous brother his entire career, Dos Caras established himself in the eyes of promoters on the merits of his own ability.

"Dos Caras is perhaps the best heavyweight of the last 25 or 30 years," opines Lucha Libre historian Jose Luis Fernandez. "He started his career as a tag team partner for his brother Mil Mascaras and mostly got to do the workload of the tag team; but, eventually he made a name for himself, and gained such a reputation through his work that he could get booked anywhere without having to rely on his brother's stardom."

92

Edouard Carpentier

World traveler, Edouard Carpentier.

Nicknamed "The Flying Frenchman," Edouard Carpentier revolutionized wrestling in the '50s and '60s with his acrobatic style. He was a main-event star and a top draw in every territory he appeared in before retiring in the mid-'80s.

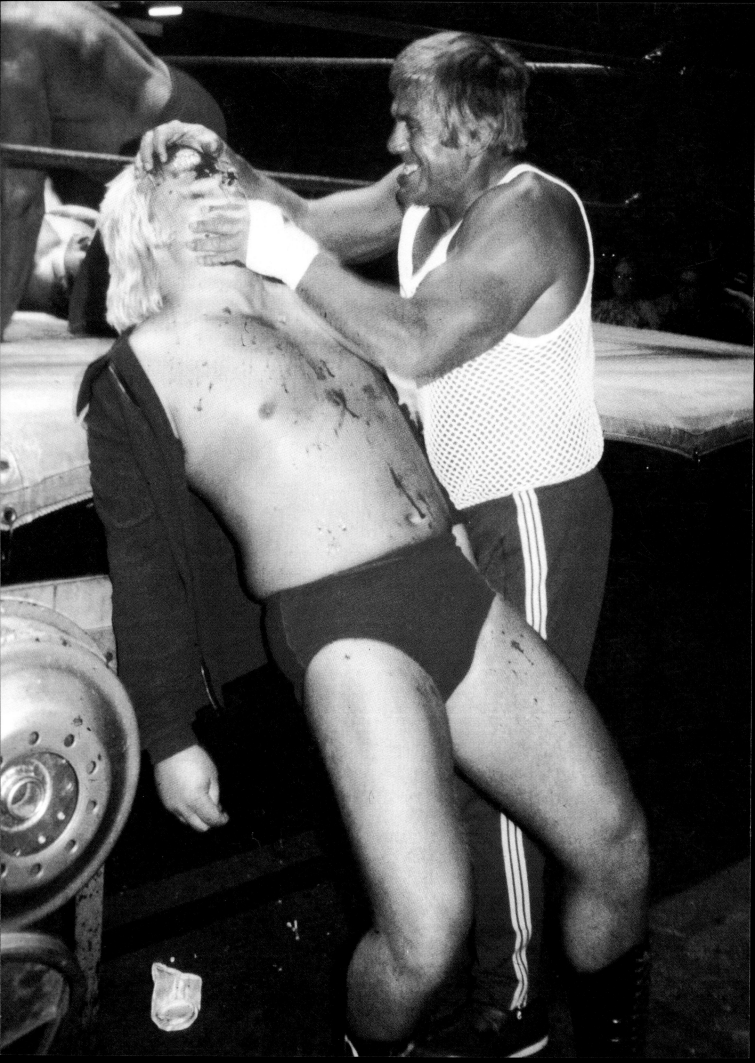

In the 1950s, when wrestling was predicated on collar-and-elbow lockups, stationary holds, and mat skills, Carpentier (born Edouard Weicz) was among the first wrestlers to regularly use high-flying moves. A former gymnast, Carpentier was a true pioneer, thrilling fans with his impressive array of flying dropkicks, cartwheels and somersaults. A gifted mat technician and renowned for his muscular physique, Carpentier helped change the landscape of wrestling in the U.S. and Canada with his aerial ingenuity, trailblazing a path for future high-flyers to follow.

Carpentier was a top draw for Montreal's International Wrestling Association in the '50s and '60s, feuding with Killer Kowalski and winning the IWA World title five times between 1960 and 1967. He teamed with Andre the Giant (known as Jean Ferre at the time) when he first entered the Montreal promotion in 1971. (The storyline had it that Carpentier introduced Andre into North America.) Alongside Yvon Robert, Carpentier became a household name in Montreal and is still considered the most famous wrestler that storied wrestling city has ever produced.

His most famous match came on June 14, 1957, against NWA World Champion Lou Thesz in Chicago. After splitting the first two falls, Thesz didn't come out for the third fall, claiming to have a back injury. Carpentier won the match, but the NWA declared that the title could not change hands due to injury and Thesz remained champion. Nevertheless, Carpentier was recognized in many territories as World Champion, a fact that was later legitimized when Thesz, still the official NWA titleholder, put Carpentier over.

Carpentier legitimized what became the AWA World title when he dropped his version of the belt to Verne Gagne on August 9, 1958, in Omaha, Nebraska. That title then went on to become unified with the AWA World title on September 7, 1963, when AWA champion Gagne defeated Fritz Von Erich in Omaha. Carpentier's World title reign also led to the World Wrestling Association World title, which was created for him in 1961 in Los Angeles.

93

Rayo de Jalisco

Mexican icon, Rayo de Jalisco.

One of the true icons of Mexican wrestling, Rayo de Jalisco was a huge star in the '60s, second in popularity only to the revered El Santo.

Jalisco (born Maximo Linares Moreno) was a master ring psychologist. Blessed with tons of charisma, he could hold throngs of rabid fans in utter captivity. Although he used parody and clowning techniques in the ring to entertain fans, Jalisco was an accomplished wrestler. His mix of comedy, solid ring work, and innovative aerial spots made him one of Mexico's biggest box-office attractions of the '60s and '70s.

Jalisco debuted in 1954 under the alias Doc Curtis. He didn't have much success under that name so in 1958 he took the moniker El Rayo de Jalisco (suggested to him by his friend, Filli Espinoza) and donned his trademark black and gold mask.

The former NWA World Middleweight Champion is best remembered as one half of one of Mexico's most famous tag teams, along with El Santo. The two masked legends won the Mexican National Tag Team titles in the mid-'60s, feuding with the greatest heel tag team in Mexican history, René Guajardo and Karloff Lagarde, in a program that is still talked about today.

His body started to break down and his skills began to deteriorate by the late-'70s while competing on Mexico's independent scene. Although past his prime, Jalisco was still a tremendous draw. On August 13, 1989, 35 years after making his pro debut, Jalisco lost his mask to Blue Demon, one of his biggest rivals from the '60s, in an historic mask vs. mask match in front of a sold out crowd at Monterrey's Plaza de Toros Monumental.

facing page: Edouard Carpentier bloodies Johnny Valentine.

All-time great, Stanislaus Zbyszko.

94

Stanislaus Zbyszko

A two-time world champion in the '20s, Stanislaus Zbyszko is one of the most important figures in wrestling history.

Born Stanislaus Cyganiewicz in Poland in 1878, Zbyszko was a world-class wrestler and a top star in Europe at the turn of the century, reputedly going undefeated in over 900 matches. He won his first world title on May 6, 1921, from Ed "Strangler" Lewis, but will forever be remembered for winning the title from world champion Wayne Munn in 1925, in one of wrestling's most famous double-crosses.

Because of his long, "boring" matches, Zbyszko's first reign as champion was a failure at the box office. The Gold Dust Trio (promoters Billy Sandow, Joe "Toots" Mondt, and Lewis) convinced Zbyszko to join their syndicate and drop the title to Lewis in 1922. Zbyszko continued to wrestle for the Trio faction, regularly putting Lewis over.

In 1925, Lewis lost the title to Munn, an ex-football player with no wrestling ability. The Trio wanted to create a new charismatic box-office star in Munn and then draw a huge crowd for a rematch where Lewis would regain the title. The Trio set up a title match between Munn and Zbyszko in order to give Munn more credibility as champion. At the same time, however, Zbyszko had already jumped to the Joe Stecher circuit behind the Trio's back. During the match on April 15, 1925, Zbyszko began shooting on Munn, scoring countless shoot pins. The referee was forced to award the title to Zbyszko to prevent the crowd from rioting. A month later Zbyszko dropped the belt to Stecher.

The Zbyszko double-cross had long-term repercussions on the industry: future promoters would always make sure to put the world title in the hands of a real wrestler who could handle himself in a potential double-cross situation.

It was because of this that many promoters backed Lou Thesz as the world champion from the '30s through to the '60s.

Zbyszko died on September 23, 1967, in St. Joseph, Missouri.

95

Sting

Sting in the Tokyo Dome as Rick Steiner and Tim Horner watch.

Sting was one of the biggest stars in wrestling from the late-'80s through the '90s, earning the nickname, "The Franchise" among wcw fans.

Although never known for a particularly strong workrate, Sting compensated with a charismatic, high-energy character that captivated fans. Born Steve Borden, Sting parlayed his tremendous popularity in the late-'80s into a tremendous career in the '90s, becoming the top babyface and cornerstone of Ted Turner's wcw. He defeated Ric Flair for the NWA World title on July 7, 1990, and went on to become a multiple-time wcw World Heavyweight Champion.

A former bodybuilder, Sting was trained by the legendary Red Bastien and Rick Bassman before making his debut in 1985 as a member of Power Team USA, which included Jim Hellwig – otherwise known as the Ultimate Warrior.

Together, Sting and Hellwig wrestled as the Blade Runners in Bill Watts' UWF. They split up when Jim Crockett bought out the promotion and dissolved it into his NWA office, but Sting stayed on, becoming an NWA regular.

It was then Ric Flair who made Sting's career, carrying

him through a 45-minute main event on live national TV as part of the first Clash of the Champions special. Ending in a time-limit draw, Flair carried the green and inexperienced Sting through what would be the best match of his career, instantly elevating him in the eyes of wrestling fans and making him a main-event star.

From September 1996 to December 1997 Sting was the hottest star in the world, basing his new stoic, dark persona on the title character from the film *The Crow*. Despite never wrestling a single match during this period, Sting was kept fresh due to several well-staged run-ins and skits. He trailed only Steve Austin in merchandise sales, and led the company through its most successful financial quarter ever.

His return match at Starrcade '97, where he won the WCW World title from Hulk Hogan, set company records for the largest pay-per-view buyrate (1.9), live gate ($543,000), paid attendance (16,052) and one-night merchandise sales ($161,961).

However, the match was mired in controversy after Hogan double-crossed Sting, changing the agreed-upon finish. In the original script, Hogan was supposed to win via a fast three-count from a heel ref, only to have the result overturned and the match continued. But referee Nick Patrick was apparently coerced by Hogan during the match, and gave a proper count. Hogan did not sell Sting's kick-out attempt. After much maneuvering, which included "trouble-shooting" referee Bret Hart punching out Patrick, the match continued, and Sting scored a submission victory. But the damage had already been done as fans walked away thinking Hogan had been screwed. WCW missed a glorious opportunity to elevate Sting from just another main event star into the hottest property in wrestling with a strong win over Hogan.

After securing one of the richest contracts in wrestling history, Sting finished out his days in the WCW by defeating Flair on the final edition of Nitro, before the WWF purchased the company in the spring of 2001.

96

Pat Patterson

After debuting in his hometown of Montreal as a teenager, Pat Patterson became one of the best workers in wrestling during the '60s and '70s.

Pat Patterson, at Cow Palace, San Francisco, 1973.

Patterson (born Pierre Clermont) was one of the most despised heels in the business for over twenty years. He was also a multi-faceted wrestler: he was an accomplished technical wrestler; an exceptional brawler who took great bumps; and a master of ring psychology, possessing brilliant interview skills.

Although a talented singles performer, Patterson is best remembered for his legendary tag team with Ray Stevens in San Francisco in the mid-'60s. Known as "The Blond Bombers," Patterson and Stevens are considered one of the greatest tag teams in wrestling history. They held the San Francisco version of NWA World Tag Team titles twice in the late-'60s, and the AWA tag titles in 1978. The two split up when Stevens turned babyface, and they went on to have a series of Texas Death matches from 1970-1971, in one of the hottest feuds in the history of the territory.

Patterson was an institution in San Francisco, capturing the U.S. title six times and winning the tag titles eleven times with eight different partners. He also won the annual Cow Palace Battle Royal – a major event through the '70s – in 1975, and again in 1981, the year promoter Roy Shire closed down the promotion.

A former WWF North American titlist, Patterson became the first WWF Intercontinental Champion in 1979 after "winning" a fictitious tournament. He lost the belt to Ken Patera the next year and went on to feud with Sgt. Slaughter – then one of the top heels in wrestling. The Patterson-Slaughter feud resulted in a series of unbelievable Boot Camp matches, including an incredibly bloody battle at New York's Madison Square Garden on April 6, 1981, which is now regarded as one of the best matches of the '80s.

Patterson retired from active wrestling in 1984 to become Vince McMahon's right-hand man and main booking assistant. Working alongside McMahon and booker George Scott, Patterson was one of the chief architects of the WWF, playing an integral role in helping it become a global phenomenon.

New Japan star during a brief stint in the NWO.

97

Masahiro Chono

A former NWA and IWGP Heavyweight Champion, Masahiro Chono was one of Japan's top stars and best heavyweight workers during the '90s.

The threesome of Chono, Keiji Muto, and Shinya Hashimoto comprised the Three Musketeers. The three of them were the backbone of New Japan Pro Wrestling during its hot years of the '90s, when they were consistently the promotion's main event stars and top box-office draws.

Chono started at the New Japan dojo on April 21, 1984, as part of a special training camp that would also produce Muto, Hashimoto, and Jushin "Thunder" Liger. Chono made his pro debut a mere six months later against fellow classmate Muto. After four years of wrestling on New Japan's undercard, Chono was sent to North America in 1988 to gain experience. Chono split his time between the Central States territory, Alabama, and Atlantic Canada before returning to Japan in 1989 to compete in a tournament to crown a new IWGP Champion.

Chono's first big break came on February 10, 1990, teaming with Hashimoto against Antonio Inoki and Seiji Sakaguchi in the main event of New Japan's second-ever Tokyo Dome show. Two months later he captured the IWGP tag belts with Muto from Hashimoto and Masa Saito, signaling his rise to the top of the promotion's pecking order. On December 26, 1990, Chono stole headlines when he wrestled and defeated mentor Lou Thesz, when the former NWA World Champion came out of retirement for one last match. It was a significant bout, since it was Thesz who taught Chono his signature STF maneuver, which was very popular in Japan.

Chono was elevated to main event status in August 1991 following New Japan's inaugural G1 Climax tournament. In the round-robin tournament, Chono defeated New Japan icon Riki Choshu, then beat Hashimoto in a sudden-death match to advance to the finals, where he took on Muto (who had beaten Vader and Tatsumi Fujinami to advance). The two young wrestlers took center stage in the finals of the G1 for the entire Japanese wrestling public to see. Having just been passed the torch with wins over New Japan's old guard, Muto and Chono put on a 30-minute mat classic that showcased their incredible athleticism. The crowd heat was electric. In the end, Chono pinned Muto, but the match was a five-star event that solidified both men's reputations as the future flag-bearers of the promotion.

Chono would go on to win the G1 in 1992 and 1994 and appear in the finals in 1996, earning the nickname "Mr. August" in the process. By virtue of his 1992 tournament win he became the NWA World Heavyweight Champion, but dropped the belt to Muto on January 4, 1993, in front of 63,500 fans at the Tokyo Dome.

Chono's career took a turn when he suffered a massive neck injury in 1992 during a match with Steve Austin. The injury would result in continuing neck problems that forced him to abandon his hard, snug working style in favor of matches that got over more on guile and careful planning.

Chono won the IWGP Heavyweight title from Fujinami on August 8, 1998, but relinquished the title a month later when he suffered another neck injury. He returned in 1999 but was not the same wrestler inside the ring. In 2001, he changed his role within New Japan, becoming a booker when Choshu was ousted from the position.

98

Dara Singh

DARA SINGH

Revered Indian idol.

India's top wrestler during the '50s and '60s, Dara Singh is a cultural icon in his native country, where he helped to popularize pro wrestling.

Singh was the top box-office draw in India during his career and was a huge star in England. An accomplished wrestler who combined excellent mat skills with natural charisma, Singh was a talented ring psychologist who was able to connect with the throngs of rabid fans who attended his matches. He later became a successful promoter, an accomplished movie producer, and prominent businessman.

Singh achieved huge crossover popularity in India along the same lines of Mexico's El Santo, appearing in major motion pictures and becoming a matinee idol. His unforgettable series of matches against Lou Thesz in the late-'60s drew huge crowds to outdoor stadiums all across India, further adding to his legend.

Before he passed away in May 2002, Thesz reflected on the lasting mark Singh left on wrestling.

"He was about my size, but very handsome and had audience savvy. There were probably better pure wrestlers in India, but he had the power to capture the imagination of the fans… Mostly his success was due to an agile mind and a great personality. Historically, he had more impact in India and England than the U.S., but he is a big part of world wrestling history."

Singh also wrestled in the U.S. and Canada during the '50s and '60s, winning the Canadian Open Tag Team titles with Yukon Eric in Frank Tunney's Toronto promotion in 1958. Still, his greatest success came in his native India where he is considered a national hero.

Singh retired from active wrestling in 1983 due to health problems.

99

Jesse Ventura

Future Governor Ventura.

Known more for his microphone skills than his wrestling ability, Jesse "The Body" Ventura was one of the seminal characters in the WWF from 1984 to 1990.

Ventura retired from wrestling in 1986, two years after a blood clot was discovered in his lung. He quickly became one of the WWF's most popular personalities, as the heel to Gorilla Monsoon and Vince McMahon's straight man act. During this time, he commentated on some of the biggest events and most important angles in history. Although not the first heel commentator in wrestling, Ventura redefined the role with his thoughtful observations and confrontational style, setting the standard by which future heel color analysts would be judged.

Ventura (born James Janos) grew up a lifelong wrestling fan in Minnesota, where he idolized "Superstar" Billy Graham. He debuted as "Surfer" Jesse Ventura in the Central States territory in 1975. Veteran Omar Atlas was Ventura's opponent in his first pro match in Cedar Rapids, Iowa. The promoter told Atlas to let Ventura throw him over the top rope and get disqualified, if he thought the rookie had promise. Otherwise, Atlas was instructed to simply beat him up.

"Omar thought he was doing well and told [Jesse] to throw him," said Omar through his wife, Charlotte. "In [Ventura's autobiography], Jesse writes that Omar, not being one of those egotistical guys in wrestling, told him 'Amigo, throw me over the top.' He also credited Omar with helping him start his career."

After a lengthy stint in the Pacific Northwest, where he was first billed as "The Body," Ventura jumped to the AWA in 1979 and formed the famed East-West Connection with Adrian Adonis. He left the AWA a few years later and bounced around between Memphis and the WWF.

Ventura quit the WWF in 1990 over a dispute concerning royalties and on April 13, 1994, a federal jury awarded him $809,958 in a lawsuit he filed against McMahon. Ventura joined WCW in January of 1992, securing a $350,000 per year contract that made him the highest paid announcer in history. He left in 1994.

By all honest accounts Ventura was not a great wrestler. But he did have tremendous charisma (that enabled him to land several major motion picture roles, including a part opposite Arnold Schwarzenegger in 1987's *Predator*) and was one the best interviews in wrestling. Nowadays, Ventura is best known for shocking pundits and politicians alike in 1998 to become the governor of Minnesota as a third-party candidate.

Golden boy Eddie Graham.

100

Eddie Graham

Eddie Graham was a top star during the "Golden Era" of the '50s and early '60s, but his true legacy is as a promoter and booker.

For over 20 years, Graham was one of the most influential people in the industry as owner of Florida Championship Wrestling, one of the most respected promotions in the U.S. With its twist-and-turn booking, compelling storylines, and high-quality matches, the Florida territory earned Graham the reputation as the best booker of his era.

Graham (born Eddie Gossett in 1930) made his pro debut as a teenager in 1947, and gained fame partnering with "brothers" Dr. Jerry Graham and "Crazy" Luke Graham. Eddie and Jerry were the top heel tag team of the '50s and

'60s, dominating the U.S. Tag Team titles. They were huge gate attractions all along the East Coast in their battles with The Fabulous Kangaroos, The Bastien Brothers, and Argentina Rocca and Miguel Perez. In the early '60s, Graham traveled to Florida, turning it into the hottest territory in the country.

Graham is best known for his unforgettable feud with Professor Boris Malenko. Graham attacked Malenko during a 1966 match, punching him in the mouth and knocking his false teeth out. In one of wrestling's all-time classic moments, Graham then began stomping on the teeth, igniting an epic feud that set the territory on fire.

A freak accident in 1968 nearly ended his career. A 75-pound steel window fell on his head while he was lacing up his boots in the locker room, sidelining him for 15 months. He suffered torn retinas in both eyes and required over 300 stitches in his face and head.

Graham was generally regarded as having the best business mind in wrestling. It was not unusual for other promoters, stuck on how to finish off a main-event program, to call up Graham for help. Graham later imparted his creativity and business savvy onto others, mentoring future bookers Bill Watts and Dusty Rhodes. He was highly respected by other promoters, who elected him NWA President in 1976, 1977, and 1978.

Eddie Graham committed suicide on January 20, 1985, after privately battling alcohol addiction for several years.

Watch Out For

The Next Ten

Legend in the making, on the left, Jun Akiyama.

Jun Akiyama

It was a hell of a way to start a career.

Seven months after first entering the All Japan training camp, Jun Akiyama made his pro wrestling debut on September 17, 1992, at Tokyo's venerable Korakuen Hall against Kenta Kobashi.

Incredibly, the reality of stepping into the ring with arguably the best wrestler in the world didn't faze Akiyama. Instead, the 22-year old rookie – formerly an alternate for the 1992 Olympic wrestling team at 220 pounds – made an impressive debut, proving to be a natural inside the ring and providing fans with a brief glimpse into what they could expect from him in the future.

Since then, Akiyama hasn't disappointed, continuing to study and learn from the likes of Kobashi, Mitsuharu Misawa, and Toshiaki Kawada, and developing one of the world's best in-ring work styles. Like Kurt Angle and the late Owen Hart, Akiyama had an inherent instinct for pro wrestling, picking up its finer points and mastering the craft with the greatest of ease. Akiyama learned the sport the hard way, in one of the most challenging classrooms

possible: the rings of All Japan Pro Wrestling, against the top workers in the world.

Years of fighting his way up the company ladder flew by and Akiyama made extraordinary progress, becoming the hottest young prospect in Japan and the performer that All Japan founder Giant Baba and booker Misawa tagged as the future cornerstone of the promotion. By 1996 he had come into his own, and had begun teaming with Misawa. The duo went on to capture the Unified World Tag Team titles. Akiyama also continued to impress in singles matches against Kobashi and Kawada, before scoring his first pinfall victory over Misawa on February 27, 2000.

If there had ever been any doubt about his future, his victory over Misawa ended it. It was a symbolic passing of the torch – much in the same way Jumbo Tsuruta handed the mantle of leadership to Misawa ten years earlier – and Akiyama began his ascent to the top of the Japanese wrestling hierarchy.

After close to eight years in All Japan, he left the company in 2000 for Misawa's Pro Wrestling NOAH group, becoming a main-event star in the new promotion and having epic matches against Kobashi and Vader. A year after wrestling his first match in NOAH, he defeated his mentor, Misawa, in a classic match for the Global Honored Crown title. It was Akiyama's first world title.

His victories over Misawa, Kobashi, and Akira Taue have solidified his standing as the premier Japanese heavyweight of the new millennium, truly fulfilling the prognostications of greatness made by Giant Baba. That Akiyama will uphold the standard of match quality that All Japan main-event matches are renowned for is a given. How long it will be before someone displaces him as the best heavyweight in Japan is the greater mystery.

Kurt Angle ties Steve Austin into the ropes.

Kurt Angle

Like Earl McCready, Verne Gagne, Danny Hodge, and Jack Brisco before him, Kurt Angle capitalized on his status as a collegiate wrestling champion and went on to become one of the top pro wrestlers of his era. Angle's seamless transition from the pinnacle of the amateur ranks to the top of the pro wrestling world wasn't surprising. Blessed with incredible ring presence, natural charisma, and an off-the-charts sense of timing, Angle – a two-time NCAA Heavyweight Champion at Clarion University and an Olympic Gold Medalist – seemed destined to scale the starry heights of pro wrestling.

After turning down a lucrative offer from the WWF in 1996, Angle signed a five-year deal with the organization in 1998 and trained under the watchful eye of former NWA World Champion Dory Funk Jr. Angle then went on to gain some seasoning in the Memphis-based Power Pro Wrestling promotion, before making his WWF debut in November 1999 on RAW.

Billed as "The Most Celebrated Real Athlete in WWF History" upon entering the WWF, the 5'9", 230-pound Angle quickly won praise from longtime fans for the way he picked up pro wrestling with such relative ease. Not since Jun Akiyama and Owen Hart had anyone become ranked among the best workers in the business so soon after his debut.

Angle quickly proved to be one of the best in-ring workers of his time, drawing rave reviews from insiders for the elegant fluidity and trademark snugness of his work. Although not a gifted orator at first, Angle quickly overcame the stumbling interview-style of his early days to become one of the most entertaining promo men in the business. He skyrocketed up the ranks of the WWF, combining incredible interview skills with a scientific, yet compelling ring-style reminiscent of the seminal NWA World Champions of the '60s and '70s.

"There's one young man that's doing super that reminds me of me, and that's Kurt Angle. He can mix it up with the big boys," says Danny Hodge, a former NWA World Junior Heavyweight Champion and three-time NCAA champion at the University of Oklahoma.

Thanks to his groundbreaking matches with Chris Benoit, Steve Austin, Triple H, and The Rock that established him as a main-event star, Angle was rewarded for his hard work in November 2000, when Vince McMahon put the WWF World title on him for the first time. After winning his second WWF World title in 2001, Angle was inducted into the National Wrestling Hall of Fame as one of the greatest amateur wrestlers in U.S. history. It's a foregone conclusion that the same will be said of his pro wrestling career once he decides to hang up his trunks for good.

Classic Chris Benoit pose.

Chris Benoit

Chris Benoit is an original star, and not the second coming of the Dynamite Kid, as so many have labeled him. And yet, when watching him wield his special brand of wrestling magic inside the ring, one can't help but draw comparisons between Benoit and his childhood idol.

The grace and proficiency with which he executes the most technical of wrestling maneuvers; the bone-crushing

facing page: Mexican action, Benoit splashes Blue Panther in Mexico City.

bumps he takes; the belief in pro wrestling as a sport, first, and entertainment, second: these were the fundamental, career-defining traits that Benoit first became aware of while watching the Dynamite Kid as a teenager growing up in Edmonton. Benoit would later attain an intimate understanding of these same traits as a student of Stu Hart's Dungeon, while training for his 1986 pro wrestling debut.

After spending his formative years in Calgary's Stampede promotion, Benoit first gained widespread notoriety as the masked Pegasus Kid while wrestling in Japan, Mexico, and Europe. Shunned by U.S. promoters because of his size (5'8" and 220 pounds), Benoit carved out his reputation on the international wrestling scene with breathtaking matches against Jushin "Thunder" Liger, the late Owen Hart, Koji Kanemoto, and Negro Casas. The startling ease with which he mastered every foreign style imaginable earned him the reputation among industry insiders as the best pound-for-pound wrestler in the business.

"When you're able to work all those different styles and grab a little bit from here and a little bit from there – and combine it into your style – it makes you different and makes you stand out," says Benoit of his experiences wrestling abroad.

Benoit used the reputation he had earned in Japan and Mexico (and his tenure in ECW in the mid-'90s) as a springboard to greater success, inking a deal with WCW in 1995. However, backstage politicians and clueless bookers conspired to railroad his career, and he lingered in mid-card purgatory. He asked for his contractual release and signed with the WWF in January 2000.

With a new lease on his wrestling career, Benoit responded by helping to elevate the standard of match quality in the WWF through his epic matches against Steve Austin, The Rock, Chris Jericho, Triple H, and Kurt Angle.

A career-threatening neck injury sustained in 2001 sidelined him, but could not dampen his competitive spirit. He began a training and rehabilitation program that will undoubtedly see him take his rightful place among wrestling's elite workers once again. Although never an established main-event star (except in Stampede and Mexico), Benoit has consistently earned a spot in consensus listings over the past 12 years as one of the world's top-ten workers, ranking him among the greatest in-ring performers in wrestling history.

Triple H

Triple H known as a ring General and backstage politician.

Triple H is the archetypal pro wrestler of the 21st century, combining solid in-ring work and excellent promo skills with a political shrewdness which enables him to manipulate any situation to his advantage.

After learning how to navigate the political waters of the WWF from Shawn Michaels, Triple H used his considerable talents – both inside and outside of the ring – to become a main-event star in the WWF. And while pundits point to his personal relationship with Stephanie McMahon as the reason for his ascendancy to the top of the WWF, his sharp wrestling skills are ample justification for his position within the company.

Trained by the famous Killer Kowalski, Triple H (born Paul Levesque) made his debut on the indie circuits of New England in the early '90s before signing with WCW. After a forgettable run there under a slew of gimmicks, he entered the WWF in 1995 as the aristocratic Hunter Hearst Helmsley. Somewhere along the line, he shed the two-dimensional trappings of the character and became Triple H – the cocky, kick-ass heel whose ring-style was reminiscent of Harley Race and Ric Flair. Triple H studied hours of Flair matches on videotape, and the results were impressive: he became a master of ring psychology and a brilliant storyteller inside the ring.

Although he had memorable bouts against The Rock, Steve Austin, Kurt Angle, Chris Jericho, and Chris Benoit, it was his series of matches against Mick Foley from 1999-2000 that established him as a main-event star. By putting over Triple H in such a convincing fashion in a series of pay-per-view main events, Foley helped to establish Triple H as one of the biggest superstars in the industry.

His career was thrown into jeopardy on the May 21,

2001, episode of RAW, when he tore his left quadricep muscle right off the bone during a heated tag-team match. Undeterred, he fought through the pain and continued for several more minutes, finishing the match, and further aggravating his injury in the process.

Eight months later, after a strenuous rehabilitation, he made his miraculous comeback, receiving one of the biggest pops in company history for his return to RAW on January 7, 2002. Although the added bulk to his upper body caused him to lose a step in the ring, he continued to perform at a high level. The comeback was completed when he won his fourth WWF World Heavyweight title against Chris Jericho at WrestleMania x8 before 68,000 fans at Toronto's SkyDome.

As The Rock spends more and more time in Hollywood, and as Steve Austin's run on top slowly winds down, Triple H stands ready to solidify his role within the WWF as the company's unquestioned leader.

The lion tamer.

Chris Jericho

Growing up as a teenager in Winnipeg, hockey was in Chris Irvine's blood. His father, Ted Irvine, was an NHL veteran of 11 years with the Los Angeles Kings, New York Rangers, and St. Louis Blues. That Chris would follow in his father's footsteps was a given.

Yet, a 19-year old-Chris Irvine enrolled in wrestling school in 1990, trading in his aspirations of hoisting the Stanley Cup for dreams of becoming the WWF World Champion. It was a dream that would be realized 11 years later when Irvine, wrestling as Chris Jericho, would capture the prestigious world title, becoming one of the brightest wrestling stars of the new millennium.

A student of the Hart Brothers School of Wrestling, Chris Jericho survived the horrors of Stu Hart's Dungeon and was instilled with a solid work ethic long before he stepped into the ring for the first time in October 1990.

After spending his early years on the Canadian independent circuit, he began to split his time between Mexico, Japan, Germany, and the Tennessee-based Smoky Mountain Wrestling promotion. As he acclimatized himself to the various foreign wrestling cultures, Jericho became one of the top junior heavyweights in the world, combining the grinding physical style he was taught by the Harts, the aerial maneuvers he picked up in Mexico, and the solid mat skills he learned while wrestling in Japan.

His international reputation and legendary matches with Ultimo Dragon, Negro Casas, and Silver King caught the attention of promoter Paul Heyman, who brought him into ECW in 1996. Later that year, he signed with WCW.

Although he wrestled all over the globe, Mexico's EMLL was Jericho's bread and butter for two-and-a-half years. Looking back now, he feels his spell in Mexico was integral to his growth and development as a wrestler.

"I loved Mexico. I was 22 years old…working six, seven, eight times a week. It was a really good experience and a good way to build a solid foundation. I still use some of that stuff and can easily draw on it in the ring whenever I need to."

After a three-year stint in WCW, Jericho jumped to the WWF in the summer of 1999. It was in the WWF that Jericho's career began to flourish, as he was given ample television time and many opportunities to hone his interviews skills. Billed as Y2J, Jericho quickly became a main-event star while engaging in a series of captivating matches with Triple H, The Rock, Chris Benoit, and Kurt Angle.

On December 9, 2001, his dream was fulfilled when he defeated Steve Austin and The Rock to capture the WWF World title. And although his title reign came to a premature end, Chris Jericho, possessing arguably the most well-rounded set of skills of any wrestler of his generation, is destined to be a major player in the industry for years to come.

All Japan's Kenta Kobashi.

Kenta Kobashi

Living in the formidable shadows cast by Mitsuharu Misawa and Toshiaki Kawada his entire career, Kenta Kobashi almost seemed like a forgotten man during his main-event tenure for All Japan Pro Wrestling.

Kobashi was one of the principal architects behind All Japan's glory years of the 1990s, helping to lead the promotion through the most profitable business period in its history. At 6'3" and 260 pounds, Kobashi is famous for performing breathtaking moonsaults, and for combining the workrate and ring skills of contemporaries, Misawa and Kawada, with brilliant facial expressions that enable him to communicate subtle storylines during his matches.

A three-time holder of the Triple Crown Heavyweight title, Kobashi distinguished himself during the '90s in the most physically demanding wrestling promotion in the world. His groundbreaking matches against Misawa, Kawada, and Stan Hansen earned All Japan the reputation as the promotion that staged the best main-event bouts in the world. His stunning ring-work and stiff working style made him one of the best heavyweights of his era, while simultaneously helping to raise the bar of pro wrestling athleticism to startling new heights.

After debuting for All Japan in 1988, Kobashi slowly made his way up the company ladder, playing a major role in the seminal Misawa & Co. vs. Tsuruta & Co. feud that set All Japan on fire from 1991 to 1993. Partnering with Misawa in 1993, the legendary duo won three consecutive Real World Tag League Tournaments and were twice crowned Unified World Tag Champions. They would eventually be recognized as the greatest tag team of the '90s. Meanwhile, Kobashi had a timeless series of singles matches with Misawa, Kawada, and Hansen that would rank among the greatest bouts in wrestling history.

His first Triple Crown title came on July 24, 1996, when he defeated Akira Taue. After enjoying two more title reigns and winning the Carnival Championship, Kobashi joined Misawa, leaving All Japan to form Pro Wrestling NOAH in June 2000. By the end of the year, the physically demanding ring-style and the years of grueling punishment began to take their toll. Shortly after a singles match against Jun Akiyama on December 23, Kobashi took a 14-month sabbatical from wrestling in order repair his ailing body. He went on to have several major surgeries on his knees and elbows, before returning to the ring in 2002.

Although currently sidelined and facing the distinct possibility that his wrestling career may be over, Kobashi still stands as a shining testament to hard work and commitment inside the ring – qualities that will no doubt ensure his rightful place among wrestling's paramount performers.

Japan's young lion.

Satoshi Kojima

It seems appropriate that Satoshi Kojima made his pro debut against Hiroyoshi Tenzan. Little did anybody know – when they stepped into the ring against each other on July 16, 1991 – that they would go on to form the greatest wrestling duo of the new millennium and revitalize tag-team wrestling in Japan.

Upon first entering pro wrestling, astute observers could see a world of potential in Kojima. After completing his training in the New Japan dojo, Kojima proved to be a quick learner inside the ring, effortlessly picking up the subtle aspects of pro wrestling. Gifted with natural athleticism, Kojima displayed excellent ring psychology in his rookie years, using intricate facial expressions to properly communicate storylines.

His first big break came on March 24, 1994, when he defeated Manabu Nakanishi in the finals of the Young Lions Cup – a sure sign that New Japan had big plans for his future within the company. At the end of the year, he left to work in Otto Wanz' CWA promotion in Austria and Germany, allowing him to learn a foreign wrestling style that he would incorporate into his ever-expanding repertoire of maneuvers.

After returning in 1996, he was put into a main-event program against then-IWGP Heavyweight Champion Shinya Hashimoto. While he was making a name for himself as a singles performer, Kojima showed his versatility by teaming with Nakanishi. On May 3, 1997, the duo won the IWGP Tag Team titles from veterans Riki Choshu and Kensuke Sasaki.

As Kojima slowly worked his way up the New Japan ladder, he began to grow more confident inside the ring, where he developed a cocky, yet charismatic attitude that perfectly complimented his athletic style. After joining the NWO Japan clique, Kojima became the understudy of Keiji Muto and began to learn from the man who led the company through its glory years of the '90s. In December 1998, Kojima and Muto won the Super Grade Tag League, another sure sign that his star was on the rise.

A month later he formed a tag team with Hiroyoshi Tenzan, winning the IWGP Tag Team titles from Genichiro Tenryu and Shiro Koshinaka at the Tokyo Dome. The duo became a regular tag team, winning the belts for the second time in 2000 (going on to hold the titles for 14 months) and quickly established themselves as the top tag team in the world thanks to their unequalled work rate. Meanwhile, Kojima continued to carve out an impressive singles career for himself, regularly challenging for the IWGP Heavyweight title and becoming a main-event star.

Kojima's partnership with Tenzan was dissolved in February 2002 when he left the company to join All Japan. Although his departure was overshadowed by the simultaneous exit of Muto, Kojima will no doubt prove to be All Japan's biggest asset, as he stands poised to become the promotion's in-ring leader for years to come.

Yuji Nagata

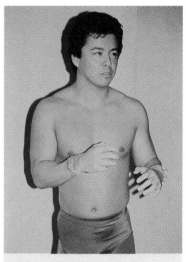

Young Yuji Nagata.

At just under 6'1" and 238 pounds, Yuji Nagata doesn't look like much at first. But then, looks can be deceiving. In the case of Nagata, anybody who mistakenly dismisses him because of his physical build isn't taking into account the size of his heart, or the magnitude of his ability.

Nagata is the fulcrum upon which New Japan Pro Wrestling has been hinged since the new century began. Nagata has emerged from his role as a bit player to become a main-event star and the in-ring leader of the promotion. In doing so, he has set the standard for match quality within New Japan with his scientific wizardry inside the ring.

His mere presence at any arena for a New Japan house show or TV taping means the difference between the event being a success or a bust. His stellar ring-work and exemplary work ethic prevented New Japan from completely falling apart during the early part of the new century, when the company was being torn apart by backstage politics.

He slowly worked his way up the company roster, impressing fans and booker Riki Choshu with his taut ring-style. Nagata was rewarded for his years of hard work when he assumed a top-tier position in New Japan, after defeating Keiji Muto in the final of the annual G1 Climax tournament in 2001.

His career took a major blow on New Year's Eve 2001, when kick boxer Mirko Cro Cop destroyed him in 21 seconds during a shoot fight as part of an Antonio Inoki live TV special. After rebounding from the crushing loss, he won the IWGP Heavyweight title from Tadao Yasuda on April 5, 2002.

With the future of the promotion now squarely resting on his shoulders, Nagata has become the new flag-bearer of New Japan, leading the struggling company on its quest to match its past glories in the new millennium.

Wrestler and contact fight star.

Kazushi Sakuraba

A legend before he even turned 30, Kazushi Sakuraba is the most successful pro wrestler to have ever crossed over into the world of mixed-martial arts and combat fighting. His success story is even more noteworthy in light of the fact he stands a mere 5'9" and weighs only 183 pounds.

Born July 14, 1969, Sakuraba began martial-arts training as a teenager in high school. He became an accomplished college wrestler before entering the pro ranks for Nobuhiko Takada's Union of Wrestling Forces International (UWFI) in the early-'90s. Sakuraba spent years as a mid-carder in the UWFI and Kingdom organizations (where he was held back because of his size) and eventually realized that he would never become a main-event star.

He left pro wrestling for mixed-martial arts and quickly established himself as one of the premier no-holds-barred fighters in the world, despite being outweighed in the majority of his matches. On December 21, 1997, he made his debut in UFC by defeating Conan Silveira in the final of a heavyweight tournament, stunning the mixed-martial arts world and providing a preview of what was yet to come.

With the backing of Takada, he entered PRIDE in 1998, and quickly turned heads by making both Vernon White and future UFC Champion Carlos Newton tap out. However, his greatest victory came on April 29, 1999, when he solidly defeated Vitor Belfort by decision at the PRIDE 5 event. Sakuraba then finished the year by defeating Royler Gracie. With subsequent wins over Royce, Renzo, and Ryan Gracie the following year, he became an instant legend in the world of no-holds-barred-fighting.

Sakuraba's upset victory over Royce Gracie on May 1,

2000, at the Tokyo Dome was an epic battle full of drama and emotion, and earned him the respect of the Japanese media. On the strength of that match, Sakuraba was named wrestler of the year by all of the major Japanese sports dailies, and finished seventh on Nikkan Sports newspaper's list of the 20 greatest wrestlers of the 20th century, finishing ahead of such legends as Akira Maeda, Keiji Muto, Riki Choshu, and Genichiro Tenryu.

Sakuraba suffered a huge loss to Vanderlei Silva on March 25, 2001, at PRIDE 13. The PRIDE 17 rematch, on November 3, 2001, saw Silva defeat Sakuraba due to a medical stoppage. Despite the loss, the rematch established Sakuraba as the greatest-drawing junior heavyweight in history, as 53,246 fans, paying $5.5 million – the largest crowd ever for a mixed-martial arts event and one of the largest live gates in wrestling history – packed into the Tokyo Dome to see the bout.

The losses to Silva notwithstanding, Sakuraba has a long career ahead of him. Sakuraba's overwhelming, very real successes not only overshadow the somewhat mythical exploits of men like Ed "Strangler" Lewis, Frank Gotch, Joe Stecher, and Lou Thesz, but also quell the myth that "small" competitors can't become main-event stars in pro wrestling.

Manami Toyota

Manami Toyota prepares to take on Akira Hokuto.

The Ric Flair of women's wrestling, Manami Toyota is arguably the greatest female pro wrestler of all time. Toyota set the world of women's wrestling on its ear

Kyoko Inoue stretches Manami Toyota as Bull Nakano watches from the ropes.

during the '90s, producing some of the best matches of the entire decade and establishing herself as one of the top workers in the world.

Toyota became the cornerstone of the All Japan Women's promotion and the top female wrestler of her era, following in the footsteps of Chigusa Nagayo, Jaguar Yokota, and Lioness Asuka. Her revolutionary ring style combined high-risk maneuvers, flawless mat holds, and a lightning-quick pace inside the ring. Toyota set a new standard of match quality within the industry, proving that women wrestlers were every bit as capable of having highly athletic, physically punishing matches as their male counterparts.

Over the years, she became renowned for working rapid-pace bouts that featured her trademark last-second kick-outs, which masterfully built her matches up to incredible crescendos of heat. Toyota's classic battles against Kyoko Inoue, Aja Kong, Akira Hokuto, and Dynamite Kansai stand as the greatest series of women's matches in wrestling history.

After debuting on August 5, 1987, at the age of 16, her first big break came on May 6, 1989, as part of the first Wrestlemarinpiad event. Teaming with Mima Shimoda to defeat Toshiyo Yamada and Etsuko Mita, Toyota managed

to steal the show with her stunning performance. Her land-mark singles feud with Yamada climaxed on August 15, 1992, with Toyota winning an epic hair vs. hair match that set her on a course for stardom. On March 26, 1995, she captured her first of four WWWA World singles titles, defeating Aja Kong for the strap.

Toyota's first reign only lasted three months, but was highlighted by a brilliant 60-minute draw against Kyoko Inoue on May 7, 1995, which drew rave reviews from fans and critics all over the world. On the strength of her leg-endary matches and mesmerizing work-rate, Toyota's name was routinely mentioned alongside Mitsuharu Misawa's during any discussion over who the greatest in-ring worker of the '90s was. That, perhaps more than anything else, speaks volumes about the astonishing magnitude of her talent.

Toyota began to slow down as the '90s drew to a close, as the years of grueling punishment in the ring began to catch up with her. Still, her influence and the contributions she made to women's wrestling are incalculable, inspiring a whole new generation of Japanese teenagers to enter the sport.

Index

AAA, 102, 103, 126, 152
Abdullah the Butcher, 24, 47, 48, 76, 84, 86, 96, 102, 106, 154, 166, 169, 177–179, 180, 181
Adams, Chris, 50, 52
Adkisson, Jack (Fritz Von Erich), 186
Adonis, Adrian, 163, 191, 199
Afflis, Richard (Dick the Bruiser), 151
Aguayo, Perro, 43, 102–103
Akiyama, Jun, 81, 201, 202, 206
Albright, Gary, 68, 112, 147
Ali, Muhammad, 23, 24, 47, 106
All Japan Pro Wrestling, 4, 18, 23, 36, 47, 48, 49, 68, 69, 70, 71, 77, 78, 81, 84, 85, 86, 87, 89, 96, 98, 105, 113, 118, 120, 123, 124, 128, 133, 150, 154, 155, 157, 166, 177, 179, 181, 187, 193, 201, 206
All Japan Women (AJW), 134, 166, 167, 209
Allen, Bad News, 90, 155
American Wrestling Association (AWA), 2, 10, 11, 13, 26, 28, 34, 35, 36, 68, 75, 82, 83, 85, 104, 105, 112, 124, 138, 142, 143, 146, 151, 154, 184, 186, 191, 195, 197, 199
Anderson, Arn, 4, 6, 138
Anderson, Gene, 2
Anderson, Ole, 2, 4, 106, 107
Andre the Giant, 17, 28, 29, 33–37, 46, 68, 104, 132, 136, 155, 170, 176, 183, 195
Angle, Kurt, 54, 72, 96, 201, 202, 204, 205
Anjoh, Yoji, 133
Arkangel de la Muerte, 89
Asai, Yoshihiro (Ultimo Dragon), 165
Assassin #1, 104
Assirati, Bert, 155, 165, 170
Asuka, Lioness, 134, 166, 167, 209
Atlas, Omar, 199
Atlas, Tony, 77
Atomic Pair, The, 40, 171
Austin, Chuck, 71
Austin, Killer Buddy, 19
Austin, Steve, 50–55, 91, 110, 136, 138, 139, 149, 158, 159, 197, 198, 202, 204, 205
Austin, "Stone Cold" (Steve Austin), 50, 72, 73
Austin, "Stunning Steve" (Steve Austin), 50

Baba, Shohei "Giant", 14, 18, 19, 20, 22, 23, 24, 36, 44–49, 68, 69, 77, 78, 80–81, 84, 85, 86, 89, 96, 108, 123, 124, 154, 166, 169, 177, 180, 186, 201
Baby Bull (Vader), 112
Backlund, Bob, 4, 23, 24, 91, 104, 124, 149, 159
Baker, Ox, 123
Barr, Art "Love Machine", 126
Bassman, Rick, 196
Bastien Brothers, 200
Bastien, Red, 196
Beauty Pair, 166
Beefcake, Brutus, 157
Beel, Fred, 63
Belfort, Vitor, 208

Benoit, Chris (Wild Pegasus), 116, 117, 155, 202–204, 205
Bernard, Frenchy, 35
Beyer, Dick (Destroyer), 18, 46, 83, 110, 143, 179–180
Biasetton, Antonino (Antonino Rocca), 153
Big Van Vader (Vader), 112, 129, 140
Bigelow, Bam Bam, 68
Billington, Tom (Dynamite Kid), 155
Bischoff, Eric, 6, 30, 31, 50, 52, 54, 91
Blade Runners, 196
Black Shadow, 41, 88
Black Tiger, 98, 100, 116, 117
Blanchard, Tully, 4, 106, 107, 138
Blanco, Angel, 158
Blassie, Freddie (Vampire), 18, 46, 70, 110–111, 154, 179, 180
Blassman, Fred ("Classy" Freddie Blassie), 110
Bliss, Mildred (Mildred Burke), 176
Blond Bombers, 142, 143, 197
Blood, Richard (Ricky Steamboat), 136
Blue Demon, 41, 43, 88, 101, 195
Blue Panther, 89
Bockwinkel, Nick, 1, 28, 35, 68, 69, 82, 83, 85, 104–105, 142, 143, 166
Bockwinkel, Warren, 104
Bollea, Terry (Hulk Hogan), 28
Borden, Steve (Sting), 196
Boulder, Terry (Hulk Hogan), 28, 34
Brazil, Bobo, 131, 154, 169, 177, 189
Brisco Brothers, the, 136
Brisco, Jack, 11, 13, 47, 84, 86, 96, 122–123, 124, 131, 190, 202
Brisco, Jerry, 122, 123
British Bulldogs, the, 90, 155, 157
Brody, Bruiser, 1, 24, 48, 68, 69, 76–77, 85, 96, 106, 150, 177
Brown, Orville, 11, 67
Browning, Jim, 65
Bruggers, Bob, 2, 109
Bruns, Bobby, 16
Brunzell, Jim, 2, 105
Bull Power (Vader), 112
Burke, Mildred, 176–177
Burns, Martin "Farmer", 62
Byers, June, 177

Cactus Jack (Mick Foley), 147, 177
Caddock, Earl, 66
Calloway, Mark (The Undertaker), 157
Canek, 78, 112, 128, 152
Caras, Cien, 102, 103
Carnera, Primo, 17, 65
Carpentier, Edouard, 12, 34, 110, 151, 176, 193–195
Carson, Don, 110
Casas, Negro, 126, 204, 205
Casey, Jim, 58
Casey, Steve, 13
Cauliflower Alley Club, 13, 105
Chochoshivili, Shota, 24
Chono, Masahiro, 13, 79, 112, 116, 120, 140, 198
Chosu, Riki, 17, 24, 48, 78–79, 85, 112, 128, 129, 132, 140, 150, 181, 198, 207, 208
Chyna, 139, 176
Clash of the Champions, 5, 7
Coage, Allen (Bad News Allen), 23
Cobra, the, 155
Coleman, Eldridge Wayne (Superstar Billy Graham), 159
Colon, Carlos 76, 77, 177,
Corino, Steve, 140
Crabtree, Shirly "Big Daddy", 170
Crockett, David, 2, 48, 109
Crockett, Jim, 2, 4, 5, 83, 106, 107, 123, 136, 143, 162, 196
Crush Gals, 134, 166, 167
Crusher, The, 47, 82, 83, 104, 124, 143, 150–151, 171, 191

Cruz, Roberto Gonzales (El Solitario), 158
Curtis, Doc (Rayo de Jalisco), 195
CWA, 112
Czaya, Emile, 17

Damian, Pedro Aguayo (Pedro Aguayo), 102
Davies, Killer, 16
de Jalisco, Rayo, 40, 41, 101, 195
Degeneration X, 139
Dempsey, Jack, 82
DeNucci, Dominic, 149
Destroyer, The, 18, 19, 46, 47, 75, 89, 110, 143, 179–189
Detton, Dean, 192
Devil Masami, 166, 167
DiBiase, "Iron" Mike, 183
DiBiase, Ted, 29, 52, 69, 75, 96, 144, 150, 183, 190
Dick The Bruiser, 82, 104, 124, 143, 146, 151, 169, 184, 191
Diesel, 139
Dillon, J.J., 4
DiPaolo, Ilio, 19
Dos Caras, 88, 152, 193
Douglas, Shane, 149
Dr. Wagner, 152, 158
Dr. X, 83, 180
Dude Love (Mick Foley), 147, 149
Duggan, Jim "Hacksaw", 125
Duncum, Bobby, 24, 106
Dusek, Ernie, 75
Dynamite Girls, the, 134
Dynamite Kid, 48, 75, 78, 90, 98, 100, 102, 116, 128, 155, 165, 170, 202, 204

Eagle, Don, 58, 75
ECW, 52, 87, 107, 149, 154, 204, 205
Eigen, Haruka, 49, 180
El Canek, 193
El Hijo del Santo, 43, 89, 126
El Matematico, 101
El Samurai, 116–117, 193
El Santo, 19, 38–43, 49, 88, 101, 126, 171, 195, 199
El Satanico, 98
El Sicodelico, 193
El Solitario, 41, 128, 158
El Universitario (Canek), 152
EMLL, 98, 102, 103, 165, 205
Espanto, 88
Esserati, Bernardo (Bert Assirati), 170
Estrada, Jose, 128
Everett, Eddie "Monster Man", 23

Fabulous Kangaroos, 200
Fargo, Jackie, 161
Farhat, Ed (The Sheik), 154
Firpo Pampiro, 177
Fishman, 102
Flair, Ric "Nature Boy", 2
Flair, Ric, 1–7, 8, 11, 25, 29, 30, 48, 50, 54, 59, 61, 72, 75, 80, 82, 84, 85, 86, 87, 90, 96, 100, 102, 106, 107, 108, 109, 112, 124, 125, 129, 136, 142, 144, 145, 155, 163, 183, 186, 187, 189, 196, 197, 204
Fliehr, Richard Morgan (Ric Flair), 1
FMW, 87, 154
Foley, Mick, 54, 72, 73, 76, 87, 147–149, 155, 158, 204
Four Horsemen, 4, 107
Freebirds, 4, 187
Friedrich, Robert, 66
Fuchi, Masa, 49, 180
Fujinami, Tatsumi, 5–6, 78, 79, 100, 102, 112, 120, 128–129, 169, 198
Fujiwara, Yoshiaki, 133
Funk, Dory Jr., 11, 22, 68, 77, 84, 86, 87, 96–97, 108, 122, 123, 124, 131, 146, 150, 179, 183, 186, 202

Funk, Dory Sr., 86, 96, 186, 189
Funk, Terry, 1, 5, 11, 68, 76, 77, 86–87, 96, 123, 124, 131, 146, 149, 154, 161, 179, 181
Funks, The 22, 47, 48, 68, 84, 85, 90, 106, 124, 154, 177
Fuyuki, Samson, 118

Gable, Dan, 62
Gagne, Greg, 2
Gagne, Verne, 2, 12, 13, 62, 68, 69, 82–83, 104, 105, 131, 136, 138, 143, 146, 150, 153, 159, 161, 165, 176, 180, 186, 190, 191, 195, 202
Galindo, Cavernario, 41, 171
Garvin, Ronnie, 4, 5
Gedo, 193
Geigel, Bob, 184
George, P.L. "Pinkie", 11
Georgia Championship Wrestling, 4
Giant Gene Ferre (Andre the Giant), 155
Giant Kimala, 181
Gilbert, Eddie, 149
Gold Dust Trio, 66, 196
Goldberg, Bill, 31, 91
Golden, Sterling (Hulk Hogan), 28, 34
Goliath, 110
Gomez, Pepper, 142, 143
Gonzales, Jose Huertas, 77
Goodish, Frank (Bruiser Brody), 76
Gordman, Black, 88
Gordon, Ray, 124
Gordy, Terry, 4, 68, 69, 81, 87, 187
Gorgeous George, 11, 13, 29, 36, 58, 74–75, 142, 153, 176, 180, 189
Gorilla Monsoon, 70, 199
Gotch, Frank, 8, 10, 13, 62–63, 114, 169, 208
Gotch, Karl, 13, 22, 23, 59, 132, 155, 165, 169–170
Goto, Tatsutoshi, 140
Goulet, Rene, 170
Gracie, Renzo, 208
Gracie, Rickson, 147
Gracie, Royler, 208
Gracie, Ryan, 208
Graham, "Crazy" Luke, 13, 200
Graham, Billy "Superstar", 35, 70, 71, 89, 107, 123, 124, 159–160, 199
Graham, Dr. Jerry, 151, 159, 200
Graham, Eddie, 106, 122, 200
Graham, Hobby, 124
Graham, Mike, 106, 107
Great Muta (Keijo Muta), 120
Great Sasuki, The, 98, 117
Great Togo, The, 19, 44
Guajardo, Rene, 88, 158, 195
Guerrera, Juventud, 126
Guerrero, Chavo, 128, 162
Guerrero, Eddie, 40, 117, 126
Guerrero, Gori, 40, 41, 158
Guerrero, Hector Eddie, 171
Guerrero, Mando, 171
Guerrero, Salvador Gori, 171
Guerrero, Salvador Jr (Chavo), 171
Guzman, Jorge (El Hijo del Santo), 126
Guzman, Miguel, 38
Guzman, Rudy, 38

Hackenschmidt, George, 10, 62, 63, 114–115
Haft, Al, 10
Hamada, Gran, 102, 165
Hamaguchi, Animal, 48, 78
Hansen, Stan, 24, 48, 68–69, 70, 71, 77, 81, 84, 86, 87, 89, 96, 105, 106, 118, 150, 181, 183, 206
Harris, Houston (Bobo Brazil), 169
Hart, Bret, 6, 17, 30, 31, 53, 65, 73, 87, 90–91, 96, 100, 102, 128, 132–133, 136, 138, 155, 158, 161, 163, 197
Hart Foundation, 90, 157
Hart, Gary, 106

Hart, Owen, 53, 90, 91, 116, 136, 139, 155, 158, 201, 202, 204
Hart, Stu, 90, 116, 155, 159, 166, 184, 186, 204, 205
Hase, Hiroshi, 116, 181
Hashimoto, Shinya, 79, 112, 116, 120, 140, 147, 198, 207
Hawk, Rip, 2
Hayabusa, 181
Hayato, Mach, 100
Heaton, Don (Don Leo Jonathan), 154
Heenan, Bobby "The Brain", 104, 143
Hellwig, Jim (Ultimate Warrior), 196
Helmsley, Hunter Hearst, 72, 139, 204
Hennig, Curt, 82, 90, 104, 105, 161
Hennig, Larry, 124, 151
Herd, Jim, 5, 6
Hickenbottom, Michael (Shawn Michaels), 138
Hild, Helen, 183
Hodge, Danny, 13, 47, 62, 122, 130–131, 171, 190, 202
Hogan, "Hollywood", 30
Hogan, Hulk, 6, 17, 20, 24, 26–32, 34, 36, 50, 52, 54, 64, 66, 73, 83, 102, 105, 112, 125, 134, 136, 144, 145, 158, 159, 160, 162, 163, 183, 197
Hokuto, Akira, 209
Hollywood Blondes, The 52
Honawa, Seiko, 166
Hori, Ayumi, 166
Hoshino, Kantaro, 89
Huerta, Rodolfo Guzman (El Santo), 38
Hulkamania, 28, 31, 83, 105
Hutton, Dick, 13, 17, 179, 184

Iaukea, Prince (King Curtis), 18, 142
Idol, Austin, 161
Inoki, Kanji "Antonio", 6, 14, 18, 19, 20–25, 28, 36, 44, 47, 48, 68, 77, 78, 79, 86, 96, 100, 108, 128, 132, 150, 169, 170, 179, 181, 186, 198, 207
Inoue, Kyoko, 167, 209
Inoue, Masao, 180
Iron Sheik, The, 2, 29, 157
Ishingun, 48, 100, 128
Istaz, Karl (Karl Gotch), 169
IWA, 89, 149, 184, 191, 195
IWGP, 24, 28, 78, 79, 112, 113, 116, 118, 120, 128, 129, 140, 146, 147, 150, 198, 207

Jannetty, Marty, 138
Janos, James (Jesse Ventura), 199
Japan Pro Wrestling Association (JWA), 17, 19, 20, 22, 23, 24, 47, 86, 89, 108, 169, 177
Jarrett, Jeff, 31, 138
Jenkins, Tom, 62, 63, 114
Jericho, Chris, 116, 155, 204, 205
Johnson, Dwayne (The Rock), 72
Johnson, Rocky, 72
Jonathan, Don Leo, 34, 70, 146, 154–155, 169, 176, 180, 191
Jones, Paul, 2, 123
Jumping Bomb Angels, 134, 167
Junkyard Dog, 125, 183

K-1, 132
Kai, Shoji, 98
Kane, 54
Kanemoto, Koji, 117, 204
Kanemura, Wing, 181
Kansai, Dynamite, 209
Kareline, Alexander, 133
Kashey, Abe "King Kong", 82
Kawada, Toshiaki, 49, 80, 81, 116, 118, 120, 150, 201, 206
Keirn, Steve, 128
Kido, Osamu, 79, 132
Kim Sin-Nak (Rikidozan), 16
Kimura, Kengo, 128
Kimura, Masahiko, 16, 17

Kimura, Rusher, 49
Kiniski, Gene, 11, 13, 47, 82, 96, 108, 124, 146
Kirby Roger, 190
Kitamura, Tomoko (Lioness Asuka), 167
Kobashi, Kenta, 49, 80, 81, 201, 206
Kobayashi, Kuniaki, 48, 78, 80, 116
Kojima, Satoshi, 206–207
Koloff, Ivan, 70, 89, 123, 189
Kong, Aja, 209
Konnan, 102, 103, 193
Korak (El Hijo del Santo), 126
Koshinaka, Shiro, 80, 146, 207
Kosugi, Shunji, 116
Kowalski, Killer, 18, 33, 34, 35, 59, 70, 76, 155, 176, 184, 191, 195, 204
Krauser, Karl (Karl Gotch), 169
Kumi, Nancy, 166

La Galactica, 166
La Ola Blanc, 158
Ladd, Ernie, 34
Lagarde, Karloff, 88, 195
Landel, Buddy, 61
Lansdowne, Lord Patrick, 74
Lawler, Jerry, 90, 105, 144, 157, 161–162
LeBlanc, Frogman, 50
LeDuc, Jos, 106
Lee, Kwik-Kik, 132
Lee, Sammy (Satoru Sayama), 98
Leone, Baron Michele, 11
Levin, Dave, 58
Lewin, "Maniac" Mark, 154, 177
Lewis, Ed "Strangler", 8, 10, 12, 13, 56, 62, 64, 65, 66–67, 75, 184, 196, 208
Lewis, Evan "Strangler", 66
Liger, Jushin "Thunder", 98, 116–117, 120, 155, 198, 204
Lisowski, Reggie (The Crusher), 150
Little Wolf, Chief, 16
Londos, Jim (The Golden Greek), 64–65, 66, 75, 153
Longson, Bill, 10, 11, 13, 171, 189
Los Espantos I, 41
Los Espantos II, 41
Los Misioneros, 41–43
Luger, Lex 6, 48, 68, 125, 157
Lurich, George, 63

Macho Man (Randy Savage), 144
Maeda, Akira, 17, 24, 36, 48, 78, 79, 100, 128, 132–133, 169, 208
Mahmout, Yussiff, 63
Maiva, Rocky, 149
Maivia, High Chief Peter, 72
Malenko, Professor Boris, 200
Managoff, Bobby, 10
Mankind (Mick Foley), 147
Manson, Cactus Jack (Mick Foley), 149
Marshall, Everett, 10, 13
Martel, Rick, 68, 85
Mascara Ano Dos Mil, 102, 103
Mascaras, Mil, 41, 43, 84, 88–89, 98, 101, 126, 153, 158, 159, 180, 193
Matsuda, Hiro, 130, 169, 190
Matsumoto, Dump, 134, 167
McCready, Earl, 183–184, 189, 202
McDaniel, Wahoo, 2, 108, 109, 187–189
McGuirk, Leroy, 190
McLeod, Dan, 62
McMahon, Vince, 4, 5, 6, 7, 17, 26, 28, 29, 30, 31, 36, 50, 54, 66, 72, 73, 83, 91, 122, 132, 133, 138, 144, 155, 157, 160, 162, 163, 183, 191, 198, 199, 200, 202
McMahon, Vince, Jr., 20, 24, 28, 35, 71, 90, 107, 111, 134, 159
McMahon, Vince, Sr., 13, 28, 34, 35, 58, 59, 61, 68, 70, 76, 89, 108, 111, 159, 170
McShain, Danny, 190
Mega Powers, 144

Mendoza, Rey, 102, 158
Meyers, Sonny, 18
Michaels, Shawn, 53, 54, 61, 65, 90, 91, 102, 113, 138–139, 149, 158, 191, 204
Midnight Rockers, the, 138
Miller, Bill, 59, 70, 83
Mirko Cro Cop, 207
Misawa, Mitsuharu, 49, 68, 78, 80–81, 84, 85, 118, 150, 201, 206, 209
Misterio, Rey Jr., 98, 116, 126
Mita, Etsuko, 209
Momota, Mitsuhiro (Rikidozan), 16
Momota, Mitsuo, 49
Mondt, Joe "Toots", 13, 59, 61, 65, 66, 70, 192, 196
Monroe, Sputnik, 86, 130
Monster Ripper, 166
Morales, Pedro, 70
Moreno, Alejandro Munoz (Blue Demon), 101
Moreno, Maximo Linares (Rayo de Jalisco), 195
Mortensen Clara, 177
Mr. Atomic, 18
Mr. T, 29, 163
Muchnik, Sam, 10, 11, 13, 47, 58, 61, 146, 171, 183, 186
Mulligan, Blackjack, 4, 189
Munn, Wayne, 196
Muraco, Don, 147, 157
Murdoch, Dick, 1, 24, 48, 106
Muto, Keiji, 79, 116, 118, 120, 133, 140, 147, 150, 198, 207, 208

Nagata, Yuji, 207
Nagayo, Chigusa, 134, 167, 209
Nagurski, Bronko, 13, 65, 192
Nakanishi, Manabu, 207
Nakano, Bull, 134
Nash Kevin, 31, 191
National Wrestling Alliance, 1, 8, 10, 11, 12
National Wrestling Association, 10
National Wrestling Federation, 23
Neidhart, Jim, 90, 139
New Japan Pro Wrestling, 13, 24, 30, 36, 47, 48, 68, 78, 79, 80, 90, 96, 98, 100, 102, 112, 116, 117, 118, 120, 128, 129, 132, 133, 140, 146, 147, 150, 155, 157, 165, 170, 179, 181, 198, 206, 207
Newton, Carlos, 208
Nielsen, Don, 24
Nitro, 47, 48, 91, 197
NOAH, 78, 118, 150, 201, 206
Nomellini, Leo, 12
NOW, 6
NWA, 2, 4, 6, 12, 13, 17, 18, 22, 23, 34, 40, 41, 46, 47, 48, 52, 56, 58, 59, 61, 64, 65, 67, 69, 75, 80, 82, 83, 84, 85, 86, 89, 96, 98, 100, 101, 102, 106, 107, 122, 123, 124, 125, 128, 130, 131, 136, 140, 142, 143, 145, 158, 166, 179, 183, 184, 186, 189, 190, 191, 195, 196, 198
NWO, 30, 79, 139, 145, 207

O'Connor, Pat, 11, 12, 58, 65, 83, 142, 171, 176, 184, 189, 191
O'Mahoney, Danno, 65, 191
Octagon, 126
Ogawa, Naoya, 25, 140
Okerlund, "Mean" Gene, 83
Olin, John, 66
Omori, Yukari, 134
Onita, Atsushi, 79, 87, 154, 181
Orndorff, Paul, 29, 112
Orton, Bob Jr., 157
Owen, Don, 180, 191

Packs, Tom, 8, 10
Page, Diamond Dallas, 145
Patera, Ken, 2, 61, 197

Patterson, Pat, 2, 36, 52, 123, 142, 143, 191, 197–198
Pegasus Kid (Chris Benoit), 204
Pena, Antonio, 102
Perez, Miguel, 153, 200
Pillman, Brian, 52, 116, 117, 155
Pilusso, Henry, 41
Piper, Roddy, 4, 6, 29, 162–163
Poffo, Randy (Randy Savage), 144
Potts, William (Whipper Billy Watson), 189
Powers, Johnny, 23
Principe Azul (Canek), 152
Psicosis, 116, 126
Purple Shadow (Bill Longson), 171
Putski, Ivan, 159
PWF, 48, 77, 85

Race, Harley, 1, 4, 11, 35, 47, 76, 82, 84, 86, 96, 102, 104, 106, 107, 123, 124–125, 151, 204
Ramirez, Huracan, 41
Ramon, Razor, 138
Ramos, Bull, 88
RAW, 47, 54, 91
Reed, Butch, 160
Rhodes, Dusty, 4, 76, 86, 106–107, 124, 129, 154, 159, 177, 200
Rich, Tommy, 4, 124, 161
Richter, Wendi, 166
Rikidozan, 12, 14–19, 20, 22, 44, 47, 49, 110, 179, 180, 186
RoadWarriors, 157, 159
Robert, Yvon, 10, 171, 189, 191–192, 195
Roberts, Jake "The Snake", 52
Robinson, Billy, 2, 82, 83, 104, 143, 155, 165, 170
Rocca, Antonino "Argentina", 12, 70, 151, 153, 176, 200
Rocco, Mark "Pollerball", 98, 116
Rock 'n' Roll Express, 138
Rock, The, 31, 54, 72–73, 202, 204, 205
Rockers, The, 71
Rodriguez, Jose Luis (Dos Caras), 193
Rogers, "Nature Boy" Buddy, 1, 10, 12, 13, 56–61, 65, 70, 108, 142, 170, 176, 184, 191
Rohde, Herman (Buddy Rogers), 56
Roller, B.F. (Ben), 63, 114
Romero, Rito, 41
Roop, Bob, 123
Rougeau Johnny, 191, 192
Rougeau, Jacques, 163
Rousimoff, Andre Rene (Andre the Giant), 33
Rude, Rick, 139
Runnels, Virgil Jr (Dusty Rhodes), 106
Ruska, Willem, 23
Russo, Vince, 7, 31

Sabu, 87, 149, 154
Saito, Hiro, 48
Saito, Masa, 48, 78
Sakaguchi Seiji, 198
Sakuraba, Kazushi, 166, 208
Salvador III, 171
Sammartino, Bruno, 28, 46, 61, 68, 70–71, 76, 159, 176
Sandow, Billy, 66, 67, 196
Sano, Naoki, 117
Santana, Tito, 144
Santel, Ad, 8, 63, 114
Sasaki, Kensuki, 118, 181, 207
Sato, Jackie, 166
Saturn Perry, 176
Savage, Randy, 6, 29, 36, 136, 144–145, 158, 163
Savoldi, Angelo, 130, 131
Savoldi, Jumping Joe, 65, 169
Sayama, Satoru, 25, 80, 98, 100, 116, 132, 155, 157, 169
Schmidt, Hans, 153

Scorpio, 193
Seikigun, 48, 100, 128
Severn, Dan, 140
Sexton, Frank, 13
Sgt. Slaughter, 197
Sharpe Brothers, The, 17
Sheik, The, 86, 88, 96, 102, 104, 109, 110, 153–154, 169, 177, 179
Sherry, Jack, 67
Shibuya, Kinji, 110, 142
Shikat, Dick, 64, 67, 184
Shimoda, Mima, 209
Shinma, Hisashi, 20, 22, 23, 24, 25, 98, 100, 128, 132, 146
Shooting, 100
Shreeve, Larry (Abdullah the Butcher), 177
Shultz, Dr. D. David, 83
Silva, Vanderlei, 208
Silveira, Conan, 208
Silver King, 205
Singh, Dara, 199
Singh, Tiger Jeet, 23, 24, 47, 48
Skyscrapers, the, 157
Smith, Davey Boy, 48, 90, 138, 139, 157
Smith, Johnny, 120, 157
Snuka, Jimmy, 4, 48, 61, 68, 143, 147, 149, 153, 163
Snyder, Wilbur, 82, 142
Song, Pak, 106
Sonnenberg, Gus, 67
Spider, The (Randy Savage), 144
Spinks, Leon, 24
Spivey, Danny, 157
Spoiler, The, 89
Stampede, 90
Stanchev, Nikola, 130
Stanlee, Gene, 153
Starrcade, 4, 5, 6, 31, 91, 107, 112, 124, 163, 197
Stasiak, Stan, 70
Steamboat, Ricky, 1, 5, 52, 80, 82, 87, 96, 100, 108, 109, 123, 136, 144, 155
Stecher, Joe, 8, 63, 64, 66, 67, 208
Steele, Gary, 140
Steele, George, 71
Steele, Ray, 8, 153, 192
Steeles, Ray, 65
Steiner Brothers, 157
Stevens, Carl Raymond (Ray Stevens), 142
Stevens, Ray "The Crippler", 1, 2, 52, 104, 142–143, 166, 191, 197
Sting, 5, 7, 31, 102, 112, 145, 149, 196
Strongbow, Jules, 18, 180
Studd, Big John, 34, 61, 176

Super Delfin, 117 16
Super Strong Machine, 48
Super Tiger, 100
Survivor Series, 5, 91, 107, 133, 139, 157, 158
SWS, 48
Szabo, Sandor, 65

Takada, Nobuhiko, 13, 79, 112, 113, 120, 133, 140, 146–147, 169, 208
Takahashi, Mayumi, 166
Taue, Akira, 49, 81, 113, 118, 201, 206
Taylor, Chris, 2
Tenryu, Genichiro, 48, 68, 69, 78, 80, 84, 85, 86, 96, 118, 120, 150, 181, 207, 208
Tenzan, Hiroyoshi, 206, 207
Texas Outlaws, The, 106
Thesz, Lou, 8–13, 17, 18, 46, 47, 56, 61, 62, 63, 67, 108, 122, 146, 153, 169, 170, 171, 176, 180, 184, 189, 191, 192, 195, 196, 198, 199, 208
Thorton, Les, 100
Three Musketeers, 198
Tiger Mask, 48, 78, 80, 88, 90, 98–100, 102, 116, 118, 128, 155, 169, 181
Tiger, The, 100
Tiza, Lajos (Lou Thesz), 8
Tokyo Pro Wrestling, 22
Tolos, John, 88, 110
Toombs, Roderick (Roddy Piper), 162
Toyonobori, 18, 165
Toyota, Manami, 134, 167, 208–209
Tragos, George, 10, 63
Triple H, 31, 54, 72, 149, 176, 202, 204–205
TripleMania, 102
Tsuruta, Tomomi (Jumbo), 47, 48, 68, 69, 75, 78, 80, 81, 84–85, 86, 96, 105, 150, 166, 201, 206
Tunney, Frank, 154, 180
Tunney, Jack, 70
Tyson, Mike, 53, 54

Ueda, Maki, 166
Ueda, Umanosuke, 48
UFC, 132, 133, 208
Ultimate Warrior(Jim Hellwig), 144, 158, 159, 196
Ultimo Dragon, 98, 116, 117, 165, 205
Undertaker, The, 54, 72, 91, 139, 149, 157
Union of Wrestling Forces International (UWFI), 13, 147, 208
Universal Fighting-arts Organization, 100
UWA, 78, 102, 126, 128, 152, 193
UWF, 36, 38, 48, 100, 112, 120, 128, 132, 133, 140, 146, 147, 196

Vachon Luna, 176
Vachon Paul The Butcher, 104, 191
Vachon, Mad Dog, 1, 82, 83, 104, 171, 190–191
Vader, 6, 68, 78, 79, 81, 112–113, 120, 125, 128, 139, 147, 149, 198, 201
Vale Tudo, 132
Valentine, Greg, 2, 4, 108, 157, 163
Valentine, Johnny, 2, 22, 108–109, 154, 169, 189
Valois, Frank, 34, 35
Van Dam, Rob, 154
Velasco, Diablo, 102
Veloz, Ciclon, 38, 40
Ventura, Jesse "The Body", 83, 159, 191, 199–200
Vera, Rolando, 101
Vicious, Sid 6, 113, 139, 157, 158
Volkoff, Nikolai, 157
Von Erich, Chris, 186, 187
Von Erich, David, 186, 187
Von Erich, Fritz, 76, 77, 82, 83, 108, 186–187, 195
Von Erich, Jackie Jr, 186
Von Erich, Kerry, 4, 159, 161 186, 187
Von Erich, Kevin, 186
Von Erich, Mike, 186, 187
Von Erich, Waldo, 70
Von Erichs, the, 52

Wagner, George Raymond, 74
Wanz, Otto, 105, 112
Watson, "Whipper" Billy, 10, 12, 75, 146, 154, 171, 176, 189–190, 191
Watts, Bill, 70, 106, 138, 183, 190, 200
WCW, 5, 6, 7, 26, 30, 31, 40, 48, 50, 52, 53, 54, 67, 68, 72, 73, 87, 91, 105, 107, 112, 117, 120, 125, 128, 136, 145, 147, 149, 165, 196, 197, 200, 204, 205
Weicz, Edouard (Edouard Carpentier), 195
Wepner, Chuck, 23
Westergaard, Jess, 63
White, Leon (Vader), 112, 113
Wilhelm, Willie, 133
William, Willie, 23
Williams, Steve (Steve Austin), 50
Williams, Steve "Dr. Death", 50
Williams, Steve, 68, 118
Windham, Barry, 4, 6
Wisniski, John (Johnny Valentine), 108
Woods, Tim, 2, 108, 109, 189
World Class Championship Wrestling, 50
World Wide Wrestling Federation, 61

WrestleMania, 26, 139, 149, 163, 205
WrestleMania I, 29
WrestleMania II, 157
WrestleMania III, 29, 36, 107, 125, 136, 144
WrestleMania IV, 5, 144
WrestleMania V, 144
WrestleMania VII, 6, 144
WrestleMania VIII, 144, 158
WrestleMania X, 138
WrestleMania XII, 91, 139
WrestleMania XIII, 91
Wrestlemarinpiad, 209
Wright, Bearcat, 142
WWA, 110, 179
WWC, 77 18, 46
WWE, 154, 172
WWF, 4, 6, 7, 24, 26, 28, 29, 30, 31, 36, 40, 48, 50, 52, 53, 54, 61, 67, 68, 71, 72, 73, 76, 78, 83, 87, 89, 91, 100, 102, 105, 106, 107, 111, 113, 122, 125, 128, 136, 138, 139, 143, 144, 147, 149, 155, 157, 158, 159, 160, 162, 183, 197, 198, 199, 202, 205
WWWA, 134, 209
WWWF, 34, 46, 56, 68, 70, 72, 89, 104, 107, 124, 159

Y2J (Chris Jericho), 205
Yamada, Flying Fuji (Jushin "Thunder" Liger), 116
Yamada, Keiichi (Jushin "Thunder" Liger), 116, 118
Yamada, Toshiyo, 167, 209
Yamaguchi, Toshio, 16
Yasuda, Tadao, 207
Yatsu, Yoshiaki, 48, 78
Yokota, Jaguar, 166, 209
Yokota, Rimi (Jaguar Yokota), 166
Yokozuna, 30, 161
Yoshimura, Michiaki, 19, 169
Young Pair, 166
Youngblood, Jay, 123, 136
Yu, Crane, 134
Yukon Eric, 176, 199

Zangiev, Victor, 140
Zapetti, Nicola "Nick", 19
Zbyszko, Larry, 28, 68, 71
Zbyszko, Stanislaus, 62, 63, 66, 67, 196
Zbyszko, Wladek, 66,